BOYS' & MEN'S ISSUES HANDBOOK

CHILDHOOD

CHRIS VOTEY

ISBN 979-8-218-16988-6

Contact me at:

https://www.boysmenissues.com

DEDICATIONS

To Clara... With the release of the hardback copy, you were out there pushing to get the world to read it. When I released it, I was quite surprised by how little attention it got, and I was ready to give up and pursue other dreams. Your dedication to my vision on the importance of my book revitalize me in a way I didn't think possible and the later release of the softbook and ebook, as well as future releases of this book, is large part thanks to you. I can never say it enough, but I will certainly try to: Thank you!

To Hannah... You were my first fan on YouTube and gave me a chance to find my voice within the movement. I wish I had listened to you all those years ago and written this book then. You are one of the hardest-working people I know in the movement, and even then, you had time to give me a great foundation.

To Vanessa... You've been a constant presence in my life, from a guest star on my channel to my co-host to the co-creator of the Lovely Ladies of Men's Issues Calendar. With your help, I reached new heights. Your friendship has meant a lot to me.

To Elizabeth... Of everyone in my life, you were the final push that led to the creation of this book. You asked me to write a protest book in response to an awful book. Not only did my book help bring awareness of the other book, but that proved to be a success. Because of you, I realized my destiny. I had to write this book. You saw in me the potential of my talent to give more to men.

To Catherine... So few genuinely understand me the way you do. I never thought I'd ever meet someone of such a like mind... of pure abstraction... someone who speaks my language. We are like Bruce Lee and Chuck Norris, two masters of distinct disciplines, able to learn and teach, building upon one another to redefine who we are. You find new ways to challenge me, and your dedication drives me forward. I look forward to what you bring to the world.

To Kassy... It's easy to take advantage of the system. Everyone needs help, and we can't always be choosy on how we get that help, especially if others depend on us. You demonstrated that there is a line we should not cross ever and fix the system instead of take it for granted.

To Warren... Myth of Male Power to the *Boy Crisis*... You led the groundwork for many decades and continue to be a voice for men everywhere. You are a giant, and I know I stand on your shoulders when I write this book. One day, I'll be a giant such as you for others to stand on my shoulders.

To Cassie... You are a very courageous person. You started a journey of the great unknown with preconceived notions. When you truly stepped into the darkness of the unfamiliar, you found a light. A light many others would run from to dishonest comfort. You questioned what you knew to be undoubted to discover what is truly undeniable. The Red Pill movie is one definite inspiration for this book. You gave me courage.

To Janice... You remain one of the most humble people I know. You have given a voice to men from within the academic sphere, a world at odds with those trying to reveal the truth. We all have a part to play in raising awareness, and you always ask yourself if I am doing enough. Let me assure you that what you've done in this world has added to this book.

To Robert... I thank you for Wiki4Men. Your website is much like this book. Cataloging resources to be used as a reference and give those new to the movement proof that what we speak of is not isolated events but a pattern of a greater truth.

To Elly... Activism takes many forms, but it's important to remember through it all to be yourself. It's too easy to get caught up in the constant negativity of those who rather destroy than build up. You made a shirt that revealed the truth of people, to focus on images made of string than the accomplishment of the entire human race. That shirt is a piece of history, and you displayed unyielding pride in your work. You give me such strength that we are not alone no matter what we face.

To Tom McCarthy, Josh Singer, and the Boston Globe Spotlight team... While the movie Spotlight was about a very specific element that hurt boys (and girls), the work done in reporting the abuse and the work done in making the film proved as one of the bigger inspirations of this book. There are too many films to name that helped me during the last decade, but this movie is perhaps the one I've watched more than any other.

And to so many others that I hope to thank in future books.

CONTENTS

AUTHOR'S NOTE

I DON'T
HATE WOMEN!!!

I n order to read this series, you must suspend your preconceptions of who and what men and boys are. That is easier said than done, as the general understanding of men is integrated into our culture. Because of this bias, some will cite this book as the *misogynist manifesto*, reading just the preview to find some tiny thing to take out of context. In fact, if you can't keep an open mind, I dare you to give me a 1-star review. Perhaps you'll write I'm some pathetic neckbeard living in my mother's basement... well the joke is on you; my mother doesn't have a basement.

Why would I want someone to give me a bad review? Simple. When someone writes such a politically biased criticism, they will accomplish two things:

1. Generate more sales for my book.
2. Proves they don't care about equality.

So yes, give me a 1-star review to make me more popular by demonstrating you hate men... unless you can keep an open mind and grant me some leeway. I will start by disclosing something vital to help put this entire book into proper perspective:

I DON'T HATE WOMEN!!!

I begin my book addressing I'm not a misogynist because my work is a by-product of the Men's Human Rights Movement (MHRM), which the media, the government, and Feminism have claimed is a hate group.[1] They portray us as a group who seek to regain what was lost by rolling back the clock to when men had absolute control and women were slaves to a man's needs. We men want to repeal the power women have fought for and won, shackle them to the kitchen. And why do they say this? Because we disagree with Feminism, and to disagree with Feminism means we hate women.

That is a gross mischaracterization of the Men's Movement. We don't desire domination over women... we simply want true equality. However, when we try to have a conversation about equality, we are immediately shut down[2] and labeled as misogynists, primarily by Feminists and the media. Ironically, while *misogynist* is considered the greatest insult, misandry (hatred of men[3]) is often seen as legitimate[4] and a badge of honor in society or permissible as a joke[5].

Personally, I identify as an Egalitarian, which is something I think all people should aspire to. An Egalitarian believes all people, regardless of labels, should enjoy the same benefits in life. To an extent, Egalitarianism means I am both a Men's Rights Activist (MRA) and a Woman's Rights Activist (WRA).[6] However, I focus more on the MHRM as I firmly believe males are being left behind. In our society today, that is a very dangerous statement to make because it goes against the mainstream narrative. Most believe men have all the privileges set forth by men for the benefit of men, better known as **The Patriarchy**.

You'll note I said WRA and not Feminism. I firmly believe both men and women deserve to get the same legal protections and empathy. I feel Feminism is not the path towards equality (or at least the present state of Feminism), as it does more harm than good. That being said, this book doesn't set out to be anti-Feminist, though it will paint Feminism in a bad light by showing the atrocities done in the name of Feminism. It is my hope Feminists will see this and alter their opinion on men's issues, as well as their own movement.

Like many others, I have lost friendships after they learned of my supporting Men's Rights. I've also been accused of being a rape apologist, crybaby, neckbeard, and a hateful bigot to my face and by Feminists online. Because of this, many within the Men's Movement hate Feminism. Believe me when I say that if I made this series directly attacking Feminism, many within the Men's Movement would cheer me on. Read this series and look at all the sources... then ask yourself: Can you blame them?

My overall issue with Feminism primarily emanates from Radical Feminists who get the most attention. Yes, not all Feminists are radicals... however, I hold the rest of the movement responsible for not calling them out. Until Feminism eliminates those who misuse the movement for their selfish needs, the Feminist Movement remains complicit in what radicals do and is, therefore, part of any blame for their actions. If, as a Feminist, you hate being lumped in with the extremists, then I **STRONGLY** recommend you do something about the radicals rather than expecting the rest of us to differentiate between the "Good Feminists" and the "Bad Feminists". Take a look at the Men's Movement: we distance ourselves from the Pick-up Artists (PUA), Red Pill (subreddit), and Men Going Their Own Way (MGTOW). Why? Because their viewpoints are not our viewpoints.

Now let me reiterate, this is not an anti-Feminist book. That might seem like a lie; after all, I do criticize Feminism. Much of this series will hold Feminism in contempt as it has set the narrative I seek to overcome. The various Feminist Movements caused many of the issues men face today. Thus, in order to discuss those issues, I must address the failings of Feminism, which will be seen as misogynistic and anti-Feminist.

Understand it is not my goal to put all blame onto women or Feminism, but where I see those standing in the way of men's emancipation, I will call it out. If you feel this will trigger you, then see this as a **TRIGGER WARNING**. I'm here to discuss reality, which means I will inadvertently hurt people's feelings.

Even I know Feminism doesn't deserve all the blame... that would be irresponsible of me. Feminism is merely a symptom of a much larger entity: **Culture**. One could argue our culture today is synonymous with Feminism as they are woven into the fabric of society, but many of the issues I address existed long before Feminism. Men exist in very narrow gender roles, from laborer to soldier, enduring back-breaking work to death in combat, all to serve the greater good of their families and country.

Feminists complain about how women have had it rough throughout history, but believe when I say: Men have it worse. It's just that the hardships men face have become normalized to the point where no sympathy is awarded to them.

The major issue of our culture is that we are quick to judge. We, as humans, crave to believe the worst about people, especially males. Males are deemed monsters in society, so anything lobbied against them must be true based on their gender alone. Funny, Feminism fights against making judgments on one's gender but is on the front line when it comes to judging males. When judging men, there is nothing wrong with the judgment; when judgment is lobbied against a female, our culture (and by extension Feminism) is ready to go to war.

Females escape persecution and are deemed innocent, even when proven guilty. They're given this privilege because they are seen as weak and vulnerable and not fully capable of their actions. They need constant protection, whereas a man can take the full brunt of anything brought against him, and we're allowed to be tougher on him.

If Feminism really looked at the world today, and I mean **REALLY** look, they would see that women have more rights and freedoms than men do. I often challenge Feminists to name five rights men have that women don't... most can't even name one that's an actual right. If they can name something, it is often something easily refuted or has already been debunked. Yet, the government and media follow the direction of Feminism of seeing men as scum.

Closing out this Author's Note, I want to leave you with one last thought before you read the rest of this book... Feminists say you cannot understand the troubles of women's suffering unless you listen to women. Then logic holds that you cannot understand men's troubles unless you listen to men. *What's good for the goose is good for the gander.* Yet, the idea of listening to a man for his issues is not only laughed at[7] in our society; in our society; Feminists have shut down our public assemblies.[8]

INTRODUCTION

Welcome to the first book of the Boys' & Men's Issues series.

The concept for this series came from the many resources available for women and girls that are denied to men and boys... from academia, support groups, shelters, books, charities, and the world itself set to help females in any way it can. This conflicts with everyone's belief that males have everything, so that's why we must give more to females. After reading this book, you will undoubtedly conclude that men have next to nothing. In truth, when males need help, they have very few resources available.

One resource men have, though believed to be bad for humanity, is the Men's Human Rights Movement (MHRM). The negative propaganda of the Men's Movement is no small part thanks to Feminism. Feminism is about empowering women, so anything outside of Feminism is automatically deemed misogynistic.

My goal is to bring together men and women as equals. I do not desire to deprive women and girls of empathy; I wish to expand the empathy for boys and men. When we expand empathy, many problems worldwide can be resolved, and true equality can be realized. By the end of this book, you will see more of the larger picture of what boys and men are fighting for and the opposition they endure.

The Reality of Men

One of the key issues men face in this world today is misandry, the hatred of men. Much of the world is guilty of this, but the biggest culprit of misandry is Feminism. Now, I do understand not all Feminists hate men; however, most Feminists tolerate those who do hate men, and all others see men as the problem of female issues. Men have all the power, men are part of the Patriarchy, the very thing Feminists fight against.

Interestingly, so many say men have all the power, and yet they seem to lack it when they try to discuss their issues. Men are often shut down, whether trying to raise points on social media or holding their own conferences. How is it we have all the power and, at the same time, lack the capability to help ourselves? The fact we're unable to help ourselves might well be proof that men don't have power. I've often heard that because no woman has been president in the US is an indication of the Patriarchy. I've also heard the Patriarchy hurt men. So I ask you, what is the purpose of the Patriarchy then if not to help men?

If we don't need Men's Rights because the Patriarchy is for men, but at the same time hurts men... Doesn't that prove we need Men's Rights?

In this series, I will present internet sources to demonstrate the reality of men. This isn't something I'm pulling out of my ass, but information that is out right now. Ultimately, my goal is to throw out vicious lies of boys and men and reveal what is actually going on. This series is what the MHRM is all about, what we fight for, and the changes we wish to see. In the Red Pill movie by Cassie Jaye[9], Feminists discussed the Men's Movement as saying it's about the fear of losing power or the need to regain it.

I will tell you here, and now, it's not about wanting power, nor trying to regain control... and the kicker... and listen carefully... *Men never had power.*

Men never had power!?

MEN NEVER HAD POWER!!?

How can that be? Most political and military leaders are men, and most CEOs are men... Men have been running society since the dawn of time, so how can you say men never had power?

Yes, most of the powerful positions in our society are indeed held by men. This is regarded as the Patriarchy. A system designed by men for men. Yet, more and more women are in political office today, and more are in leading positions in the corporate world. Kind of a flawed system if the Patriarchy allows women to undermine men's power by giving power to women. It certainly pokes holes in the Patriarchy theory.

This top view of men in our society is one of the biggest failings of Feminism, also known as **Apex Fallacy**. They look at the elites and see men there, then identify that all males in society have this privilege. Most men throughout history had to work, often with little concern for their life. Do you think those working dangerous jobs cared about who was in office when he risked his life to put food on the table for his family? I'm not saying women didn't have their challenges throughout history, but to suggest that because a man was president meant that society favors men is erroneous.

Men were required to put their lives on the line, and their families would suffer without them if they died. This includes the military. Women getting the right to vote is considered the most significant achievement for our world. Yes, women had to wait until after men got their right to vote in the US[10] (about 70 years after), but did so without the requirement of military conscription. In the UK, however, men and women[11] got their right to vote after the completion of World War I. This means that men and women simultaneously got the right to vote in the UK. This also means that most British soldiers were fighting for a country while lacking the right to elect their leaders. Some privilege.

The Greatest Sin of All

The 1977 hit song "The Greatest Love of All", the first line reads:

I believe the children are our future.

It's a wonderful sentiment. The children of today will manage the world of tomorrow. However, if we look at the children of today and see how they are treated, we might need to revise the lyrics to:

I believe girls are our future.

To be a boy today is to be born with the sin of being a male. Everything I enjoyed as a child is taken away from the boys of today. In its place is the idea that the only thing permissible for boys is what is suitable for girls. That might sound like an exaggeration, but it's not; I am being quite serious.

Within education, boys are treated as defective girls; anything a boy might like to do is restricted, and he is demonized for wanting it. Moreover, the school will remind him that his gender is responsible[12] for all the atrocities in the world. It is his gender that has held women back and done awful things to them. Every boy needs to give up their "privilege" to compensate girls today for yesterday's crimes. At the end of this book, I want you to consider an important question:

Why should any boy today remain a boy
if it is so wrong to be a boy?

<u>Keep In Mind</u>

If there is anything I want you to take away from this book, it is this simple truth: males desire the same respect as females. We want balance in humanity. Anything that would be seen as wrong for men to do would also be seen as wrong for women to do. Likewise, if women are celebrated for an action, men should also be celebrated for the same action. In a truly equal society, women and girls are held responsible for their actions and are required to face the consequences.

Understand, my writing on male victims is by no means an effort to negate female victims, a common argument I hear from those outside the Men's Movement. Someone needs to speak about the issue of men and boys. Even if those most affected by any issue are females, it doesn't mean we stop speaking of males. Focusing on just females means they get all the support and resources, and males must remain invisible.

ABDUCTION

Around 8 million children are declared missing worldwide. In 2020, there were nearly 400,000 open cases of child abduction, with 46% of the victims being boys.[13] Other locations include shocking statistics[14]:

- **Australia**: 20,000 children go missing each year

- **Canada**: 45,000 go missing, with:
  - 10,868 boys never found
  - 8,185 girls never found

- **UK**: 112,853 children

- **China**: 200,000 children
  - China officially recognizes 10,000 abductions
  - US State Department estimates 70,000
  - Vast majority were boys, often sold to crime syndicates and families wanting a male heir.

There are two main types of abductions: the victims know the abductor, and the victims don't know the abductor. The known abductor is family or a friend of the family, and the second is known as **Stranger Abduction**.

Despite how often the media reports on Stranger Danger, the rate of Stranger Abduction is relatively low, representing 1% of total abductions in the United States.[13] Despite the low amount of Stranger Abduction, this chapter will focus just on that.

Female Perpetrators

As a society, we are so focused on men being the only perpetrators of Stranger Abduction we're not on the lookout for female offenders[15] because we don't think women are capable of this action. As a result, many women get away with it. I will acknowledge that most sources state that men are more likely to abduct children via stranger abduction.

Georgia Tann

An example of a woman getting away with child abduction is Georgia Tann. Starting in 1924, she coerced mothers into giving up their children, and if that didn't work, she would kidnap children. She would then sell the children for what is now known as a black-market adoption. It's estimated that by 1950, she had a profit of $1,000,000 USD ($12m in 2022).[16]

I'm sure many of you will point out black-market adoptions were not illegal at the time, so technically, she didn't break any laws. However, her practices launched an investigation and led to laws being created. It does seem, however, that she was not focused on any particular gender.

Theatre Abduction

An instance you may be unaware of is Queen Elizabeth I[17] allowed boys to be kidnapped and forced to work in theatres to perform for audiences. The theatres were given licenses for this practice, taking boys off the streets and hurting them should they not obey (i.e., whipping). Additionally, there were legal protections that prevented parents from rescuing their sons.

There are also strong indications that boys were required to perform sexually explicit plays (often playing the part of females), which meant they were raped or otherwise sexually abused. In fairness, this was likely a common practice during this era and not specific to Queen Elizabeth. I would like to see more research done on this issue. And yes, the Queen didn't actually conduct the kidnappings herself.

Please note that I wrote this section years before Queen Elizabeth II died, with her death occurring around the time of my final proofing prior to publishing. While Queen Elizabeth I and Queen Elizabeth II are two distinct women, I don't want anyone to accusing me of denigrating the honor of Queen Elizabeth II.

Fetal Abduction

A rare form of Stranger Abduction is known as Fetal Abduction. This occurs when a pregnant woman is kidnapped when giving birth and goes through a crude cesarean section to remove the baby. Only about half of the mothers and fetuses survive.[18]

The majority of perpetrators are women incapable of having a baby. They are likely to befriend the mother or take a baby when they see an opportunity to take one. They often prepare ahead of time with a fake pregnancy to explain to friends and family why they have a new child in their lives. Some go as far as self-genital mutilation to replicate injuries suffered during childbirth.

While there hasn't been a lot of study on this phenomenon, there have been many cases of women raising kidnapped children. Some children learn the truth, usually in adulthood. We can only imagine the psychological damage done to a child to know that who they called mother were criminals who stole them from their actual parents; time they won't ever get back.

Male Perpetrators

Bacha Bazi

Similar to the theatres mentioned in the last section, we see cultures in the Middle East that use boys for entertainment. It's a cultural practice known as Bacha Bazi.[19] Young boys are kidnapped and forced to dance for men while wearing dresses before they are brutally raped. Now Middle East governments and the Taliban outlaw Bacha Bazi, primarily because homosexuality is against the law. However, it is rarely enforced under the law as many powerful men engage in this activity, which allows the practice to continue.

During the documentary, "This is What Winning Looks Like"[20], Ben Anderson films a US Marine speaking to a police chief about the practice, in which he states that this is not an act of homosexuality; instead, it is part of their culture. Additionally, he claimed this act is consensual and that the boys want it to happen and was further quoted, *"If [my commanders] don't fuck the asses of those boys, what should they fuck? The pussies of their own grandmothers?"*

From 2010 – 2016, the US Military reported 5,753 acts of human rights violations in Afghanistan, primarily that of boys being raped. This report should have caused America to cut off aid. No such action occurred. Instead, the US Military took the stance of ignoring it, and any soldier who made any complaint about it had their career ruined. This includes Captain Dan Quinn[21], who beat up an Afghan commander who had a boy chained to his bed and lost his command.

Hijra

An even worse instance of Non-Custodial Abduction is that of boys in India. Hijra[22] is another word for eunuch, which is the removal of the penis against their will. For most of the modern world, it is not something practiced anymore, except in places such as South Asia, primarily India and Pakistan. This form of genital mutilation primarily happens to boys, but it also can happen to young men.

In this practice of castration, boys are kidnapped, given opium, their genitals removed, a stick placed in their abdomen (so as not to allow closing of the area), and provided no water to prevent urination. If they survive all of that, they are celebrated as a Hijra. Some houses of Hijras require that the victim injure their ass so that it bleeds, having their first "menstruation". They then can return home, though some are auctioned off.[23]

It is believed that there are two million Hijras in India, to the point that the Indian government recognized Hijras as a third gender. However, more than just the forced removal of their genitals, they are considered the lowest of castes, often beaten by people who look down on them. Also, being the lowest caste, they lack opportunities to find work and become sex workers. As sex workers, their male clients primarily engage in anal sex, which the clients don't perceive as being gay, as they're the ones who are doing the penetration.[24]

No, no, no, you have it all wrong.

Only some were castrated and they volunteered to have it done,
others were simply born without genitals or were born the wrong gender.

Any mention of India's Third Gender ruling is met as a positive in certain communities, but these same communities easily gloss over the castration issue, either downplaying it or not mentioning it at all. I'm baffled anyone would choose to live in squalor and be regarded as the lowest of the low. Perhaps some choose it, but more than a million???

In truth, no serious research has been done on this community, and the rate of kidnapped boys is unknown. Personally, even if it is one boy out of a million, that is one boy too many. The rate is suggested to be as much as a thousand boys castrated yearly.[25]

Boko Haram

When the conversation of Boko Haram comes up, we immediately think of Michelle Obama and the campaign #bringbackourgirls.[26] This was the hot topic item for 2014, with politicians and celebrities holding signs demanding the return of kidnapped girls.

By May 2014, it became Twitter's most tweeted hashtag at 2.3 million tweets; by 2016, it totaled 6.1 million tweets. Vigils around the world were made at the 100-day mark from the kidnapping.

By the world's response, you would think that all kidnappings by Boko Haram would be that of girls. We live in a patriarchy, and the needs of males come first, right? So the lack of attention to males must mean there is no problem, right?

Wrong. Wrong wrong wrong wrong. The exact opposite is true; extremist organizations have kidnaped far more boys than girls.

You're making that up.

If that was true,
I would have heard about it on the news.

Not only did it happen, but the world ignored it before and after the #bring-backourgirls campaign. Some even attempted a #bringbackourboys campaign, initially started for 3 Israeli boys[27] who went missing but eventually used to raise awareness of the kidnapped boys in Africa, which gained no traction.[28]

Again, we live in a Patriarchy, and girls' needs are ignored.

Boko Haram is responsible for kidnapping over 10,000[29] boys over a three-year period (276 girls were taken from Chibok in 2014, which sparked #bringbackourgirls). Many were indoctrinated and became child soldiers, while others became slaves.

A documentary about four boy soldiers titled *"Trained to Kill: How Four Boy Soldiers Survived Boko Haram"*[30] gives us great insight into what boys go through. While I will go over **Child Soldiers** later in this book, I will point out that these boys describe an environment of some of the most outstanding human rights violations in history. They were forced to hunt and behead people, then bathe their hands in the blood. These boys were beaten, raped, and starved. They would be forced to do this to other boys and kill infants.

The world knew Boko Haram was a threat, and no one cared... until girls became victims. In fact, months before the kidnapping of girls at Chibok, soldiers came to a school. The soldier told the girls to go home and become wives while the boys were barricaded in a building. That building was set on fire. Any boy who escaped was gunned down.[31]

Worse yet, was the lack of media attention. Within two months, the world would be outraged about kidnapped girls, but next to no media outlet raised even a whisper of the atrocities that happened to these boys.

And why should it? Not like we live in a patriarchy that puts men's needs above women's.

This, right here, is absolute proof that we don't live in a Patriarchy, as there is more concern for women and girls than boys and men. I mean, ask yourself, what has to happen to boys for the world to take notice? What has to happen to boys for the world to intervene as they did for the 276 kidnapped girls?

And it's not like this stopped. Boko Haram still kidnaps both boys and girls, with 330 boys kidnapped in 2020.[32] The few times it is mentioned in the news, there seems to be a deliberate effort by the media to erase male victims. Should something happen to boys, it will always be read as kids. This is primarily in the headlines, but entire articles may suppress the gender of the victims. Don't believe me... look at the list on the next page:

- **Daily Mail**: Boko Haram claims it is behind the abduction of hundreds of schoolchildren in Nigeria on Friday[33]

- **Al Bawaba**: Why Did Boko Haram Jihadists Kidnap 300 School Kids?[34]

- **ABC News**: Boko Haram has abducted over 1,000 children, killed more than 2,000 teachers[35]

- **CNN**: UNICEF: Boko Haram has kidnapped more than 1000 children in Nigeria[36]

- **Al Jazeera**: Boko Haram claims kidnapping of hundreds of Nigerian students[37]

- **The Organization for World Peace**: 330 Students Kidnapped – Is Boko Haram Expanding?[38]

- **New York Post**: Boko Haram claims abduction of students in northern Nigeria[39]

- **Dawn**: Boko Haram claims kidnapping of hundreds of students in apparent turn in Nigerian conflict[40]

Many of these articles are from 2020, and despite so many of us pressing the conversation that boys are more affected by Boko Haram[41], the media does its best to only focus on girls. The media makes concerted efforts to erase male victims, only mentioning them when *absolutely* necessary. Some sources out there do raise awareness, but they are minor publications compared.

ABUSE

Who will cry for the little boy, lost and all alone?
Who will cry for the little boy, abandoned without his own?
Who will cry for the little boy? He cried himself to sleep.
Who will cry for the little boy? He never had for keeps.
Who will cry for the little boy? He walked the burning sand.
Who will cry for the little boy? The boy inside the man.
Who will cry for the little boy? Who knows well hurt and pain.
Who will cry for the little boy? He died and died again.
Who will cry for the little boy? A good boy he tried to be.
Who will cry for the little boy, who cries inside of me?

– Antwone Fisher

Both boys and girls experience abuse in their childhood, often by their parents. We recognize as a society that hurting children is bad, but like most things, we tend to focus on when girls are abused versus boys. This is especially true when women who've committed a crime will have their childhood cited[42] as justification for her actions as "she was abused as a child". Whereas for men, child abuse is par for the course and can never be used as an explanation for adult misconduct.

13

Simply:

Men Bad; Women Good.

Put another way:

Boys Bad; Girls Good.

Beyond the BBGG dichotomy, another challenging aspect of child abuse is how countries define abuse. Even though there are similarities, the World Health Organization (WHO) mandated a definition[43]:

> *Child abuse or abuse constitutes all forms of physical and/or emotional ill-treatment, sexual abuse, neglect or negligent treatment, or commercial or other exploitation, resulting in actual or potential harm to the children's health, survival, development, or dignity in the context of a relationship of responsibility, trust, or power.*

Even then, a good definition is elusive because of how researchers or authorities define child abuse. The challenge is how to identify when abuse occurs, from the intention of an adult to the physical signs of abuse children might have. The problem when examining an adult's motive is that one's culture or personal morals may not perceive it as harmful, even if the action negatively affects a child. Much of the literature on child abuse is based on if the adult's intentions were malicious.[44]

In this book, we will focus on the effects that happen to children, how it might alter their development into adulthood, and whether there was any ill intent behind the action. Accidents do happen, and that's not an indication of abuse, but ongoing activities without consideration of their short- or long-term consequences are abusive.

I will note here that Sexual Abuse will be discussed in greater detail in the **SEXUAL ABUSE** chapter. As you will see, the rates of Sexual Abuse compared to other forms of abuse are relatively low. Paradoxically, the **SEXUAL ABUSE** chapter takes up half the book.

Perpetrators

I had an abusive step-father who took great delight in causing me pain. He damaged me emotionally and psychologically. It took a long time to overcome. Prior to joining the Men's Movement, the experience left me biased that men were the ultimate abusers. I mean, if he was this bad towards me, how many other men are just as bad, if not worse? I hadn't really considered if females could be as abusive as him. I now understand that not only can women be abusers, but in many ways... much worse.

Now, despite what is commonly believed, most perpetrators of child abuse are, in fact: Mothers. It's not to say that fathers can't be abusers, but children are more likely to receive abuse from their mothers.

In 2020, out of 634,939 reported relationships to abuse victims, mothers as the sole perpetrator were 221,372 cases (38%). Fathers as the sole perpetrator represented 138,803 (24%). Mothers and Fathers acting together represented 20.7%. As we can see, there are other combinations of stepparents and non-parents, but these figures represent the minority of perpetrators.[45]

If it takes a village to raise a child, it takes a village to abuse one.

– Mitch Garabedian (Stanley Tucci) "Spotlight"

Table 3–14 Victims by Relationship to Their Perpetrators, 2020

Perpetrator	Victims	Reported Relationships	Reported Relationships Percent
PARENT	-	-	-
Father Only	-	138,803	23.6
Father and Nonparent	-	6,910	1.2
Mother Only	-	221,372	37.6
Mother and Nonparent	-	37,064	6.3
Two Parents of known sex	-	122,015	20.7
Three Parents of known sex	-	955	0.2
Two Parents of known sex and Nonparent	-	5,230	0.9
One or more Parents of Unknown Sex	-	1,292	0.2
Total Parents	-	**533,641**	**90.6**
NONPARENT	-	-	-
Child Daycare Provider(s)	-	2,013	0.3
Foster Parent(s)	-	1,990	0.3
Friend(s) and Neighbor(s)	-	3,961	0.7
Group Home and Residential Facility Staff	-	1,080	0.2
Legal Guardian(s)	-	1,726	0.3
Other Professional(s)	-	1,187	0.2
Relative(s)	-	32,037	5.4
Unmarried Partner(s) of Parent	-	19,370	3.3
Other(s)	-	18,966	3.2
More Than One Nonparental Perpetrator	-	2,504	0.4
Total Nonparents	-	**84,834**	**14.4**
UNKNOWN	-	**16,464**	**2.8**
National	589,141	634,939	107.8

Based on data from 50 states.

45

Several behavioral characteristics have been linked to understanding perpetrators' need to cause abuse. Parents who abuse their children are more likely to have low self-esteem, poor impulse control, and anti-social behavior. Neglectful parents may also have difficulty with life decisions such as marriage, having (more) children, or seeking/staying employed. Abusive parents often have unrealistic expectations of how to care for children. Parents will become irritated and annoyed by their children's behavior due to not living up to expectations. This can further result in being less supportive, affectionate, playful, and responsive to children's needs.[46]

As you might imagine, higher abuse rates are seen in poorer communities with high levels of unemployment and overcrowded housing. High levels of poverty often have fewer resources and amenities for families to get support or for children to have services to ensure their safety within their homes.[47]

Victims

The abuse may be brief, but the trauma lasts a lifetime.
-American Society for the Protection & Care Of Children

Most presume the overwhelming victims of Child Abuse are female. Much of the research in this area tends to identify gender only when females are the majority of victims. When victims are nearly equal, or boys are the majority, many studies will try to hide gender using gender-neutral terms. It is difficult to find studies that target boys specifically, often requiring the use of older research.

In general, the younger children are, the more likely they will suffer abuse. Children under the age of five are 74% of all victims and 25% under one.[48] Of all children who suffer abuse, 85% suffer from only one abuse, with 61% of those being neglect, 10% physical abuse, and 7.2% sexual. Of the 15% with more than one abuse type, Neglect and Physical are the most common combination.[49]

Regarding gender, reports find that 52% of child abuse victims are girls, with 48% being boys.[50] The significance of this statistic is that it is easy to say the majority are girls, which is technically true, but by a margin of 4% —this misunderstanding results in boys becoming invisible victims.

<u>Neglect</u>

Unlike physical or sexual abuse, where something is actually done, neglect is failure to do something.
-Kathleen Kendall-Tackett

We'll start with the most common form of abuse. While all forms of abuse are neglect, to one degree or another, this section will focus on just the lack of basic needs. The unfortunate thing about neglect, beyond the abuse and long-term effects, is that it doesn't get as much attention as it should. Physical and sexual abuse tend to take center stage.

Child neglect is the failure of an authority figure (i.e., parent) to provide amenities, including food, clothing, shelter, health services, safety, and proper discipline.[51] Note that I say proper discipline, as improper discipline is a form of physical or psychological abuse. In fact, not giving discipline for misconduct is a form of neglect.

Signs of neglect for children are those who are often sleepy, dirty or have poor hygiene, poorly dressed for weather conditions, wearing the same clothing often, depressed, withdrawn or anti-social, destructive behavior, substance abuse problems, poor living conditions, and inadequate medical or dental care.[52] Additional signs may include begging for food and money, and stealing.[53]

Some of these warning signs can be challenging, as children in a perfectly loving home can steal, get dirty, or wear the same thing often. So how do you differentiate between typical childhood experiences and neglect victims? Usually, it is not one thing; instead, a collection of red flags that point to neglect. For a series of behaviors to be designated neglect requires an investigation.

Neglectful parents often suffer from substance abuse or mental disorders. For instance, parents that are alcoholics will spend most of their money on alcohol rather than food for their children, causing their children to go hungry. As mentioned before, poorer families tend to be more abusive, but not all abused children come from low-income families. A well-off family can easily provide basic needs for children and their substance abuse problems. So, the most common factor of neglect in the home once finances are removed is depression amongst parents.[54]

Long-term effects of neglect can result in a lack of executive function, attention, processing speed, language, memory, and social skills. It's also been found that suffering from neglect can cause disorganized attachments and a need to control their environment, with an increase of aggressive or hyperactive behaviors which disrupts attachment to caregivers, instead replacing it with distrust. This will lead to later difficulty if forming/maintaining relationships, whether friendship or romantic.[55]

While neglect is the most common form of abuse, there is still a lack of understanding of how widespread it is. This is a problem of definitions, as countries have their own way of defining it and even parents and children define it differently. This means that while neglect may happen, some communities or cultures may not view it as abuse, and it goes misreported.[56]

More than how it is defined, there is the issue of degrees. Rarely do children suffer from one type of neglect, often suffering from several subtypes.[57] To truly understand neglect, we must analyze the various types of neglect to gain a comprehensive picture of how children suffer from the inaction of others.

Physical

Physical neglect is what we can directly see. This can be in the clothes children wears: whether they are constantly dirty, not fitting properly, or not having the proper clothes for when it rains or during cold seasons. This can also be hygiene issues, such as children looking dirty or having a foul smell. These kinds of things affect not only children's personal health but also their mental health, as the children will be laughed at and likely isolated from other children.[58]

One example of physical neglect is the case of the Collingswood Boys. In 2004, adoptive son Bruce was rummaging through garbage cans looking for food at a neighbor's home. The police were called and found a boy who was 45lbs and 4 feet tall, believed to be 7 years old. Later, Bruce was confirmed to be 19. He was not only extremely malnourished but shoeless and covered in bruises. In the home, the police found his brothers: Michael age 9 and 23lbs, Terrell age 10 and 28lbs, and Tre'Shawn age 14 and 40lbs.[59]

The adoptive parents claimed this was because of medical problems and not neglect on their part. Their church community proclaimed them model parents, taking children no one else wanted. The adoptive mother pleaded guilty and was sentenced to seven years in prison but only served a single year.

Bruce gained 100lbs within a year.

Medical

Medical Neglect is difficult to determine. This may result from parents either being ignorant of the importance of modern medicine (i.e., faith-based healing) or simply lacking insurance. Negligence doesn't necessarily require a parent to have the motive to harm their children. However, as health insurance can increase over time, it is hard to hold a parent in contempt if they cannot afford it.[60]

Lacking dental care can also be another form of medical neglect, but this is often because of costs. Dental care is for those well off as even dental insurance often requires out-of-pocket costs, which prevents many poorer families from getting their children dental care.[60]

The major concern of medical neglect is when there is actual intention not to use modern medicine to help treat preventable issues and instead rely on alternative forms due to religious or political doctrine.

Educational

Educational neglect is the failure of a caregiver to regard children's educational needs, including school attendance or preventing children's time to study. This can also include any form of homeschooling in which parents neglect to provide a standard curriculum. Failures in education can result in children being held back or expulsion from school, which can have later consequences on their livelihood.[61]

Another aspect of Educational Neglect is teachers' inability to recognize children suffering from abuse. Teachers spend a great deal of time with children outside their homes and can see indicators that might represent a bad home environment. A sudden drop in homework or test scores can indicate something going on. Parents' lack of involvement in their children's education or low aspirations is equally a cause for concern.[61]

The problem with reporting abuse seen in children's performance is that tardiness, sleepiness, hyperactivity, and delinquency can be due to problems with the school system or a terrible teacher.[61] There's a reason kids don't like school. In a future book focused on Education, it will be shown that there is a grading bias against boys. Teachers often view boys as defective girls, and males can easily be seen as just bad students rather than having negligent parents. This is an example of Educational Neglect.

Emotional

Emotional Neglect is when children don't receive affection or nurturing. This is likely caused by an emotionally unavailable parent, resulting from substance abuse issues, narcissism, or other mental health problems.[61]

Emotional Neglect can also occur if a parent has difficulty accepting children's identity or if they are disabled. Parents often yearn for their children's future, even before they're born. Failure to meet expectations can cause refusal to nurture their children. This can be especially true for Tigering Parents (or helicopter parents) who want their children to achieve academically or to do well in sports. When children achieve the level of success their parents desire, they are praised, but when they cannot live up to their standards, they are shunned.[62]

Emotional neglect can be difficult to detect, especially with Tigering parents, as children's physical needs might be met.[61]

Supervisory

Supervisory Neglect, or leaving children unsupervised, deals with children who are put in a situation at risk of physical, emotional, and psychological harm because parents are not there to help. All children are unique; some mature early, especially girls over boys, and can handle time away from an authority figure, while others cannot.

Whether children are suffering from Supervisory Neglect depends on the following[60]:

- If the children have a disability
- Lacking the ability to make judgments on own behavior
- Length of time children were left unsupervised
- Hazards in the children's environment
- Children's comfort levels during time unsupervised
- Accessibility to an authority figure for support or emergency
- Children's accessibility to doing homework or having fun
- Whether responsibilities given are age appropriate

Parents have to work to support their family. This can easily mean working long hours, especially if they live in a poorer community, work multiple jobs as they lack higher-end skills, or are a single parent. If they lack the financial means, it may prevent hiring a babysitter for the time they need. Parents may instead "employ" the oldest child by taking on babysitting, whether or not they can handle it. This means the oldest child must make sacrifices of socializing outside of school or getting homework done if there is too much home responsibility. I'm not here to judge situations in the home, only to note that if children are denied access to a caretaker and have to become adults during their formative years, it can cause difficulties later in life.[63]

A more extreme form of Supervisory Neglect is abandonment. While there are steps one can take to give children to the state, many children are abandoned in other ways that can harm children. Should children grow up beyond the abandonment, they are likely to have emotional and psychological problems later in life.

Physical

When it comes to Physical Abuse, there is a very thin line between discipline and abuse. Many cultures believe in hitting children for discipline, such as spanking. Despite the cultural differences, discipline can quickly change into abuse. Many might remark their own disciplinary punishments in childhood and that they turned out just fine, arguing that it's not abuse. In contrast, others will see any form of violence as just that: violence.

Physical abuse is violence children receive that may or may not result in physical symptoms. Unless reported by children or a 3rd party, physical abuse can easily go undetected, even if there are visible signs. Physical symptoms of abuse can consist of bruises, welts, burns, and lacerations.[64] These can be visible injuries, though children may be encouraged to wear clothing to cover signs of abuse. A more clever abuser may cause damage that normal clothing would typically conceal.

A doctor's examination will undoubtedly see external and internal injuries consistent with abuse, including damage to organs, bones, or symptoms of PTSD or Traumatic Brain Injury.[65] To avoid doctors from seeing abuse, an abuser may prevent children from going to a doctor, crossing over into *Medical Neglect*.

Physical abuse is not just a parent physically hitting children or throwing things at them. Physical abuse can also include corporal punishment, such as teachers spanking children at school[66], which still has some support, though there is limited information on how often teachers hit students. A study in 2009[67] in India's Andhra Pradesh and Telangana states that 78% of 8 years old and 34% of 15 years old were physically punished at least once. There were similar reports in Ethiopia, Viet Nam, and Peru.

Another form of physical abuse can include shaken infant syndrome, resulting in a baby's death or cause neurological problems later in life.[68]

Emotional

Emotional Abuse is the exploitation of emotions to affect children's well-being. The difficulty of Emotional Abuse is that it is quite similar to Psychological Abuse and even Wikipedia links them to the same thing.[69] Emotional Abuse is more defined as the coercive behavior of an authority figure to undermine self-confidence or alter how someone regulates their emotions. This can be seen as name-calling, shouting at them, or talking down to them to make them feel stupid.[70]

Emotional Abusers know what they have done is wrong and understand they caused the problem after the fact and may continue with emotional manipulation in begging for forgiveness. Psychological Abusers display Bipolar Disorder or Narcissistic behaviors that continue to believe they are justified in their actions or it is the fault of others.[71]

Emotional Abusers can change, Psychological Abusers won't.

Emotional abuse can come from various sources, including parents, teachers, coaches, and even other adults. It's one thing to be shouted at for doing something wrong. The lesson here becomes, you don't want to be yelled at, don't misbehave. It's another thing when the behavior is constantly used at the drop of a hat, and other methods of correcting behavior or ways of encouragement are disregarded.[72]

Emotional abuse is not a single incident but a series of events. Various forms of Emotional abuse include verbal abuse, domination, manipulation, intimidation, humiliation, threats, insults, blame, excessive criticism, isolation, and rejection.[73]

Psychological

One of the hardest things in discussing abuse is most of us who experienced it seem to go on to have healthy lives. That while yes, it was horrendous... we moved on. It's not uncommon for those who suffer and recover to look down on those who don't. This may be a defense mechanism or simply a lack of empathy.

Perhaps the most common type of psychological abuse is gaslighting. Whether to make children doubt how they perceived things or admit to doing things they didn't do.[73] This is something I can personally relate to, as my stepfather would require me to confess to his accusations, resulting in more severe punishment should I continue to deny it. I've long suspected that many of his accusations were covering up his misdeeds, to get me to confess to things he did so he wouldn't get in trouble with my mother.

Gaslighting can also be excused as humor. That the actions were not abusive because it was a prank or a joke, telling the children "just kidding" and further telling them "not to be so serious". This can undermine children's feelings.[73]

One notable example of this was the former YouTube channel FamilyOFive, in which the parents made a mess on Cody's (youngest son) bedroom floor, then accused the child of making the mess. They scolded Cody for the m and threatened punishment if he continued to deny it. Cody was in tears. Once they revealed the prank, they told him he should calm down and just laugh it off, which he wasn't able to do. Instead, he was screaming at his parents for being horrible.[74]

Psychological abusers rarely see their actions as abusive or wrong. Or, they don't feel they are the cause of the abuse that results, that the children did the bad action and therefore needs to be punished for it. No matter what the Psychological abuser does, they don't see themselves as doing wrong; they are a good person. However, an abuser may give an apology, but said apology is simply a ruse and will most often result in no change of behavior.[73]

<u>Other Types of Abuse</u>

- Covert Incest
- Parentification
- Faith-Based
- Malnourishment
- Misandry
- Factitious Disorder Imposed by Proxy
- Sibling Abuse
- Substance Abuse
- Witnessing Domestic Violence

Rates of Abuse

According to a report in the US in 2020[75]:

- **Neglect**: 76.05%
- **Physical**: 16.49%
- **Sexual**: 9.37%
- **Psychological**: 6.41%
- **Medical**: 1.99%
- **Sex Trafficking**: 0.15%
- **Other**: 5.97%

The same report logged 618,399 children suffered 720,048 abuses.[76] Of the abuses reported, less than 60,000 children were sexually abused, which doesn't compare to neglect and physical abuse (at 79.43% combined). Yet, sexual abuse garners the most attention. Understand that I, in no way, am saying sexual abuse shouldn't get attention, but how many victims go invisible because of misallocating resources based on a faulty premise?

Fatal Abuse

Abuses, such as physical and neglect, can lead to death. Other kinds, such as psychological, don't directly lead to death. Even though over time someone could die due to abuse suffered at an early age (i.e., suicide), Fatal Abuse focuses on death that occurs as a direct result of abuse.

In 2020, the total child death rate in the US from abuse was 1,750, which was a drop of 80 deaths from 2019.[77] From 2015, there was a 5% increase[78] and a near 89% increase from 1995 at 925.[79] In 2020, 68% of deaths were under 3 years of age and 46% were younger than 12 months.[77]

Exhibit 4–C Child Fatalities by Sex, 2020			
Sex	Child Population	Child Fatalities	Child Fatalities Percent	Child Fatalities Rate per 100,000 Children
Boys	29,732,915	890	60.1	2.99
Girls	28,490,819	584	39.5	2.05
Unknown	-	6	0.4	-
National	58,223,734	1,480	100.0	N/A

80

Let this table sink in for a moment: Boys are more likely to die as a result of child abuse than girls—a 60/40 split. Not to take away from girls, but this begs the question: why isn't this discussed more? Of all abuses addressed, such as pedophilia with a heavy female focus; the fact boys are more likely to die from abuse is rarely brought up.

Worst of all, the death of children is not routinely investigated, and autopsies of bodies are not always carried out. Now you might say, *"Impoverished countries have fewer resources"*, but this is also seen in more prosperous countries as well. Around the world, there is a problem in recognizing cases of infanticide. Now, if there is a reinvestigation, a child's death is likely ruled a homicide.[81]

The worldwide yearly rate of child homicide is around 95,000[82], with 77% between 15 – 19 and 23% between 0 - 14.[83] This number is probably low because of the under-reporting or lack of investigation.[84] What does this mean? There might well be even more cases of children dying because of child abuse, which falls through the cracks. This issue requires that all children's deaths be investigated with stricter protocols to determine the cause of death. I would love to believe that the total number of deaths of children due to abuse remains relatively low, but that remains unknowable unless things change.

Of course, these are statistics that one can turn a blind eye to. So let us put some faces to these numbers of boys dying because of abuse:

- Ghanson Debrosse, 3, was tortured to death by his mother. Florida DCF had run-ins with the mother in the past, including battery against the boy's father, and would threaten to throw the children at the father.[85]

- Malachi Lawson, 4, was reported missing by his mother until she confessed that she and her female partner killed her son and put him a dumpster.[86]

- Rhuah Candido, 9, was murdered by his mother and female partner after botching a gender reassignment by removing his penis in their home. They then decapitated the boy and tried to use a barbecue grill to dispose of evidence.[87]

- Jameel Penn Jr and London Williams, 1 and 2, were placed in an oven by the mother and turned it on. The mother then did a video chat with the father to show him what she had done.[88]

- Zachary Andrew Turner, 1, featured in the documentary "Dear Zachary", was murdered by his mother, who also murdered Zachary's father. She drugged the boy and took him to the ocean, where she drowned herself and the child. Zachary's grandparents on his father's side fought to gain custody of the children but failed as the courts showed bias towards the mother.[89]

- James Hutchinson, 6, was abandoned in the middle of nowhere by his mother. James had grabbed onto his mother's vehicle at the last second and was dragged off. Later, she drove back to find him with a head injury on the road. She threw the body in the river with the help of her boyfriend.[90]

- Sakurako Hagi and Kaede Hagi, 3 and 1, were locked inside a home by their mother in Osaka, Japan, for several days. A work friend who hadn't seen the mother for days went over and noticed the smell and called the police, who found both children dead.[91]

I'm sure someone out there will try the line, *"You're just focusing on women. Chris Votey is a misogynist who thinks men don't murder their children"*. Yes, I picked seven horrible cases featuring female perpetrators and didn't mention male perpetrators. Had I mentioned a male perpetrator, I feared the response would be, *"Well, of course, men are bad"*.

As discussed earlier in **Perpetrators & Victims**, mothers are more likely to be abusive than any other group, including fathers. The same is true for Fatal Abuse: mothers are more likely to kill their children. Even with all this evidence, people can quickly forget that women can be just as evil as men. So yes, I went for shock value, hoping to wake people up to reality.

Table 4–4 Child Fatalities by Relationship to Their Perpetrators, 2019

PERPETRATOR	Child Fatalities	Relationships	Relationships Percent
PARENT	-	-	-
Father Only	-	212	14.2
Father and Nonparent	-	26	1.7
Mother Only	-	435	29.2
Mother and Nonparent	-	149	10.0
Two Parents of Known Sex	-	337	22.6
Three Parents of Known Sex	-	3	0.2
Two Parents of Known Sex and Nonparent	-	25	1.7
One or More Parents of Unknown Sex	-	1	0.1
Total Parents	-	**1,188**	**79.7**
NONPARENT	-	-	-
Child Daycare Provider(s)	-	26	1.7
Foster Parent(s)	-	10	0.7
Friend(s) or Neighbor(s)	-	9	0.6
Group Home and Residential Facility Staff	-	3	0.2
Legal Guardian(s)	-	8	0.5
Other(s)	-	75	5.0
Other Professional(s)	-	36	2.4
Relative(s)	-	56	3.8
Unmarried Partner(s) of Parent	-	22	1.5
More than One Nonparental Perpetrator	-	3	0.2
Total Nonparents	-	**248**	**16.6**
UNKNOWN	-	**55**	**3.7**
National	**1,491**	**1,491**	**100.0**

Based on data from 43 states.

92

Analyzing the table, we know 60% of fatalities from child abuse are boys, and nearly 50% of perpetrators are Mothers acting alone or with a partner. This right here is why this book is so necessary, as this goes against conventional wisdom. We dare not think women capable of such an atrocity, yet the statistics state otherwise.

**When we face reality,
we can do more to help children
who die from abuse.**

Problems of Being a Male Victim

The great thing about the human brain is neuroplasty, the ability for children to heal from adverse events, so long as they are given the necessary support to recover. Should children experience abuse and get treatment before adulthood, chances are good they will go on to have a healthy life. Lacking treatment, or having a delay until adulthood, results in many problems that will be detrimental to their livelihood.[93]

The problem of being a male victim pretty much starts in our infancy. While many would claim there are no differences between males and females, there are, in fact, distinctions. Females mature faster than males by at least two years. An eight-year-old girl is as mature as a ten-year-old boy. That is until the teen years when boys surpass girls mentally. This isn't a denigration of boys; just a biological fact.[94]

At birth, boys smile less than girls and are more irritable. Males also engage in less self-comfort and less excitement. Girls appear to be less vulnerable to interactive stress. Boys are more likely to be emotionally reactive when they see their mother's face. Boys are also more likely to use facial expressions to be angry or fussy and to desire to be picked up more. What this indicates is that boys have greater difficulty with self-regulating their affective state.[95] The study I referenced does not take into consideration if boys were circumcised, which may well be significant in male brain development.

Male brains develop slower and are more susceptible to trauma than girls. Girls, from birth to maturity, handle stress better than boys[96], until male maturity when men surpass women.[97] Now in our culture, more resources are given for any trauma females endure. In contrast, boys are told to "man up" or suppress their emotions, essentially being denied the help they need in handling their trauma, which they need extra support because of slower brain development.

Studies on child abuse erase or passively mention male victims, focusing solely on female victims. Mental health professionals apply a female-centric model of victimization when addressing their male patients, resulting in failure to get the help they need.[98]

In summary, while boys and girls are about parity as victims of abuse, boys are less likely to receive help for their abuse. This results in psychological and/or emotional problems in adulthood. To which, their behavior is attributed to Toxic Masculinity or the fault of testosterone. Ironic, isn't it? Females dislike the stigma that their emotions are attributed to their hormones but have no problem equating unacceptable male behavior to their hormones.

Later Effects

It's hard to pinpoint the direct result of child abuse. Everyone reacts differently to their abuse, with some living a healthy life and not experiencing any problems. Some are unaware they are suffering, and others attribute their suffering as a normal part of life. When discussing the later effects of child abuse, one will note the lack of direct correlation, or rather "Correlation does not imply causation". The best we can do is show patterns of behaviors and hypothesize what effects one is most likely to have based on one of the following reasons: health-harming behaviors, social detriments of health, and neurological genetic pathways.[99]

Any abuse endured generates some negative aspects in adult life, but studies show that the more trauma and abuse children experience, the more complications they have in later life. Complications include low life potential, risky health behavior, premature death, and chronic conditions.[100] I myself have suffered a great many abuses at the hands of my step-father and look at the results of my life, both good and bad. I am left wondering how much of what I've endured is life choices or the abuse I suffered. How might my life been changed had I not been a victim of childhood abuse?

The following are the likelihoods of what one is likely to suffer in adulthood, whether from one type of abuse to several. These are compared to children who suffered no abuse at all:

- 4 times more likely to develop diabetes[101]
- Up to 20 years reduce life expectancy[102]
- 6 times more likely to receive treatment for mental illness[103]
- More likely to commit domestic violence[104]
- 1.6 times more likely to have bone fractures[105]
- 7 times to be an active smoker[106]
- 18 times to be an alcoholic[107]
- 4 times more likely to have COPD[108]

Telomeres

"One thing you can't hide is when you're crippled inside."
-John Lennon

What are Telomeres, and how do they relate to child abuse?

I will start by saying that this changes everything we know about what it means to be human. A quick explanation is to imagine your DNA as a shoelace. Telomeres would be the hard plastic at the end of the lace (called an aglet) to prevent fraying. A better explanation is that telomeres are gibberish DNA code that protects DNA during cell division. Each time a cell divides, the telomere shrinks.[109] Most cells divide once a day for about 60 days.[110] At the end of the 60 days, cells no longer divide as the telomeres are too short (or gone), but many cells still carry out their function (known as Senescence).

This explains why our bodies age. As our cells stop dividing, our bodies begin to fail, or rather because the rate of cell replacement decreases, the body doesn't rejuvenate. An example would be wrinkles.

The shrinking of telomeres is how we measure the biological age of an organism.[111] The less telomeres you have, the older you are on a genetic level. This means a greater likelihood of medical problems associated with old age, such as dementia, heart disease, Alzheimer's, and many other things. Now telomere shrinking is a natural function of our body, but other things can cause telomeres to shrink. Such as smoking, a poor diet, or even stress.[112]

And what is more stressful than abuse itself?

No matter the type of abuse, it is bad across the board. As children suffer abuse, it causes their telomeres to shrink. Put this into perspective: if telomeres indicate our actual age and child abuse can cause our telomeres to shrink[113], then that means that those who suffer abuse are technically older than their non-abused peers.

Child abuse affects us physically, psychologically, and genetically. In the first part of **Later Effects**, I theorized it might be lifestyle choices that lead to those who suffer later effects, but shrinking telomeres may well explain many effects seen in adulthood. At birth, you might be genetically predisposed to have heart issues later in life, and with the premature reduction of telomeres, you may experience those issues earlier in life.

Only in the last few years has there been a surge of studies to understand telomeres and explore whether they can be repaired so that we might live a longer, healthier life despite any life events that cause drastic shrinking. So far, the studies suggest that a healthy diet and exercise[114] may be the key, as well as a good night's rest.[115]

As I mentioned, we still know very little about telomeres, especially how stress affects the length. What is known is that those who have suffered child abuse have shorter telomeres and that a drastic shortening results in "old age" health problems before reaching old age. And if boys are less likely to get help for their abuse, it might well explain why men are more likely to die at an earlier age than women or more susceptible to heart disease.

CHILD LABOR

If we can't begin to agree on fundamentals, such as the elimination of the most abusive forms of child labour, then we really are not ready to march forward into the future.

-Alexis Herman

When discussing child labor, the prostitution of little girls is immediately brought up. And as bad as prostitution is for girls, it overshadows how boys are affected by child labor. While boys are also affected by the sex trade industry (as discussed in **SEX TRAFFICKING**), there is much more to the conversation than sex; about how boys are used as cheap labor. This section will focus on the non-sexual aspects of Child Labor.

It's important to distinguish between **Child Labor** and **Child Work**. Child Labor is essentially slavery, whereas Child Work teaches life skills, such as responsibility, as a part of growing up. The critical difference is how important education is concerning their work responsibilities. Child laborers rarely go to school, hindering their ability to mature and develop naturally into adulthood.

I acknowledge that many products I use are likely products produced by child labor, and my judgment of it might make me seem like a hypocrite. I won't make an excuse for that, but I will state that it is not always easy to know which products are made by children, as corporations can lie. I want all child labor eliminated in favor of child work, in which education is the most essential aspect, and they still have access to a childhood. I take the opinion that one is not truly mature enough to enter the adult world until the age of 18, and one is not an adult until they're 21.

One challenge to this issue is economics; countries rely upon child labor as it offers distinct advantages over adult labor. Corporations can offer products at reduced prices thanks to employing children, and switching to adult laborers will increase costs and could put the company under.

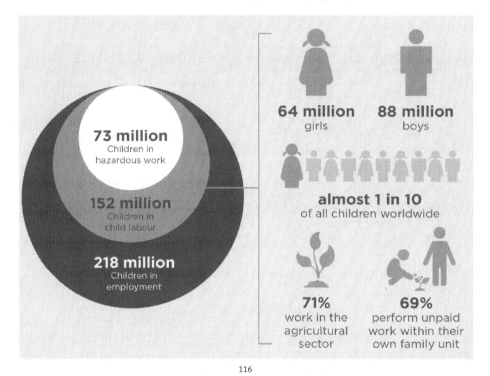

64 million girls

88 million boys

almost 1 in 10 of all children worldwide

71% work in the agricultural sector

69% perform unpaid work within their own family unit

73 million Children in hazardous work

152 million Children in child labour

218 million Children in employment

116

Another challenge is children choosing to work. Those choosing work will start part-time and still attend school but eventually drop out. Reasons for dropping out include providing for their family and being more respected for their work efforts than academic achievements. This may come from added pressure from families, as some parents feel it is a child's duty to serve the family above their own needs.[117]

Another reason for choosing work over schooling may be that going to school becomes too costly. Some families desire children to go to school, but supplies such as clothing, books, and transportation cost money, even if the school itself is free. This is not only a tragedy but continues the cycle of poverty as being able to read, write, and do arithmetic, along with critical thinking, is vital for everyone to prosper. Many children lack most, if not all, of these skills when they work.

Prevalence

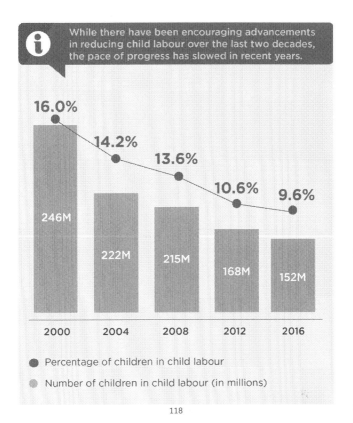

While there have been encouraging advancements in reducing child labour over the last two decades, the pace of progress has slowed in recent years.

16.0%
14.2%
13.6%
10.6%
9.6%

246M
222M
215M
168M
152M

2000   2004   2008   2012   2016

● Percentage of children in child labour
● Number of children in child labour (in millions)

118

Unfortunately, Child Labor is still quite prevalent, as it is estimated that 1-in-10 children worldwide engage in child labor. This equals about 160 million children. Some regions can be as low as 1-in-20 or as high as 50%. Generally, the more impoverished a nation is, the greater likelihood of child labor. Fortunately, the rate of Child labor has declined since 2000, and we may see a time when this is no longer an issue. Based on the graph above, there has been a 38% decrease over 16 years, averaging a 2% per year. At this rate, it very well could be at 10 million children in 80 years.[118]

A report in 2013 sampled 253,300 Child laborers (which included hazardous work) and found that 61% were boys. Of all children, 62% were between the ages of 5 – 14.[119] Another report in 2019 estimates that 152 million children are involved in child labor, with nearly half in hazardous work. Boys make up 58% of all children engaged in child labor.[120]

History

"There can be no keener revelation of a society's soul than the way in which it treats its children."
-Nelson Mandela

When we think of Child Labor, we think of it as a problem concerning the 3rd world. Many forget that once upon a time, nations of the first world had issues with Child Labor, which required reform to abolish. Places such as the United States and the United Kingdom once treated workers as 3rd world countries do today, such as poor working conditions and no benefits. Undervaluing employees was done under the belief that the lower cost for workers, the more profit overall.

Understanding the history of child labor in first-world nations can give us insights into the mindset of children and their employers today. One resource, groundbreaking for its time, is the Sadler Report[121], which interviewed children in the 1800's about what they endured, from dangerous work to savage beatings for not keeping up with the quotas.

During the Industrial Revolution, employers would hire mothers and children together, as fathers already had jobs. Children were often hired for factories and mines, as they could more easily access areas of machinery that adults could not.[122]

In a 1900 census, it was estimated that 1.8 million children ages 10 – 15 were employed, making up 18% of the total workforce in the US. The rates of children working increased every decade until World War 2, with 60% of child workers in agriculture by the 1910's.[122]

Like today's children, many preferred work over school. This was because of the respect they received in their home for making money. It was also because they didn't enjoy schoolwork, and back then it was legal for teachers to utilize corporal punishment.[122]

Beyond factory work and mining, other kinds of jobs children performed were selling newspapers on street corners, breaking up coal, and chimney sweeping. Usually, these jobs would not pay the children but would provide room and board. If children were paid, it would be 10% of what an adult would earn for the same work.[123]

Businesses could treat children as slaves, abusing them as they saw fit. Adults were difficult to control as they might fight back if provoked, but adults are bigger than children, so they were easier to manipulate. Businesses could keep children locked up and force them to work long hours. In their minds, they were doing the children a favor, as they'd otherwise be on the streets starving. During the Industrial Revolution, there were few government regulations and oversight, so companies could treat their workers however they wanted. This meant that injury was a certainty and that places like mines could have inadequate ventilation, leading to medical issues.[123]

Ending child labor in the US was a concerted effort. The most significant opposition was, of course, businesses wanting cheap labor. Not to mention the families that needed the income their children could bring home. Ironically, the Great Depression proved to be a saving grace for children. Jobs became scarce for adults, and since children were paid substantially less, they were more likely to have jobs. President Franklin Delano Roosevelt's New Deal focused on giving out-of-work adults jobs through federal oversight.[124]

The Fair Labor Standards Act was passed in 1938, which put limitations on minimum wage and how many hours an employee could work, including restrictions on child labor. That wasn't the first attempt at limiting child labor.[123] In 1916, Congress passed the Keating-Owns Act, which set children under 14 unable to work in factories and under 16 unable to work over eight hours in a mine. Unfortunately, the US Supreme Court ruled the act unconstitutional.[125]

Of course, having laws and enforcing laws are two different things. Ending child labor required technological developments, such as improved machinery replacing the repetitive tasks done by children. Besides technology, states mandated more years of schooling as a prerequisite to holding a job, lengthening the school year, and enforcing truancy laws.[124]

Types of Labor

Fifty-nine percent of child labor is in agriculture, followed by 32% in the service industry, 7% in the industrial sector, and 7% in domestic work.[126] Despite the attention it gets, Child Sex Labor (or Child Trafficking) represents a small minority of overall child labor.[127]

There is an extensive range of labor by children throughout the world. This is a short list of the most commonly produced products by children[128]:

Alcohol, Amber, Bamboo, Bananas, Beans, Beef, Blueberries, Brazil nuts, Bricks, Carpets, Carpets, Cashews, Cattle, Ceramics, Charcoal, Chestnuts, Coal, Cobalt, Cocoa, Coffee, Copper, Corn, Cotton, Diamonds, Electronics, Emeralds, Fish, Footwear, Furniture, Garlic, Garments, Glass, Gold, Granite, Grapes, Hogs, Jute, Leather, Limestone, Matches, Olives, Peanuts, Pineapples, Poppies, Poultry, Pyrotechnics, Rice, Rubber, Rubies, Salt, Sapphires, Sesame, Sheep, Shrimp, Silk, Silver, Soap, Soy, Sports Equipment, Strawberries, Sugarcane, Sunflowers, Tantalum, Tea, Textiles, Timber, Tin, Tobacco, Tomatoes, Tungsten, Vanilla, and Zinc.

Forced Labor

When my mother died I was very young,
and my father sold me while yet my tongue
could scarcely cry "Weep! Weep! Weep! Weep!",
so your chimneys I sweep and in soot I sleep.

-William Blake

Forced Labor is characterized by work through coercion. The coercion can be during job recruitment, to keep the job, or maintain a level of performance. An estimate in 2016 found that 4.3 million children were in Forced Labor. Of that, 1 million were in commercial sexual exploitation, with the remaining 3.3 million in other kinds of labor. The number may very well be higher than reported as the use of forced labor is often illicit, and measures are taken to keep it hidden.[129]

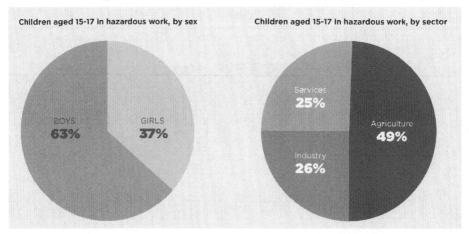

130

Hazardous Work

While many jobs have a level of danger, hazardous jobs are those with a higher degree of danger, requiring safety policies to reduce injury or death. There are few to no policies regarding Child Hazardous Work, as children are expected to perform no matter what. Because of the lack of safety, children face health issues that can interfere with the development of education, physical and psychological well-being, and social skill.[131]

A recent report found that 73 million children are involved in hazardous work, with 63% being boys. About half of all dangerous work by children are in the agriculture sector.[130]

Dangers

Child labor robs boys and girls of their childhood. It does this by not only exposing children to dangerous environments but also to limited education. Being worker drones and not seen as children, they will lack mental and social growth and easily be exploited for sexual and economic work throughout childhood and adulthood.

Of course, getting paid is an essential aspect of working. A child's wages are often used against them, whether as a means of coercion, replacing broken items, or even being late for work. Most times, they don't need a reason to take it, they just do it and there is nothing a child worker can do about it.[132]

A significant danger concerning the workplace is violence. Violence in the home can lead children to run away and wind up in child labor. Since runaway children don't have a safe haven to return to, they can easily be exploited by their employers, which results in forced labor, recruitment by gangs, labor/sex trafficking, or other exploitation. Employers can also use violence to coerce children to work, but children may receive attacks from co-workers. Older children are more likely to be abused by an employer than younger children, which causes older children to be violent towards younger co-workers.[133]

Chemical exposure is another thing to consider. Many jobs require the use of chemicals, and children are rarely informed of their dangers. Child laborers can be exposed to pesticides on crops after spaying and be absorbed into their clothing or pollute drinking water. Other chemicals can be mercury for gold mining and diesel fumes from generators.[134]

These brutal environments, hazardous working conditions, and abusive employers and co-workers can lead children to suffer from psychological trauma, including anxiety, stress disorders, and depression. Given that there is no regulation or some form of health insurance, this will lead children to escape through drugs, which will cause more suffering and decrease their life expectancy.[135]

Other dangers not so apparent are working in stationary and/or confined spaces for long periods, poor lighting that can affect vision, poor ventilation and mold exposure that can damage the lungs, and crowded environments that can easily spread disease.[136]

There are a wide range of injuries and other medical issues that result from unsafe work environments, including[137]:

- Muscular Deformities
- Respiratory Infections
- Sore Throat
- Skin Rashes
- Cancer
- Brain Damage

United States

While the US has a history with Child Labor and eventually made laws to protect children, it doesn't mean that it is no longer practiced in the US. The US continues using Child Labor, and those children face many dangers mentioned in this section.

Most illegal workers come to the US hoping to make money to survive and send home. Since they are in the US illegally and desperate for any amount of money, it is too easy for businesses to force them to live and work in deplorable conditions and to justify any reason to give them a small wage.[138]

The reason for such small wages is due to expenses being deducted from their pay, such as rent, drugs, equipment use, or anything else perpetrators can think up to justify giving a minimal wage. And not talking about the US Minimum Wage guaranteed to citizens; we're talking about illegals earning $1 USD a day.[138]

There are over two million farms in the US. It is estimated that there are 2.5 million laborers, with 2 million being males. It's not so easily discernable which are forced laborers or not, but it's believed that of the migrant workers, up to 90% are males, with 75% being boys transported from Mexico. Rather interesting, Latin American farm workers in the US nearly match the number of African slaves working on US farms in the 1850s.[139]

The threat of deportation often keeps boys in line, but also threats and acts of physical violence, psychological torture, and rape. They must adhere to strict rules, and any slight infraction can dole out the most severe punishments.[138]

They are exposed to poisons and pesticides at a rate of five times more than any other industry with no means of safety gear, causing permanent injury, disability, and death. Worse is that a large percentage live without running water and adequate shelter and are often forced to work and sleep in contaminated clothing.[138] Other industries beyond farming that use slave labor include restaurants, nursing homes, private homes, construction sites, and factories.[140]

Education

We will not end child labour until every child is in school, and we will not succeed in ensuring every child is in school until we eradicate child labour.

– Kailash Satyarthi

Many across the world place importance on employment over education. Some boys can combine a part-time job with an education, at least at first, but due to demands placed on them, they eventually drop their education to work full time.[141] Demands from family isn't always the reason for dropping out of school, as schools can be inadequate to educate children due to a lack of funding. Schools can also demoralize children, resorting to physical or psychological abuse at the hands of incompetent teachers.[142]

Another reason for dropping out of school is the high costs for attending school. Places like Panama can provide free public education but require families to buy books and supplies and arrange transportation. If a family cannot pay these costs, children cannot attend school.[143]

Entering the workforce early in life can develop work-related skills, whether they can remain in that field or bounce around from jobs as they open and others close. On the one hand, entering the workforce seems more beneficial than spending time in school. However, there is a limitation on how much one can earn when lacking an education. Then again, if one doesn't have the financial means to go to college, then doing well in education seems to be a moot point. Except that the companies that will hire children will often only hire children, which means workers can age out their job.[144]

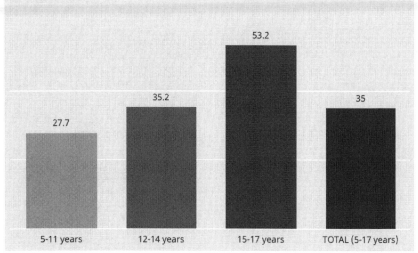

Percentage of children aged 5 to 17 years in child labour not attending school, by age

145

Children in child labour and attending school

78.3 million

Children in child labour and NOT attending school

36.1 million

146

Prevention

Perhaps the one thing that has helped the reduction of child labor more than anything else is technology. Technology replaces children's productivity with more efficient automation, making children obsolete. While this sounds like a perfect solution, it has two fundamental flaws.

1. Modern technology leads to the unemployment of workers unqualified for other vocations.

2. Other businesses that cannot afford new technology will hire children to compete.

As remarkable as technology is at cutting back child labor, it requires additional solutions to end it.

Legal Reform is the forefront of child labor. Many groups are pushing governments to enact policies to ban the use of child labor. Of course, just making a law is not enough to prevent the use of child labor. Agencies within a country must be tasked to enforce their laws.[147]

Country leaders have stated an interest in helping, but there is still slowness in adoption because of economic shocks. Many corporations rely on cheap labor, and the government tolerates the practice as jobs bring economic boosts. Thus, in order to prevent child labor, these countries must find ways of dealing with poverty and unemployment so children are not needed to work. Unfortunately, every country's needs are unique, which requires different solutions. Some solutions that have been suggested include: health insurance, support services, family leave, and accessible childcare.[148]

Education is perhaps the most crucial in the efforts to eliminate child labor. Of the 650 million primary school-age children in the world, about 40% cannot read or write, even though many have spent a few years in school. Making education a priority is a method of reducing poverty.[149]

For the rest of us, try not to buy products made from child labor. Unfortunately, that is easier said than done. Many products today are deemed necessary for daily life in the first world. And there are no reliable means to discern whether a product is the byproduct of child labor. More than that, companies do their best to hide their use of child labor and have so many subsidiaries that you may try to avoid a company and still be using one of their products without realizing it. Hopefully, trying to be mindful consumers, we can boycott companies of child labor so that if they desire to keep our business, said companies will use adults labor only.[150]

CHILD SOLDIERS

They who use children to fight their wars have lost their future.
-Christopher D. Votey

We hear about groups around the world that are anti-peace, doing whatever they want because no one will stop them. The primary focus for many is that men perpetrate these atrocities. And they're right. But there is a tiny caveat to consider: many of these men were once child soldiers who were abducted and coerced into fighting a war. Through propaganda, these children eventually became true believers.

I will start by saying that there are children who volunteer for an army and those who are kidnapped. While children volunteer via recruiters, these children shouldn't be considered voluntary, as they don't understand the full implications of their decisions, and their recruiters will also lie. Moreover, once they're in, they can't just leave. For those reasons, I treat forced and voluntary children as the same, children coerced into war.[151]

One might expect it more sensible to recruit adults to make an effective military. Children, however, are proven more invaluable. Reasons include: being easy to capture, easier to manipulate, eat little food, don't get paid, lack a developed sense of fear, and those in a position of power can turn them into sexual slaves.[152]

Understand that this section does not dismiss the human rights violations carried out by soldiers, even if they were recruited as children. Nor is this "throw the book at them" type of charge. This section points out a big problem in this world that, like so many others mentioned in this book, is largely ignored. Perhaps if more action was taken, there might be less death in this world.

Prevalence

In the entirety of human history, militaries worldwide have used children as soldiers. Today, roughly 40% of the world's arms organizations utilize child soldiers.[153] From 2012 – 2019, the use of child soldiers increased by 159%[154], with an estimate of 300,000 children serving in state or rebel militaries (though that is considered a low estimate), with 60% being boys.[155] Reasons for the recent surge of child soldiers and the use of girl soldiers (or even younger boys) are the proliferation of lighter weapons and the increasing rate of child poverty.[156]

As a result of more children being used, the focus on child soldiers has shifted from primarily a boy problem to now a girl problem. My 60% reference comes from the UN report titled *"4 out of 10 Child Soldiers Are Girls"*. The UN does its best to report on how females are mistreated throughout the world, meaning that the plight of males is largely ignored.

Painting what is otherwise a child issue as a female problem results in everyone wanting to engage in prevention methods. Many assume that a girl's role is entirely sexual and thus needs immediate attention. They fail to understand that in insurgent groups, boys and girls do various tasks, including: fighting, intelligence gathering, portering, messengers, cooking, and other general jobs, including "sex work". Yes, both boys and girls can be raped.[157] Rape is often frown upon in these militaries, but it doesn't stop it from happening.

In 2010, the US released a report under the Child Soldier Prevent Act (now called the "CSPA list") and found that six countries make use of child soldiers. This list limits military aid to countries that use child soldiers within their country.[158] A report in 2021 listed 15 nations, including for the first time a NATO member, Turkey. Those countries are: Afghanistan, Burma, the Democratic Republic of Congo, Iran, Iraq, Libya, Mali, Nigeria, Pakistan, Somalia, South Sudan, Syria, Turkey, Venezuela, and Yemen.[159]

It is wonderful the US is taking steps to combat this problem, or so it would seem. The CSPA gives the President of the United States the authority to grant waivers. Waivers are granted to countries that use child soldiers if it is determined that doingso serves "national interests," reinstating some or all military aid. Both Barack Obama and Donald Trump have issued waivers for countries that employed (or have within their border) child soldiers between 2010 - 2020. Countries on the CSPA list with a partial or full waiver are: Afghanistan, Cameroon, Congo, Iraq, Libya, Nigeria, Somalia, South Sudan, and Yemen.[160] As a result, more than $4 billion has been provided to various countries that are on the prohibited list.[161]

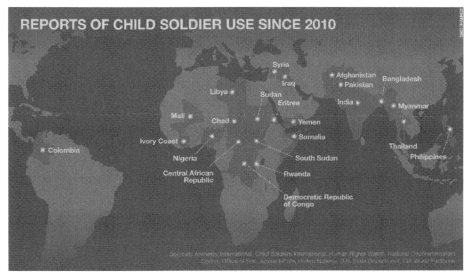

162

Impact

The impact on children actually starts before recruitment. Children growing up in poverty are more likely to be recruited into militaries, whether voluntary or forced. Child volunteers may feel it is a far better life than to be in the fields or on the streets begging. The promise of food and a place to sleep is a powerful incentive when you lack both. Unfortunately, what they're told is far from the truth.

Another reason for child volunteers is the lack of schooling. Often schools get destroyed by war, or schools are repurposed as barracks for the military. Armed conflict denies an education to children, which will cause children to join the military. If a school remains open, it is visited by recruiters who spread propaganda and misinformation.[163]

Child soldiers who survive have a more challenging time healing from the ravages of war. We must remember one of the key differences between an adult and a child is that adults have fully developed brains. An adult brain is better equipped to handle stress, while a child's brain is not. Child soldiers deal with stress, exposure to combat, shelling, acts of abuse, torture, rape, watching the death of friends, being held in detention, insufficient care, lack of safe drinking water and food, and inadequate shelter.[164]

The lifelong impact of the severe war conditions and overall maltreatment of children can leave deep mental scars. Their superiors will train in cruel ways to indoctrinate them so children can kill enemies without remorse.[165] In order to encourage children to follow orders, children are given drugs to desensitize them to the atrocities they conduct or witness.[166]

Fortunately, some Child Soldiers are rescued... others escape and hope not to get caught. Child soldiers who flee are often arrested for desertion, tried before a court, and sentenced to prison.[167] Whether they escape or remain in service for the rest of their lives, the number of psychological problems include: post-traumatic stress disorder, depression, anxiety, substance abuse, suicidal behavior, social withdrawal, low self-esteem, loss of trust, excessive guilt, hostility, and aggression.[168]

Child soldiers returning to society can be met with animosity. They are looked down upon for what they were forced to do, almost like they had a choice. Child soldiers forever live with the trauma and war crimes, which complicates reintegration into society. This stigmatization, whether of family, peers, or themselves, can cause former child soldiers to detach from society and end up rejoining the military.[169]

If children do find a stable home, education can be challenging. Their time spent in the military meant not receiving a proper education. Moreover, their response to the abuses they suffered can cause them to stop developing mentally. In many ways, whatever age they were when joining the military, they remain at that point or possibly even regress. This can lead to a lack of confidence in schoolwork, especially in trying to catch up to companions, or put into remedial classes. These children are likely to drop out.[170]

Prevention

Preventing children from being used as soldiers is not a straightforward task. It generally starts with poverty, and we need to change the living standards of these countries. Children need to be children and to develop at a normal rate to become healthy adults. Unfortunately, people will always fight, and there is collateral damage resulting in the impoverishment of civilians.

Short of changing the wellness of countries, some steps can be taken to ensure children are not recruited/kidnapped. Perhaps the most obvious is for first-world governments to stop supporting countries with child soldiers. Some countries depend on the support they receive from other nations. Of course, it is not as simple as that, and the need to provide continued support for these countries deals with a lot of politics. However, said countries have less incentive to make changes if we keep giving them waivers. Even then, many of these militaries are outside government control, and many end up tolerating the practice. Why change your conduct if you're rewarded either way?

Several organizations are in place doing their best in preventive measures. Mostly they are raising awareness and getting celebrities involved. Others are trying to rehabilitate former child soldiers to reintegrate into society, so they don't rejoin militaries and repeat the horrors done to them to other children. And some organizations are attempting to educate children in poverty-stricken areas for a chance to have a purpose in life.[171]

I know I paint a rather bleak picture of the prevention of child soldiers, but I want to give credit to the efforts in place. Without those organizations mentioned above, things would be much worse today. Countries that once ago used child soldiers no longer do so. In fact, utilizing children as soldiers is now considered a war crime, and a few people have been convicted for using child soldiers.[172]

Perhaps it is just a matter of time before this problem is resolved, but it worries me that the problem has gotten worse in the last decade. Now, more focus is put on girls, and the empathy given for them as soldiers has been non-existent throughout history for boys. That is very worrisome.

CHILD GROOMS

Child Marriage is a marriage before the age of 18. The United Nations Human Rights Council identifies it as *'a harmful practice that violates, abuses and impairs human rights'*.[173]

Hearing the term Child Marriage, one is likely to think of the barbaric practice of marrying girls off to men... essentially rape. Unfortunately, many cultures today engage in this practice. You may be unaware that boys are also forcibly married to girls their age, younger girls, or adult women. As with Child Brides, Child Grooms are deeply rooted in religious traditions. Many places that practice this rite have laws that make it illegal, although most don't enforce it.

Only in the last few decades has there been an acknowledgment that boys marry young, even though actual reports have been limited. However, it was believed that because countries are patriarchal societies; boys benefited from early marriages.[174] To generate a report without proper investigation is nothing more than political bias that girls have it worse. The blatant intolerance of researchers caused organizations and programs that help child brides to not categorize boys as being affected by child marriage.[175] A full examination in the last few years shows boys are negatively impacted.[176]

This chapter will reveal the actual benefits and disadvantages to boys, from lacking agency, being unprepared, and dropping out of school to raise their family.

Prevalence

In 2019, UNICEF underwent an in-depth analysis of child grooms for the first time ever. The report stated that 115 million men worldwide were married before 18, with 23 million (20%) married before 15. In comparison, 765 million women were married before the age of 18, making up nearly 90% of child marriages.[177]

Child Grooms are most prevalent in sub-Saharan Africa, Latin America, Caribbeans, South Asia, East Asia, and the Pacific.[178] Central African Republic has the highest prevalence of child grooms at 28%, with Nicaragua and Madagascar at 19% and 13%, respectively.[177]

Region/Country grouping	Percentage of males aged 20–24 years who were first married or in union before age 18	Range of values	Percentage of regional male population with data
Latin America and Caribbean (n = 9)	8.3%	1.6–19.4%	20.5%
East Asia and Pacific (n = 15)	5.9%	0.0–12.3%	20.8%
Eastern and Southern Africa (n = 17)	5.0%	0.6–12.9%	77.0%
South Asia (n = 6)	4.3%	1.0–10.3%	99.1%
West and Central Africa (n = 23)	4.0%	0.6–27.9%	99.9%
Eastern Europe and Central Asia (n = 10)	1.8%	0.1–3.8%	23.1%
Middle East and North Africa (n = 2)	0.2%	0.2–0.6%	22.3%
Western Europe (n = 0)	n/a	n/a	0.0%
North America (n = 0)	n/a	n/a	0.0%
Least developed countries (n = 41)	**5.4%**	**0.0–27.9%**	**89.8%**
Total (n = 82)	**4.5%**	**0.0–27.9%**	**51.4%**

179

In the UK, child grooms account for 20% of forced marriages but are believed to be a much higher rate. Unfortunately, due to the lack of awareness of male victims, there are minimal resources available on the true prevalence.[180]

The world looks to boys as the reason Child Brides exist. A data collector stated:

"There is also a need to focus on young boys and to convince them not to marry before 21 years. If boys agree to marry only when they are 21, then young girls will not get proposals from them till they are of the legal age. This will automatically raise the age at marriage."[181]

This is a limited understanding of the problem, but advocates against child brides honestly believe boys are ultimately responsible. They fail to take into account the social pressures boys have. It's not as simple as blaming an entire gender; instead, you must convince various cultures to change.

Age

The age range varies across different countries, but generally boys between 6 – 8 are promised to be married, and by 13 – 15 is when the bride moves into the groom's home. The initial promise is somewhat comparable to engagement in western societies, but this is treated more as a first marriage, with the second marriage involving co-habitation and consummation. The time between these ceremonies (in Nepal called Saadhi and Gauna, respectively) can be from 1 to 8 years.[182]

In some instance, there is no first or second marriage, but a single marriage at a young age.[183]

Laws

Many countries have laws about the age of marriage, often at 18+. In some countries, it is 20[184], but parental permission may allow males to get married at 18.[185] People who engage in child marriage are breaking the law, but it continues to be done as these laws are rarely enforced. Local leaders often adhere to local traditions and religious rites and may, in fact, take part in the practice of forced marriages.

Whom & When

As mentioned before, researchers believed due to patriarchal societies, child grooms had full agency on if they would marry, to whom they would marry, and when they would marry. New evidence shows this is not the case.[186]

While cultures require a boy's consent to marry, it is assumed that he will do it out of familial/religious obligation. Any reluctance by a boy is met with pressure and/or coercion to follow the tradition. Boys themselves have stated they felt they had no choice but to consent. It is the parents where the decision-making power lies, from whom it will be to when he will do it.

A boy's lack of agency is at odds with the notions of male privilege in these societies. Instead of privilege, he must do as his family wants and not have the right to choose for himself. This is not to say that males don't enjoy more privileges in these societies than girls do, but it is not a zero-sum game that males have all the privileges and girls have none. In many ways, males are not unlike girls, as they both lack agency when deciding their futures. These cultures put a lot of stock into marriage, and boys grow up wanting to get married. However, boys want to get married, but only when they are ready (often finishing school). Boys desire to marry who they choose rather than their bride being selected by their family.

Interesting is the response of religious leaders. They give rise that boys are of full agency and can decline should they choose. A boy himself is at fault if he marries young and is fully aware of its effects and the law. As a result, there is no such thing as forced marriage, and a child is weak if they feel pressured by their family to do it.[187] Yet, religious leaders also state that to be a good man, one must follow the rules, religion, caste, and accept decisions made by parents, and respect all elders. To that end, they should also marry who their parents pick out.[188]

So boys have the full agency to not get married and are weak for agreeing to it when it is not their wish, but to be a respectable member of their community and religion, they must do as their parents choose for them. Talk about contradictions... you are free to make choices as long as you make the choice we want you to.

Forced Responsibilities

Once a boy is married, he is required to take on the full responsibilities of marriage. They are the head of their household and are expected to take care of their family. Of course, boys are given no preparation or instruction; they are just expected to know what to do. In this way, a boy lives with the privilege of his new status and the oppression of his situation. He will live with his family and get help, though that doesn't mean it will be the best advice.

What makes this especially hard is that his dreams or goals are put on hold (likely indefinitely) so he can find work. This often means leaving school to work, especially if he must migrate. [183] This leads to depression and anger that their dreams were stripped from them.[189] The best way he can provide for his family is to finish schooling and get a higher education, leading to a higher-paying job. Instead, he will get an entry-level job that will pay little, leaving his family in poverty.

<u>Reasons for Marriage</u>

Traditions are a big part of why boys feel they must get married. After all, his parents married young, and his grandparents, and his great-grandparents, and great great great... the tradition goes a long way back. So who is he to break the tradition now? In essence, unless they want to be ostracized from their family and community for breaking tradition, they, too, must adhere.

Assets

In many cultures, women have no access to family assets should the patriarch die. The only way they (and any daughters they have) can be supported is if a male heir is married and has a male heir. A mother won't wait for her son to marry when he desires it, as he could die before his would-be marriage. Instead, she will arrange for him to be married as soon as she can to ensure her family's future.[190]

Family & Religion

Family is a crucial factor in our lives. For those we love, we will do anything to support and protect them. They care for us; the least we can do is give back when necessary. For child brides and grooms, family is often the reason for marriages. Without your family, one has no future in many of these cultures.

Religion and family are intertwined in many cultures. As children follow their parents' religion, giving to their family and faith bestows significant benefits in their local community. One essential link is the belief in an afterlife.[188] Grandparents (or dying parents) feel they won't be allowed into heaven unless their boys marry. This puts pressure on boys not wishing to disappoint their family or betray their religion, despite their reservations.[189]

Even if boys disobey family wishes, they are still met by religious expectations as to why they didn't honor their family wishes. It's not just their family they feel pressure from, but all aspects of their local community.

Poverty

Impoverished families may be unable to support their children and push them to get married to get them out of the house. They may also push for their child to get married at a much younger age to offset the cost of a dowry (money a family pays to the bride's family).[183]

Another way poverty affects child grooms is family-run businesses. A boy getting married may add to help with household chores as free labor. Bringing a bride into the home and having children will help the family in the years to come.[191]

Ironically, pushing boys to marry leads them to drop out of school, which denies them access to higher-earning jobs. Child marriages continue the cycle of poverty that if families waited for boys to be financially ready or more mature, they could break the cycle of poverty and improve their life-styles through the success of their children.[181]

Sex

Teenagers have sex. This is true across the world. And sometimes, this results in pregnancy. A pregnancy in patriarchal societies can bring shame to a family, both for males and females. Parents may insist on child marriage if a pregnancy results to hide the pre-marital indiscretion. Child marriage can also be a preemptive measure if suspected that teen pregnancy could happen.[191]

Another unfortunate reason is if the parents of a boy know or suspect their child is gay. They fear the shame of their child not marrying and will arrange for them to get married to hide what they perceive as an embarrassment.[192]

Domestic Violence

In fairness, child brides and child grooms face different challenges. Child brides face pregnancy in their teens,[193] causing them to drop out of school and live with the groom's family, raising the children along with other domestic responsibilities. They also face being victims of family violence.

An unfortunate result of child grooms is the creation of mental health problems in giving up their hopes and dreams by being coerced into marrying. They have to work dead-end jobs with little chance of advancement. They're likely unable to read and write. And for the promise of better pay, migrate to a country unable to speak the local language. This leads to depression. And since they are boys forced to be adults, they lack the means to handle their stress. Worse, they live in a society where admitting weakness makes you less of a man. All of this is a perfect recipe for an angry, abusive husband.[194] That said, there is no excuse for Domestic Violence.

The best way to stop a boy's domestic violence towards his wife is to allow him to grow into a man rather than be forced.

Sex

In these cultures, you can't have sex until you're married, and one of the key responsibilities in marriage is having children. Many believe boys want to have sex, and being a child groom means having all the sanctioned sex they want. However, not all boys want to have sex, and given the taboo nature of discussing sex, so few know how to have sex.[183]

Incest

Once upon a time, families would arrange for cousins to marry. Only in the last hundred years did the western world stop this practice. Many generations of incest marriages can cause poor outcomes for families and children. In countries that practice child marriages, it's not uncommon for cousin to marry. The rationale is marrying family members strengthens the family. Many children find the practice disgusting and would avoid it if they could. As one father put it, *"Home-made yoghurt is more digestible than someone else's curdled milk."*[194]

Social Status

In the past, when comparing child brides and grooms, it was presumed that because of the patriarchy and girls suffer a great deal, then boys must inherit from being married at a young age. I could say that is absolutely wrong and only point out the negatives of child grooms, but that would be intellectually dishonest. There are, in fact, benefits boys receive.

Positive

Understand that by positive, I don't mean that any part of this is good. Child marriage is an evil practice that should be outlawed. However, I use positive here in what boys feel they gain in giving in to their family's decision to marry at a young age.

Places in the first world value marriage and raising a family, but it is nothing compared to patriarchal societies. To be a man, one must be married, have children, and work.[195] In a survey, boys were asked if a man was the head of a company if he was a man. The general response was that if he's not married, he's not a man.[196]

In these cultures, parents see their son as a man when he takes on the duties of a husband. Earning money makes boys more trustworthy. Parents' view of their son can be night and day, from unmarried to married, no matter his age. His having a family earns their trust and respect. Refusing to get married earns their disdain.[196]

Some boys use their marriage status to their advantage. Knowing how important it is to their family, they can use their needs against them. Suppose he is promised to a girl but seeks to marry another. In that case, he can impregnate her, so the family has no choice but to agree to it to save face.[197]

Married boys can also access things unmarried men cannot, such as getting a condom from the local clinic. As a result, unmarried men will state they are married to get a free condom.[198] This demonstrates that the only sanctioned form of sex is marital sex, and unmarried boys must lie to get access to protection.

Negative

Many of the negatives have been mentioned, from being thrown into the deep end of adulting[199], discontinuing education, and giving up one's dreams. While marriage makes one a man, unmarried males gain access to higher levels of education with the potential for higher earnings. This is something that parents who support this custom don't really understand, often devaluing education for religion and traditions.

Married boys who continue to go to school are likely to be teased and bullied by unmarried boys. Unmarried boys look down on married boys' families as uneducated and of bad culture.[200] This shows that if boys had a choice, they would choose education over early marriage. Therefore, married boys must hide their status to avoid embarrassment.

Boys who marry young may stay in school, but most drop out eventually. The appeal of school is to get a high-earning job down the road. Of course, that's not the only goal of boys. Some boys want to do something more artistic, which can be done as a single man. Raising a family means little to no disposable income.[201] Perhaps fortunate, exposure to non-married boys disappears when they leave school and work a low-income job and are likely surrounded by boys and men who also married at a young age. It's easy to forget what you once desired if you're not constantly reminded of what you lost.

The ultimate negative is that it adds to the cycle of poverty. Families remain confined in their corner of the universe and will stay there so long as they keep marrying off their children. Those that break the cycle often end up improving their situation.

Reporting

Being within a patriarchal society, boys constantly fear appearing weak. Asking for help is seen as the ultimate weakness, and they must appear to have everything under control, which they most often don't. This means that breaking out of the system through 3rd party resources takes a real will of effort to overcome their upbringing.

Add to that, this is regarded as a female-only problem... so there are few resources available should a boy wish to escape. Refusal to follow family wishes may result in being locked up, physically and sexually abused, and forced to move to other countries. Lacking resources for boys and the risk of severe inhuman punishment shows why boys are less likely to report being a child groom.

Long-Term Effects

Only recently has there been any disclosure of child grooms. It was previously thought to be an insignificant problem that was to the benefit of a boy in his status within a patriarchal society. We now know that any benefit gained is done so at a tremendous personal cost. However, there is little empirical data on how it affects men long-term. Once again, the prevailing thought is girls have it worse... always.

With what evidence we have, from giving up dreams to the cycle of poverty, there must be a powerful psychological impact. Boys are likely depressed, lonely, and suicidal. Throughout the world, boys are more likely to commit suicide than girls. Especially in these regions, since they are taught no coping methods for their pain.[189]

Prevention

So, how do we stop this? Can we stop this? Should we stop this?

This is another culture, and they're justified by their viewpoint. It allows the continuation of their family and gives a sense of accomplishment that their family remains strong into the unknowable future. This is important to them and has been practiced for a long time. One could argue it is our westernized viewpoint that we think we know better than a people's history.

What a bunch of bullshit.

We need to stop this. Cultures change for the needs of the world around them. Holding onto an ancient rite because people of yesteryear did it doesn't mean it is a good reason for it to continue. This hurts people, specifically boys, for an empty promise of fulfillment.

Boys forced to marry shouldn't be looked at as beneficiaries of a patriarchal society. Instead, boys should be viewed as victims of a traditional system dating back eons that serves no function in the modern world. It strips boys and men of agency to perpetuate a family's desire. Boys and Men are fragile as Girls and Women, and all are victims of this practice.

Fortunately, this practice has decreased over time, but it will remain until more is done by governing bodies to protect those demonized for having a voice. Steps have already been put into place to address the concerns of child marriage, including:

- Convention on the Elimination of All Forms of Discrimination Against Women
  - In Article 16: The betrothal and the marriage of a child shall have no legal effect, and all necessary action, including legislation, shall be taken to specify a minimum age for marriage

- Universal Declaration of Human Rights
  - States that consent cannot be 'free and full' when one party involved is not sufficiently mature to make an informed decision about a life partner

- Convention of the Rights of the Child
  - Doesn't address child marriage directly; it mentions the right to freedom of expression, the right to protection from all forms of abuse, and the right to be protected from harmful traditional practices

- Convention on Consent to Marriage
- Minimum Age for Marriage and Registration of Marriages
- African Charter on the Rights and Welfare of the Child
- Protocol to the African Charter on Human

Much of the efforts for child marriage are directed toward girls. However, rather than just creating new organizations to help boys (which we should still do), it is just as easy to get these organizations to also address child grooms.

There are several grassroots movements taking hold, such as Tipping Point[202] and Mahalaxmi Janajagriti Yuba Pariwar (Mahalaxmi Awareness Youth Club). They address child marriage in Nepal, including child grooms. Initially, these groups would try to convince parents and other family members to stop. Failing that, approach the child bride and groom to dissuade them. This also led to failure.[189]

In retrospect, arguing the morality of an action rarely sways people. You don't succeed by telling people they're bad; you must show them how much better life can be when they make different choices. This is why groups in Nepal changed their methodology to focus on peer support. Boys see the better life when talking to peers who aren't married.[189]

Of course, it is not just showing families; it is showing communities and countries there is a better way. However, doing that takes time and resources, and we must show the world that this is worthy enough to address. Trying to solve the problem by only focusing on one gender will never resolve the issue. Maybe we can one day stop child brides, but that will cause women to be forced to marry boys for the continuation of the family and culture. We solve the problem only when we stop both Child Brides and Child Grooms.

Schools and NGO's are helping, trying to push anti-marriage and pro-education for children. The good news is that child marriage rates have decreased in the last 25 years as fewer parents follow their parents' traditions.

Governments need to enforce the laws that prohibit child marriages. It may not need to result in arrest, but having to pay a fine and dissolve the marriage seems like a step in the right direction. Make the act so costly that families will adapt to the change. Of course, this will create a conflict between church and state, but over time, that should die down.

Every child has a right to a childhood.
Every child has a right to develop naturally.
Every child has a right to grow up.

BODY IMAGE
& EATING
DISORDERS

Boys and Men with eating disorders!?
They have body image issues!?

Many presume that Body Image and Eating Disorders are problems only females deal with. It's well known in our culture that women are bombarded with unrealistic beauty standards, which cause them to have low self-esteem. It might surprise you that men experience the same problems as women.

Unfortunately, there is not a lot of research on male BI and ED. The few times boys are mentioned is primarily used to compare boys to girls to show that girls have it worse. Studies that do focus on boys use methodologies designed exclusively for girls. There's some useful information out there, but I will state here and now that more research needs to be done.

Stigma

With what research is available, the consensus is around one-third of those affected by ED are males. Unfortunately, because Health Services treats this as a female-only problem and the under-reporting of males, there is a likelihood that even more male victims exist.[203]

Part of the problem in the under-reporting of males is the stigma. First, there is a stigma of mental health that asking for help indicates "you're crazy". Second, because BI and ED are treated as females-only issues, males facing it see themselves as having "female problems". Males fear others will ridicule them for having a "female issue".[204] Much of the fear is from the opposite sex, fearing not being seen as masculine for potential relationships with females.

Whether it is being "crazy", being seen as having "female problems", or being unattractive to the opposite sex, these stigmas are the majority reason of males not reporting their BI and ED.

Prevalence

Forty-six percent of girls and 26% of boys have significant distress about their bodies, while only 12% of girls and 17% of boys are satisfied with their bodies. This tells us that nearly 83% of boys and 88% of girls dislike their bodies. This is significant because as children grow into adults, they experience a lot of change. Unfortunately, due to their immaturity, children and teens are not unlike geese, with an established pecking order to bully anyone considered weak or undesirable. The message of the ideal body is received from the sexual attractiveness of opposite sexes, the media, the fashion industry, coaches, and parents.[205]

A lifetime prevalence of male ED is as high as 3.1%[206]. That might seem low, but presuming the worldwide population is 8 billion and males being half that, that is 248 million males. Or within the US, assuming 350 million, half being males, that is 5.4 million. 3% is a lot.

It is also known that rates among homosexual males are higher than among heterosexual males. Generally, gays are more focused on losing weight, whereas straight males tend to desire muscle gain.[206] For this reason, when looking at ED and BI, we should make weight loss and muscle gain two separate issues rather than treating them as a single issue or try to divide among sexuality.

A mean of ages reveals that male ED is 14.7, with the onset at around 13.4 years. Fortunately, boys are less suicidal concerning ED and BI, less somatization, obsessive-compulsivity, interpersonal sensitivity, and anxiety. However, males still engage in binging, vomiting, laxative and diet pill use, or substance abuse to keep their calorie count down.[207]

I would stress more studies be done on suicide rates related to ED and BI as it is known that between 15 – 17, boys commit suicide anywhere from 3 – 5 times greater than females, and while that could be for a variety of reasons beyond body issues, I wouldn't be surprised if there was more of a link.[208]

Causes of Male BI

While boys and girls experience BI issues differently, it is agreed that they start around 9 – 14.[209] Up to 50% of early adolescent boys experience BI concerns, desiring a leaner or muscular physique. Many studies have linked media as the reason for boys' BI, as cartoons, magazines, and video games portray muscular men as the idealized man.[206] Many would like this to be the extent of male BI; justifying this as a reason to remove such imagery as examples of toxic masculinity.

While I agree they influence young boys and teenagers, many of these studies don't consider other more likely causation factors. Perhaps the most significant contribution to male BI among children and teens is verbal and physical bullying. While girls might get harassed for being too fat, boys are likely to get harassed and receive beatings for being too fat or skinny.[210] If boys appear weak, they are likely to get bullied. Boys, just like girls, may also get harassed for appearance, leaving boys to believe they are unattractive.[211]

Anorexia

Anorexia Nervosa (AN) is eating very little (often skipping meals) to achieve lower body weight. Primarily, the fear of gaining weight or fat.[212] AN can leave people believing they are fatter than they actually are.

In understanding ED, it is best to look at family dynamics. Most studies focus on the dynamics of mother and daughter, but the few studies on males with AN found that most grew up in single-parent homes, and their fathers either lived in separate houses or were dead.[213]

Within single-parent homes of boys with AN, they found a climate offering limited autonomy from overcontrolling mothers. It is believed that with highly protective mothers, boys do not learn the confidence for self-initiated behaviors as their independence is compromised. Now, this isn't blaming mothers only, as overbearing fathers can also contribute to AN pushing their sons to pursue sports. This can also lead to Muscle Dysmorphia, a condition similar to AN in which males believe their muscles are smaller than they actually are.[213]

Puberty itself can be another reason for AN behaviors. Puberty for boys can cause significant weight gain, leading to boys starving themselves to compensate.[213]

Paradoxically, many people's attitudes toward AN are ambivalent. While the negative is clearly seen, some suffering from it has noted its positive aspects. This has led to the Pro-Anorexia (Pro-Ana) movement.[214] After all, slender girls are associated with greater sex appeal than bigger girls. And while some fetishize heavier females, most girls desire to be thinner. I mention a paradox, as some pro-ana communities are a place for those with AN to gather for social support to end AN, while many others want a place to learn new ways of losing weight.[215]

Because of the social stigma that AN is a female problem, males often turned to pro-ana communities to find acceptance. Males are also invisible in the Pro-ana communities as well because society assumes these communities are female only. Some males join these groups to recover. Other males did so for alternative ways to lose weight.[216] The one thing males got from these communities were social acceptance; mostly from other males.[217]

Obesity

One of the key reasons males develop BI issues is because they want muscles. This allows them to be attractive, to have popularity, and to compete in sports. Unfortunately, not enough studies have been done on muscle dysmorphism in adolescence. Another BI issue is males being overweight and wanting to get to average weight or gain muscles. Either way, children with obesity develop ED.

Those considered obese are often harassed, such as being pushed, hit, kicked, or named called. Worse than that is the social exclusion, such as group activities on the playground or having fewer reciprocal friendships.[218]

In my opinion, boys have it worse. Obese women are often fetishized with a subculture designated as *Big Beautiful Woman* (BBW). With the exception of the *Dad Bod* subculture, which is slightly over average, there's very little appreciation for overweight males. Growing up, teens are aware of these realities, and while both genders want to lose weight, there is a certain social safety net for girls that boys do not have.

Much of the research into boys with obesity is linked to behavioral problems such as ADHD and depression.[219] This is problematic for boys as it is seldom that their behavioral problems are examined, as they may act out due to bullying or societal acceptance. Instead, it is easier just to claim that ADHD and depression are contributing factors to obesity.[220] Certainly, when one is depressed, they want to eat more to receive happy chemicals in the brain. All of this comes down to noticing a symptom and assuming one leads to another without further investigation. Obesity, especially for boys, is a complex problem.

Long-Term Effect

When it comes to ED, children are disrupting their body's routine maintenance, which has consequences. For starters, starving yourself over long periods can mess with the endocrine system. The endocrine system deals with hormones. About 20% of malnourished males can become infertile.[221] Beyond infertility is the loss of sex drive. Teen boys have a strong desire for sex, but starving themselves reduces testosterone, which takes away the desire for sex or reduces their performance.[222]

Another concern is osteoporosis. Osteoporosis deals with low bone mass, making bones fragile. Females are more at risk than males, as estrogen can affect bones. Because ED affects the endocrine system, males have lower testosterone and thus are likely to develop osteoporosis.[222]

While there hasn't been any significant research on males who puke, use diuretics, binge eating, or use substances, males are affected by Bulimia. Whether male or female, puking means your food expels from your stomach, as well as stomach acid and bacteria. That upchuck cocktail, if done over several months, can lead to teeth erosion.[223]

Prevention

The prevention of ED and BI starts with culture. First, we must improve awareness of boys' and men's Mental Health problems. Unfortunately, much of psychology today is Feminist focused, which makes it difficult for males to seek help. We need to remove the stigma of males seeking help. I know from firsthand experience that many boys and men want help. ED males shouldn't need to go to a pro-ana group to feel accepted for what they're going through. Groups that will more likely encourage them to continue rather than to stop.

Second, medical, psychology, and academic communities need to recognize that men can suffer from ED and BI. This begins by paying attention to its warning signs and symptoms and not presuming it is not an issue because they are male.

Third, to develop ED identification specifically for boys and men, rather than judging them as would-be girls. It's established that males have their own BI and ED issues. Classifying by gender will allow us to see it quicker in boys who suffer from it and intervene before it becomes problematic.

We need to see more media representation of males with BI and ED issues. Suppose a show properly depicts a male with self-esteem issues going to extremes to meet his desired body image and starving himself. In that case, more males might feel that what they are going through is not unique to them.

ADHD

The degree to which the psychiatric community is complicit with abusive parents in drugging non-compliant children is a war crime across the generations, and there will be a Nuremberg at some point in the future.

–Stefan Molyneux

Studies using children for Attention Deficit Hyperactive Disorder (or Attention Deficit Disorder) often have twice as many boys than girls. However, the final results often combine boys and girls into a single statistic.[224] This means that it is difficult to say anything conclusive about how ADHD affects boys. Fortunately, there are some studies I can use to gain insight into this condition.

I will start by saying that ADHD is an actual thing that affects all children. I will also state that not every boy who acts like a boy is a candidate for ADHD. In addition, girls can be diagnosed, but due to cultural biases, they are often overlooked.

Prevalence

In the US, 9.4% of children have ADHD. Based on US population, that is about 6.1 million.[225] Of that, 4.3 million (71%) are boys and 1.8 million girls (29%). This is about 2.4 boys for every 1 girl, which is a strong sug-

67

gestion that boys are overdiagnosed for ADHD, and quite possibly, girls are underdiagnosed.[226]

By age[225]:
- 54% are 12 – 17
- 39% are 6 – 11
- The rest are younger

Symptoms

The fundamental symptom of ADHD in boys is hyperactivity. And boys are more energetic than girls, but hyperactivity is not enough to diagnose one with ADHD, though it is a trait most focus on. To be diagnosed with ADHD, a child must be symptomatic in two categories: inattention and impulsivity. Furthermore, children must have six or more symptoms in each category for at least six months, the symptoms must be present before the age of 12, present in two or more settings, symptoms interfere with maintaining schoolwork, and the symptoms are not better explained by another disorder.[227]

A symptom not mentioned in the DSM-V is aggression. Aggression is often seen in ADHD children, though boys and girls express aggression differently. Girls have more of a handle on their emotions, and their aggression is indirect; they are more manipulative in getting what they want, even with authority figures. Boys are more openly defiant to authority. Girl's ADHD is more tolerated or overlooked compared to boys.[228]

Social interaction becomes a challenge for ADHD children. Boys being unruly is likely a means of over-compensating for their inability to communicate; better to be disruptive than to be seen as defective. Medication only helps with core behavioral symptoms and doesn't address social deficits. Lacking this ability can lead to future anti-social or psychotic behaviors, abuse of drugs, and possible criminality.[229]

Misdiagnosis

In the movie "Charlie Bartlett", after Charlie gets beaten up at his new school, his mother insists on him seeing a psychiatrist. During his session, Charlie gets up on the furniture, revealing his fantasy of talking to a crowd. Charlie is full of energy. Then, after deflecting the conversation about his father, the doctor prescribes Ritalin, hoping it helps with the concentration problem. As Charlie points out, *"You mean, if I take the medication, and it helps me concentrate; you'll know I have ADD?"* I'm not a doctor, but Charlie doesn't have ADD or ADHD.

Despite how commonplace, ADHD is not so easily diagnosed. Yet, boys seem to get diagnosed with it at the drop of a hat. It might seem the film mentioned above is purely fictional in how boys get prescribed for it, but given the rates of boys, I can believe it to be true. Several things cause a boy to get treatment for ADHD that may, in fact, be wrong. It is easier to just say ADHD to see if the medications help than to take the time to investigate actual problems.

More than that, what is seen as problematic behaviors may in fact be what is considered normal for a boy. Boys and girls are different from each other, but rather than adapt to how boys are, it is easier to just say they have problems that need to be corrected.

Below are some possibilities of what leads to misdiagnoses.

Teacher Bias

Part of the problem is the inability of educators to handle disruptive behaviors. This is important as the insistence of an authority figure often leads to a child being diagnosed, with doctors considering that more than their own observations. The challenge is that while mothers feel capable of handling their disruptive children, studies have shown that teachers feel less capable of dealing with disruptive behavior.[224]

This, unfortunately, creates a bias against boys in the education system. Disruptive boys are assumed to have ADHD. Educators insist that medications be used to correct behaviors.[230]

Teachers' inability to handle boys is not seen as a detriment against her; boys are naturally bad and need help to be normal. It must be stressed that while a teacher might push for an ADHD diagnosis, this may not reflect a boy's actual problem, instead revealing the teacher's bias. This proves teachers need more specialized training on handling boys as a prerequisite to becoming a teacher.[231]

One key aspect of the DSM-V that is often overlooked is school/work performance. A boy could have many symptoms described for ADHD and excel academically. If this is the case, the child doesn't have ADHD. Only when their productivity suffers is it ADHD.[232]

Immaturity

All children mature at different rates, so it can be easy for teachers to see all their students at the same level of development. Any outliers to maturity are regarded as mental issues. However, in a classroom, immaturity may result from age differences.

In the US, the age for school admission is five. Some children might not be eligible for the school year because they won't be five for a few more months and must wait for another year. They are nearly six years old when they enroll in school. Other students might just barely turn five to make the cutoff point for school enrollment.

So in kindergarten, we've got children who just turned from four to five, and children aged five and soon will become six. Just by the numbers, the six-year-old is hypothetically 20% more mature than the five-year-old. However, a teacher can easily forget that and see some of her students as more mature than others. Studies have shown that this age difference results in higher ADHD diagnoses for boys whose 5th birthday occurred before the entry cutoff. The youngest of boys are 70% more likely to be diagnosed with ADHD.[233]

Mood Disorders

One challenge is that different disorders can be mistaken for ADHD. It begs the question, how can doctors and teachers be so certain one has a Mood Disorder with inattention versus ADHD with mood problems? Long answer short, they can't.[234]

ADHD and Mood Disorders, such as Bipolar, are quite similar to each other, sharing several symptoms[235]:

- Mood Instability
- Outbursts
- Restlessness
- Talkativeness
- Impatience

A major difference between the two is Mood Instability. While I noted this as being similar, they are still distinct. ADHD can have sudden mood swings that dissipate quickly, whereas Bipolar mood swings can last upwards of a few weeks. Bipolar children, during their Mood Instability, can appear as kids with ADHD.[235]

Trauma

As I mentioned in ABUSE, boys handle trauma differently from girls. Worse, it tends not to get reported, and so few look for the signs of it. Trauma is more than just abuse suffered; it may also result from living in poverty or a family going through a divorce, along with neglect, violence, and substance abuse among parents. Children suffering from more than one Adverse Childhood Experience are likely to be diagnosed with ADHD. It might be true, but dealing with trauma can also result in symptoms similar to ADHD, such as PTSD.[236]

AUTISM

Like ADHD, Autism is something that affects boys more than girls. Imagine if it were affecting girls more, how much more we'd hear about it, that it was some sort of pandemic. I will not delve too deep into what Autism Spectrum Disorder (ASD) is, but discuss the issue that boys are more affected.

Prevalence

Eighty percent of those with ASD are boys, or 4.2 boys for every one girl.[237] The source questions if that number reflects the actual cases of ASD, indicating it may be as low as 3.5 to 1.[238] The research stated girls are misdiagnosed or can be diagnosed later in life.[239]

Nearly 2% of all children are on the spectrum for Autism, which amounts to 1.36 million children in the US.[240] With 80% being boys, that is 1.09m vs 272,000.

In 1970's, CDC's rate of Autism was 1-in-5000, in 2002 was 1-in-150, and 1-in-68 in 2012.[241] In 2010, the CDC stated 1-in-52 for boys and 1-in-252 for girls.[242]

This begs the question, are things getting worse for children? Possibly. However, there may be a better explanation, though it is a partial one at best.

Studies show that since the 2000's, the rate of diagnosing for intellectual disabilities has decreased whereas autism has increased. Autism is looked upon as a spectrum, so it makes sense that it encompasses a wide range of intellectual disabilities. I won't say this is good or bad, but it does give an explanation as to why the rate has rapidly increased over a 40-year-period.[241]

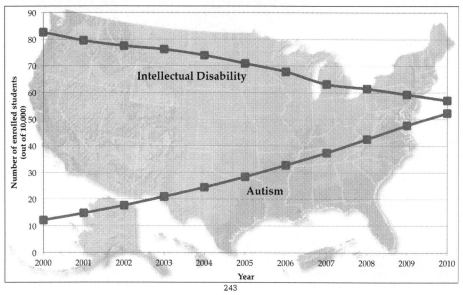

243

ADHD Misdiagnosis

In ADHD, I went over some common things that may seem like ADHD but could be something else. ASD may well be one such diagnosis, especially Asperger's. Both diagnoses have children who are fidgeting, struggling in social interactions, and becoming easily upset. This is important as the treatment for ADHD and ASD are different. A misdiagnosis of one for the other could do more harm than good.

X-Chromosome

What do males and females have in common? The X-Chromosome. For females, they are XX, and for males, they are XY. Since both males and females can have autism, it stands to reason that the mutations that cause a child to have autism must come from the X-Chromosome. And if males are more likely to have it, perhaps the male X is the culprit. Except males get their X from their mother as they take Y from their father. So if the mother's X is the culprit, why don't more girls have Autism?

A study in 2015 found that while Autism affects boys more, it is the mother's X-Chromosome that is likely responsible.[242] But girls receive the same X-Chromosome from their mothers... why aren't they just as affected. We need to remember that girls also get an X from their fathers.

Another paper in 2015 found that 80% of your most active genes come from the father's chromosomes. For boys, this makes sense, as most of our gender genetics derive from Y, with X filling in the gaps. This could explain why boys are more susceptible to the genetic mutations of X. Girls, however, are more likely to use the X of their father than their mother, so any genetic mutations from the mother's X is not activated. Of course, her father got his X from his mother, which explains why girls can still have ASD.[244]

Now this is a very complex subject and you shouldn't just take what I say as the end-all, be-all on this matter. But the point I draw here is that boys are more susceptible to ASD because of their mothers, and girls are less susceptible to it because of their fathers. Imagine how the conversation would be if it was found that a genetic disorder that affects many girls was caused by their fathers. Not saying either parent should be held ultimately responsible. Still, my point with this is that we're in this together. We should work together to resolve this, not dismiss this because it affects boys more than girls. As we see throughout this book, we only care when something affects girls more.

Circumcision

Beyond the X-Chromosome, there is another possible explanation as to the rate of Autism that might explain why it predominantly affects boys. While the rates of circumcision have decreased over the years, many boys still have their foreskins removed, a practice unheard of in girls in the first world. In fact, in the US, there are laws against the practice being done to girls[245], whereas there is no legal protection for boys.

Circumcision (referred to as Male Genital Mutilation (MGM)) is absent from this book, although it would make perfect sense to include it. If I were to write a chapter on it, I'd imagine it would be just as long as **SEXUAL ABUSE**, which takes up half the book. At some point, I will make a book specifically for this issue.

As I mentioned in **ABUSE**, MGM may be responsible for changing boys' behavior to being more needy and less able to handle stress early in their development. I also discussed how stress can be a reason for Telomere shrinking. From altered brain states to damaged DNA, this strongly suggests conditions such as Depression, ADHD, and ASD may be linked to MGM. The primary reason for this connection is that higher rates of ASD appear in countries with the highest rates of MGM, such as the United States. Obviously, because females can also have ASD, then MGM is not the only cause of these mental problems. However, since it is unknown what causes ADHD or ASD, it remains an observation rather than a direct cause.[246]

Opposition to the connection to MGM have pointed out the practice's decline over the last 40 years, yet, the rate of ASD has increased. As discussed in this chapter, ASD diagnosis has increased as other cognitive disorders have decreased. I stress that MGM is but one possible explanation for ASD, not the only culprit. There is an argument to be made that MGM be outlawed, and should it be, what is the likely outcome of ASD?

SEXUAL ABUSE

[Rape is] nothing more or less than a conscious process of intimidation by which all men keep all women in a state of fear.

–Susan Brownmiller

If you read the book cover to cover, one commonality you will notice is the lack of research, government statistics, and coverage in mainstream media. Boys as victims are not something that tugs at the heartstrings; thus, there is a reluctance to report anything vital about boys' sexual abuse. Girls do tug at the heartstrings, so we are inundated with research, statistics, and coverage of how Sexual Abuse and rape is a gendered problem.

Interestingly, a counterargument given to the official stats is that many incidents of abuse and rape go unreported. This means the problem is far worse than academia, government, and the media report. It is identified that we live in a Rape Culture.

I actually agree with this, but not how it is presented to the world.

Rape Culture is defined as a large percentage of women experiencing rape in their lifetimes. Feminists will often cite that the vast majority of rapes go unreported. This is based on FBI statistic of 85,593 rapes reported in 2010 and CDC data collection of 1.3 million incidences of rape in the same year, suggesting that 95% of rapes went unreported.[247]

However, when pointed out that males are raped, the "not all victims report abuse or rape" is not considered for males. Instead, advocates argue that males cannot be raped,[248][249] glorifying what happens to boys,[250][251] or saying that it is a vast minority of cases and is not worth deeper consideration.

It's quite tragic that when it comes to sexual abuse, females are given so much latitude, and males are essentially ignored as victims. Whether the rate of female sexual abuse is as high as believed, the rate for males is highly unreported and uninvestigated.

What is truly unknown at this time, is whether or not males and females are sexually abused in equal numbers. Many studies allude to the possibility that they are, and some even indicate males could be raped more than females. But that goes against the narrative. Let us undo the narrative and discuss truth.

This chapter will focus on how boys are victims of rape and other sexual abuse. Many would accuse me of taking the focus away from women and girls, citing me as a monster. Even pointing out that identifying women as perpetrators also makes me a monster.

In a truly egalitarian society, males, as victims of rape, would stand shoulder-to-shoulder with female victims.

Overview

No one comes running for young boys who cry rape.
– Kevin Kantor, "People You May Know"

In order to understand **Child Sexual Abuse** (CSA) and, more specifically, **Boys' Sexual Abuse** (BSA), we must first know that it is more than physical assault; it is also emotional and psychological. CSA includes exposure to pornography, sexual exhibitionism, perverse activities, and viewing of sexual acts, along with sexual contact from fondling, oral-genital contact, and intercourse.[252]

Just like rape amongst adults, the sexual assault of children has a skewed public definition that focuses on penetration as a necessary component of rape. Since women have no penetrating organs, they often escape as perpetrators of rape, even of boys.[253] Of course... men can rape boys. In our society, there is no question about men being perpetrators, as they're the ones with the penis. And because men have penetrating sexual organs, they're the only ones perceived as capable of rape by the public, academia, law enforcement, government, and Feminism.

During the rise of Feminism came the belief that rape and CSA were linked to masculine practices and were further proof of gender inequality. From Feminist's perspective, masculinity is the intersection of desire of those who are vulnerable and powerless, and dominating them to feel true to themselves.[254] Since this is seen as a gendered issue, many presume that the motivation for men raping girls is power and dominion on the weak through fear and threat.[255]

Motivations for rape are more than just having power; there is sexual gratification and the sense that you're doing something terrible that you know you shouldn't and getting away with it. Perhaps it is power and sadism for men to attack children, but pleasure and taboo excite people to act without regard for the damage they do or the laws they break.

But this is not a gendered issue; this is *"ignore half the population of society as perpetrators to fit a narrative"*. Women can be perpetrators, and penetrating organs is not the requirement for rape. So then, what is the motivation when women commit a sexual attack? The answer: Same as Men.

OMG, he said that women can rape.
He said they have the same motivations as men.

No, no... women don't rape... and if they did,
women do it for different reasons...
they have to; they're women.

This chapter will be the longest in this book and likely the most significant instance of injustice because:

- Boys are assumed to always want sex
- Males are deemed unrapeable
- The only form of rape is that which is done by men
- Boys are considered lucky if they have sex with a woman
- Female predators face lesser prison sentencing vs Male predators
- Rates of rape for boys are much higher than is generally believed
- Later events of male misconduct are never linked to the abuse they suffered in early life
- Female misconduct is often linked to early-life abuse
- Over 70% of all teachers are female
- Females believe they can get away with rape

Failure of Research

Before diving in… I know that so many will say to me, "Why didn't you look at x" or "Why did you avoid the research on y" or insistence that I am ignoring research to present my case. First, I'm one man doing this. I wish I could hire a research team. Second, I found a lot of research stating boys are a minority of victims. Looking at those studies, I felt they didn't do enough to make their case.

To that end, I want to show the dishonesty I find in much of the research by looking at two widely used sources to paint the picture of rape. Understand that I am not casting a dark shadow over all academia, as research papers are fundamental to our knowledge base and something I use myself in this book. However, we shouldn't take all reports at face value. Instead, we need to look deeper into how they form their conclusions and if there is any misconduct to get the desired results.

To put it more succinctly:

Don't automatically believe
the researcher's conclusions.

Seems odd… I tell you to use research papers, yet not to believe them. Well, research papers have great information, and the conclusions they draw from previous works and their present study can be groundbreaking. However, there is a presumption that anyone doing research and publishing a paper should automatically be believed in their conclusions. People believe researchers are infallible, not unlike people's trust in doctors, especially if their findings confirm people's preconceived conclusions.

Researchers could be 100% correct in their conclusion and can also be 100% wrong. The question is: Are they wrong because of bad science or ignorance? Or are they wrong because they've attempted to fraudulently represent their work to say something other than what their actual data says?

To clear the confusion, I am going to look at two research papers:
- CDC Intimate Partner Violence in the United States (2010/11)
- Long-Term Consequences of Childhood Sexual abuse by Gender of Victim

Actual science is skeptical, and the concept of Believe Science is politically motivated by people who don't understand science. Every paper I looked at; I was skeptical. I have nearly 5,000 resource files for this book. And believe me, I looked at all of it. I wish I could use all of it.

Perhaps my conclusions are wrong. I encourage you, the reader, to double-check to see if I got something wrong, and I may change my book if you can make a convincing argument.

256

2010/11 CDC Study

Although considerations of male victims is within the scope of legal statues, it is important to restrict the term rape to instances where male victims were penetrated by offenders. It is inappropriate to consider as a rape victim a man who engages in unwanted sexual intercourse with a woman.

— Mary P. Koss[257]

The "Intimate Partner Violence in the United States" was a study conducted in 2010 and 2011 by the CDC.[258] Regarding rape, it is estimated 19.3% of women and 1.7% of men have been raped during their lifetimes, or 92% of victims of rape are female.[259] This statistic has been used quite often that women are the overwhelming victims of rape, with a small percentage being male.

However, Cathy Young with Time Magazine noted a flaw in the study[260]:

*An estimated 43.9% of women and 23.4% of men experienced other forms of sexual violence during their lifetimes, including **being made to penetrate**, sexual coercion, unwanted sexual contact, and noncontact unwanted sexual experiences.*

Focus on the bold, **being made to penetrate** was considered other forms of sexual violence. This study specifically excluded force to penetrate from the rape definition. To quote Cathy Young[260]:

And now the real surprise: when asked about experiences in the last 12 months, men reported being "made to penetrate"—either by physical force or due to intoxication—at virtually the same rates as women reported rape (both 1.1 percent in 2010, and 1.7 and 1.6 respectively in 2011).

In other words, if being made to penetrate someone was counted as rape— and why shouldn't it be?—then the headlines could have focused on a truly sensational CDC finding:

Women Rape Men
as Often as Men Rape Women.

Unfortunately, in response to Cathy Young, many have argued men being forced to penetrate is not the same as women being penetrated. In other words, women have it worse, always.[261] However, for a world adamant about women needing help and men being responsible for all bad things, they prove their point by miscategorizing data to get the conclusion they believed it should be. Hold onto that thought for a moment.

1-in-4 & 1-in-6

I next bring up the statistic of 1-in-4 women and 1-in-6 men, a staple statistic in American society. These statistics give people two impressions:

- Far more women than men get raped.
- The rate of men who get raped is relatively low.

It's a fair assessment, as 1-in-4 means 25% of all women, and 1-in-6 means 16.67% of all men. However, this is flawed. These statistics come from the study "Long-term consequences of childhood sexual abuse by gender of victim".[262] This quoted statistic is flawed because the study wasn't about rape... it was about sexual abuse. You might say, "what's the difference?" or "aren't you just splitting hairs?". After all, they are interchangeable, right?

Table 2. Prevalence (%) and characteristics of childhood sexual abuse by gender

	Men (n=7970) %	Women (n=9367) %
Type of sexual abuse		
Touched in a sexual way	13.2	22.5
Forced to touch an adult	8.1	7.9
Attempted sexual intercourse	7.3	8.6
Completed sexual intercourse	6.7	5.6
Any type of childhood sexual abuse	16.0	24.7
Severity of sexual abuse[a]	(n=1276)	(n=2310)
No intercourse	58.2	77.1
Intercourse	41.8	22.9
Sex of perpetrator[a]		
Male only	51.0	91.9
Female only	20.8	2.1
Both male and female	18.3	3.6
Not specified	9.9	2.4

263

Well... no.

Sexual abuse is any negative sexual interaction covering a wide range of things, from flashing body parts to showing pornography. Both examples are not rape. Put another way, all rape is sexual abuse, but not all sexual abuse is rape.

The study asked four questions to 17,337 men and women: During the first 18 years of life, did an adult, relative, family friend, or stranger ever:

- ...touch or fondle your body in a sexual way?
- ...have you touch their body in a sexual way?
- ...attempt to have any type of sexual intercourse with you (oral, anal, or vaginal)?
- ...actually have any type of sexual intercourse with you (oral, anal, or vaginal)?

Many use this study to look at the lifetime prevalence of men and women. In actuality, the study asked about people's childhood experiences. Moreover, it wasn't reporting on rape, and yet that is how many others have interpreted the results. Of course, it's not the researcher's fault, as they didn't use the word rape.

The study shows that 1-in-4 women are likely to have experienced sexual abuse in childhood. And, 1-in-6 men are likely to have experienced sexual abuse in childhood. Wait a minute... the last question was about sexual intercourse and if it was done. So the study does have something to say about rape.

Looking over this chart from the previous page, we can see where it states **"Any type of childhood sexual abuse"**, where the 1-in-4 number (24.7%) and the 1-in-6 (16%) comes from. Above that is **"Completed sexual intercourse"**, which gets lost in the other three. And interestingly, males have a higher rate than females.

Looking at the numbers, 6.7% roughly translates into 1-in-15 and 5.6% into 1-in-18. So, 1-in-15 men were raped as children, and 1-in-18 women were raped as children. As small as that seems, approximately 10.8 million men and 9.5 million women in the United States were likely raped as children. And with that, we can see that 53% of childhood victims of rape are males. Yet, many research papers find that the vast majority of victims are female (when looking at sexual abuse as a whole).

Quite amazingly, using the research paper's own numbers, I proved that people's incorrect perception that over 60% of rapes happen to women is nearly 50/50 parity between boys and girls.

Conclusion

Thanks to Cathy Young, she found that "made to penetrate" was left out of the rape analysis to incorrectly show that the vast majority of rape victims are women and the vast majority of perpetrators are men.

Thanks to Tom Golden for his article on Men Are Good[264], we see the researchers didn't report on their findings on completed intercourse (aka, rape) and focused instead on just CSA, which led to the world thinking that 1-in-4 women get raped in their lifetime.

One difficulty in finding statistics on BSA is that so many studies are heavily biased against boys to show that girls are the majority of victims. Here's my question with the second study: If it were found that more girls were raped compared to boys, would that result have been made public? Looking at the CDC study and trying to fudge the numbers, I imagine that, yes, they would have. Since it turned out males were the larger percentage of victims, the paper chose not to discuss rape at all. Instead, they just went with the data that confirmed their narrative. Unfortunately, we live in an era where people just read the headlines to get their facts. So few take the time to look over any study to find flaws and gladly accept it as is.

Two of the most prevalent studies used to shape our collective knowledge about rape are shown to be the exact opposite of their perspective conclusions. And overlooking 5000 studies for this book... time and time again, I saw this bias that girls and women have it worse and thus not looking at boys and men. Or trying to obscure gender to leave the lasting impression that females have it worse. News Flash:

Males and Females Get Raped in Nearly Equal Numbers

Prevalence

Many don't consider sexual abuse as something that happens to boys. Boys, especially in their teens, want sex. As a result, any sexual encounter for boys is ultimately positive; thus, not really abuse as much as sexual experience. This is seen in the general population, academic studies, government agencies, the media, Feminism, and even non-profit organizations. It's distressing that programs designed to help children do so only from a female-centric viewpoint. Girls have it worse, and men are always the perpetrator.[265]

For the longest time, it was believed that male bodies were impenetrable, inviolable, and indestructible. Boys and men couldn't be sexually assaulted as males have all the power in society. This power grants them the ability to decide when sex happens. So if they have sex, it is because they wanted it. Males are never victims of sex.[266]

If there are any conclusions that boys can be abused, it is always as the vast minority of victims. A study in 2009 (on the next page) did a meta-analysis of 65 studies covering 22 countries found that 20% of women and 8% of men had experienced CSA.[267] This shows that 71% of victims of CSA are female.[268] As we see in the chart on the previous page, many of these studies were conducted in the 70's and 80's.

Studies can also be deceptive in the representation of boys. Studies that can show boys suffer at a greater rate than is generally believed may be merged with female victims and report on the rate of children as a whole.[269] Sometimes, boys who might be a victim won't be put in official reports, such as the child services in Scotland not correctly classifying 80% of boys in official reports (versus 25% of girls).[270]

Table 2
Prevalence Rates for Sexual Abuse among Males

Authors	Sample	Prevalence %
Canada		
Badgley (1984)	General Population Health Survey	14.0
Violato and Genuis (1992)	Canadian university students	14.0
United States		
Finkelhor et al. (1990)	American National Survey	16.0
Condy et al. (1987)	American college men	16.0
Fromuth and Burkhart (1987)	American undergraduate students	24.0
Stein et al. (1988)	American Community Sample	12.2
Urquiza (1988)	American undergraduate students	32.0
Cameron et al. (1986)	American National Survey	16.0
Risin and Koss (1987)	Males under 14 years of age	7.3
Condy et al. (1987)	Male prisoners (abused by female perpetrators only)	46.0
Groth (1979)	Adult male sex offenders	33.0
Petrovich and Templer (1984)	Adult male sex offenders (abused by female perpetrators only)	59.0
Johnson (1988)	Boys (4-13) who sexually abused	49.0
Britain		
Baker and Duncan (1985)	British National Survey	8.0

271

When it comes to prevalence, we must understand that boys are inclined not to report sexual trauma as they are aware society won't see them as victims. Even more problematic is that many boys don't understand that their sexual encounters were abusive, instead seeing it as a good thing. This is significant as a researcher may ask a boy if they were "sexually assaulted" and a boy says no, but if asked if they had "sexual contact/touching" with an adult, they very well could say yes.[272] Moreover, many victims don't report their victimization for upwards of 20 years (some longer than that). Even reporting it later in life, it is not included in crime statistics.[273]

Many sources have a wide range of figures, but no matter the prevalence of boys... girls always end up having it much worse. Maybe this is a truth of life or poorly constructed studies built on biases and assumptions. Many studies I will introduce you to will show that the rate of BSA is much higher than society believes.

United Nations International Children's Emergency Fund (UNICEF) reports that 150 million girls and 73 million boys are victims of sexual violence.[274] I don't know where UNICEF got its numbers, but that amount of boys is more than the population of the UK. That many boys don't move the needle in the majority of people's empathy that this is a problem worthy of consideration.

There has been an increase of reports worldwide, with the UK reporting a 60% increase of CSA from 5,557 in 2011 to 8,892 in 2015.[275] This, of course, is what is reported to the police. Which begs the question: is this an increase in CSA, or an increasing in reporting CSA? This is important because most studies failed to properly report the prevalence of CSA, so there is a likely chance that the rates are staying the same with more and more victims reporting to the authorities.[276] Unfortunately, we have no way of knowing which is the case.

The onset of sexual abuse can start at any time, but most ages appear between 8 – 11. Age can often reflect whether incidents of abuse were intra-familial (younger) or extra-familial (older), though boys experience more sexual abuse the older they get.[277]

Because this is a global problem, it will be best to break this down by country to better understand the full scope of this problem. It's important not to look at various countries as "that is their culture, not mine", as that will take away from the problem. As this is a worldwide problem, it can often reveal something about human nature and its prevalence in many places that try to hide it.

Something to keep in mind as you read the rest of this section and the chapter... researchers have a tendency to differentiate between penetration and the touching of genitals. At first this makes sense, as the touching of genitals is not as traumatic (but still terrible) versus actual penetration... but that differentiation only applies to girls but is used for boys as well. For girls and women, while the outer part of the vagina can be touched, she can also be penetrated by a penis, fingers, tongue, or foreign object. With the exception of the penis, any other method of penetration may be recorded as attempted rape, or like the penis, recorded as completed rape.

Boys' genitals cannot be penetrated (except for the urethra), and the only time they can experience penetration is with oral and anal sex, though neither is considered genital touching. A penis can be touched similarly to a vagina, whether with hands, mouth, foreign object, rubbing of genitals, or forced to penetrate. All of these are categorized as genital touching, often not counting towards attempted rape or completed rape. Refer to the CDC study that put made to penetrate as other sexual abuse. This may explain why boys report genital touching more than girls, and girls report higher rates of attempted and complete rape. I put the onus on the researchers for not exploring the full context of sexual abuse in greater detail.

Australia

In a 2000 study, 323 male inmates for sexual offenses were interviewed. Of single crime offenders, 55% reported being sexually abused as children, while mixed-type offenders reported 73% being victims of BSA. Extra-familiar offenders (sexually abusing non-related children) were more likely to engage in intercourse as young children.[278]

The average age from the first incidence to the last was 9 – 12. The rate of disclosing their abuse to others was, on average, 13 years after their last abuse. Only 27% of offenders who were sexually abused received some form of counseling after disclosure. Forty-six percent of those receiving counseling had previously received counseling for depression (24%), substance abuse (18%), family problems (14%), and anger issues (13%).[278]

The total victim pool of these molesters was 1,010, with 748 victims being boys (74%) and 262 girls (26%). Of the 323 convicted males surveyed, only 52% admitted to at least one offense against a child. In contrast, all the others averaged about 5.5 children per perpetrator. According to the researchers, boys account for 52% of officially recognized (in Australia) victims of sexual abuse. The researchers theorized boys are victimized at such a greater rate than what is reported, indicating boys under-report their abuse.[279]

Based on statistics of reporting, 92% of intra-familial offenders targeted girls. 47% of extra-familial and 43% of mixed-type targeted girls. This tells us that girls are more likely to be sexually abused within their family, and boys are more likely to be abused by someone outside their family.[279] Because of this, girls are overrepresented by official reports as they make up 73% of victims. When looking outside family abuse, boys are slightly more the victim than girls, and when the offender has abused multiple victims, it is more likely the victims to be male.[280]

Let's consider the previous paragraph and the researcher's conclusion regarding underreporting of male victims... there may very well be more parity between male and female victims. However, only male offenders were looked at.

UK

In 2020, police records showed over 83,000 CSA offenses, a 267% increase from 2013. One in four cases involved a perpetrator under the age of 18.[281] Another study looking at reports from 2008 – 2014 found that of 9,042 victims, 33% were male.[282]

Canada

In 1984, the Canadian government published the Sexual Offenses against Children, dubbed the "Badgley Report". This report found that 33% of males and 50% of females had been the victims of unwanted sexual touching in their lifetimes, with 80% happening during childhood. The total population of Canada is over 38m.[283] That is about 6.3m males, with 5m being abused during adolescence. This is also 9.5m women, with 7.6m being girls during their abuse. Boys represent around 40% of victims under 18.[284]

Mexico

Looking at upper secondary schools in 2013, 7% of boys and 5% of girls reported sexual insults from classmates within the last 12 months. Four percent of boys and 3% of girls reported being forced into sexual behavior.[285]

China

	Lifetime prevalence				Preceding-year prevalence			
Victimization	All (N = 18 341)	Boys (n = 9773)	Girls (n = 8568)	P*	All (N = 18 341)	Boys (n = 9773)	Girls (n = 8568)	P*
Child sexual victimization (total)	8.0%	9.3%	6.6%	<.001	6.4%	7.8%	4.7%	<.001
Sexual assault by known adult	3.8%	4.5%	3.0%	<.001	3.0%	3.9%	2.0%	<.001
Nonspecific sexual assault	3.4%	4.3%	2.4%	<.001	3.0%	3.9%	2.0%	<.001
Sexual assault by peer	2.6%	3.2%	1.9%	<.001	1.8%	2.1%	1.4%	<.001
Rape (attempted or completed)	2.2%	2.5%	1.9%	.01	1.8%	1.9%	1.6%	.26
Flashing/sexual exposure	2.5%	2.9%	2.1%	<.001	2.1%	2.4%	1.9%	.02
Verbal sexual harassment	2.9%	3.5%	2.2%	<.001	2.5%	3.0%	1.8%	<.001
Statutory rape and sexual misconduct	2.8%	3.4%	2.1%	<.001	2.0%	2.5%	1.4%	<.001
Forced exposure to pornography	3.4%	4.4%	2.4%	<.001	2.4%	3.2%	1.5%	<.001
Nude photographs being taken unwillingly	2.0%	2.5%	1.4%	<.001	1.5%	2.0%	0.9%	<.001
Nude photograph(s)/video(s)being uploaded on the Internet unwillingly	2.0%	2.4%	1.6%	<.001	1.5%	1.9%	1.1%	<.001
Private parts being watched	3.1%	4.1%	2.0%	<.001	2.4%	3.1%	1.6%	<.001
Being forced into commercial sex	1.6%	2.0%	1.1%	<.001	1.3%	1.6%	1.0%	<.001
Child sexual victimization (excluding "statutory rape and sexual misconduct")	7.8%	9.0%	6.4%	<.001	6.0%	7.3%	4.6%	<.001
Other types of child victimization								
Conventional crime	57.1%	59.0%	55.0%	<.001	43.1%	44.7%	41.3%	<.001
Child maltreatment	28.1%	28.8%	27.3%	.03	21.7%	22.2%	21.0%	.06
Peer and sibling victimization	32.6%	36.9%	27.7%	<.001	25.3%	29.3%	20.8%	<.001
Witnessing and indirect victimization	40.3%	38.6%	42.3%	<.001	32.7%	31.7%	33.8%	<.001
Property crime†	51.1%	51.9%	50.1%	.01	38.0%	38.8%	37.1%	.02
Physical assault‡	45.0%	50.6%	38.7%	<.001	34.1%	38.6%	29.1%	<.001

Table II. Prevalence of child sexual victimization and other child victimization by sex (N = 18 341)

[286]

A 2013 report of 18,341 adolescents was asked about CSA. Fifty-three percent of respondents were boys. The average age was 16 years old. Eight percent of children reported lifetime prevalence, with 6% within the last 12 months.[287] The three most common forms of CSA (lifetime/last 12 months)[288]:

- Sexual Assault by a known Adult   (3.8%/3.0%)
- Non-specific Sexual Assault   (3.4%/3.0%)
- Forced exposure to pornography   (3.4%/2.4%)

From the survey, 1-in-10 boys (9.3%) reported child sexual abuse versus 1-in-15 girls (6.6%).[288] With the 1.4 billion people in China, males have a slight majority with 723m vs females 689m. That is 67m males and 45m females in China that were abused as children, with 60% of victims being male.[289]

Researchers believe the reporting for boys is higher due to mainland China's 1-child policy, which recently changed in 2015.[290] If the one child was a girl, parents expected their daughter to stay under their strict supervision. This may reduce the rate of sexual victimization but would also prevent reporting of females. As with many cultures, female virginity is more valued than male virginity.[288] Boys are likely to face less strict supervision than girls, making them more vulnerable to strangers.

Kuwait

Kuwait did a nationwide sample of 4,467 high school seniors from gender-segregated schools, with 48.6% being boys averaging around 17 years old.[291] Of the study, 8% of boys and 9% of girls claimed someone had sexually attacked them. The sample also asked about verbal threats of sex, which 6.4% of boys and 5.5% of girls reported receiving. Other forms of abuse include unwanted sexual exposure (22.2% boys; 8.9% girls) and someone touching their sexual parts (21.1% boys; 14% girls). The vast majority of perpetrators were extended members of their families.[292]

Of the estimated 4.5m total population, 61% are males.[293] This means that 219,490 males and 154,881 females were assaulted in adolescence. Males make up 58% of total victims. This calculation, like many in the prevalence section, uses simple math. A more detailed study needs to be conducted.

Syria

We hear a lot about Syria in the news, especially about the rape, sexual torture, and sexual servitude of Syrian women and girls. It could lead one to think that this is a gendered problem as very little is reported on how men and boys have been targeted for sexual violence. Nor do we hear about refugee males who flee to neighboring countries and are likely to face poverty, economic exploitation, sexual violence, and sexual exploitation.[294]

What is not reported in the media for male Syrian sexual violence victims includes[295]:

- Forced to perform sexual acts on others, including family
- Forced to perform sexual acts on the dead
- Force to watch sexual violence on others
- Castration and sterilization
- Genital shocks
- Forced masturbation on self and others
- Object insertion into the urethra
- Oral and Anal Rape of objects, including: rifles, sticks, and broken bottles

Haiti & Kenya

A comparative study of men in Haiti, Kenya, and Cambodia looked at the rates of sexual violence. I left Cambodia out as the rate of male sexual violence was low. Of the 1459 Haitians and 1456 Kenyans, 23% and 14.8% (respectively) reported incidences of BSA. This included unwanted touching, unwanted attempted sex, pressured sex, and forced sex.[296]

Boys experienced non-consensual sex in Haiti 8.8% and 3.5% in Kenya. The rate of a perpetrator of rape being a family member was 1.5% and 10.7% (respectively), indicating that the majority of unwanted sex was perpetrated outside the family.[296]

South Africa

Around 127,000 males were asked if they had experienced forced sexual assault in the previous year. By age, they responded[297]:

10: 14.0%	15: 11.0%
11: 10.0%	16: 11.0%
12: 9.8%	17: 11.9%
13: 9.5%	18: 12.8%
14: 10.4%	19: 13.0%

In the table below, males were likely between 6 – 17 when the first abuse happened, with a mean age between 14 – 16. Girls were 4 – 17, with the mean age being 13 – 15.

SCHOOL SURVEY						
Type of Abuse	Males			Females		
	Min.	Max.	Mean	Min.	Max.	Mean
Sexual abuse by known adult	6	17	14.24	4	17	13.03
Sexual abuse by unknown adult	13	16	15.70	8	17	14.46
Sexual abuse by a child or teen	9	16	14.25	7	17	14.03
Forced sexual intercourse (actual or attempted)	11	17	14.88	9	17	14.41
Sexual exposure	10	17	14.00	10	17	14.43
Written or verbal sexual harassment	12	17	14.48	12	17	14.79
Sexual experience with an adult	11	17	15.29	11	17	15.30

298

Overall, two in five male school children by 18 reported being forced to have sex, mainly by a female perpetrator in urban areas and male perpetrators in rural areas. There was also an association between verbal insults received and beatings with sexual abuse.[299] Boys reported sexual abuse at 37% vs 34% for girls. The mean age for first sexual abuse experience for girls was 14 and 15 for boys.[300]

Sexual act	Male	Female	Urban	Rural	TOTAL PREVALENCE
Another child or teen make you do sexual things against your will	10.9%	7.8%	9.8%	8.4%	9.4%
Anyone try to force you to have sex	9.1%	14.5%	12.9%	8.6%	11.7%
Anyone make you look at their private parts/ masturbation/ pornography	17.6%	7.8%	14.2%	9.5%	12.9%
Sexual things with anyone 18 or older	15.8%	15.5%	16.5%	13.7%	15.7%

301

This chart shows us that boys are overwhelmingly likely to be forced to do sexual things by another schoolchild and be forced to look at sexual body parts. Girls were more likely to experience attempted rape. Boys and girls were nearly at 50/50 for experiencing sexual activity (consensual and non-consensual but abuse nonetheless) by someone over the age of 18.[302]

A home survey was done asking (nearly) the same questions. When questioned about being forced to touch private parts, having their privates touched, or being raped by a known adult, 3.8% of boys from school and

24.5% from home reported that the abuse was still ongoing. Compared to girls for 9.7% at school and 14.3% at home that it was still ongoing.[303]

Of children who actively engaged in sexual activity with an adult, girls were more likely to report ongoing sexual experience. Boys in school reported that 27.2% had ongoing sexual experience versus boys at home at 54.7%.[303]

Palestine

Sexual abuse of female and male students by an immediate family member: rates at three periods of age (at least once, in percentages) ($N = 652$)

Age and gender / Acts of sexual abuse	Sexual abuse at age:								
	Under the age of 12			12–16 years old			Over the age of 16		
	Total	F	M	Total	F	M	Total	F	M
1. Touched you against your will.	6.6	6.3	7.2	2.2	2.8	1.2	1.9	2.5	0.8
2. Tried to kiss or hug you in a disturbing way, against your will.	4.0	3.3	5.2	1.1	1.8	—	1.2	1.5	0.8
3. Kissed or hugged you in an upsetting way, against your will.	3.6	3.3	4.1	0.8	1.0	0.4	0.6	0.8	0.4
4. Kissed various parts of your body (not just your face) against your will.	0.5	0.5	0.4	0.8	0.8	0.8	0.3	0.3	0.4
5. Exposed his or her genitals.	3.5	3.3	4.0	1.7	1.3	2.4	0.8	0.8	0.8
6. Tried to force you to expose your genitals.	0.9	1.3	0.4	0.5	0.3	0.8	0.5	0.5	0.4
7. Tried to force you to touch his or her genitals.	0.9	1.3	0.4	0.9	0.8	1.2	0.5	0.8	—
8. Touched your genitals against your will.	2.9	2.3	4.0	1.7	0.8	3.2	0.5	0.3	0.8
9. Forced you to touch his or her genitals.	0.9	1.0	0.8	0.6	0.5	0.8	0.2	—	0.4
10. Forced you to sit on his or her lap to fondle you.	1.5	2.0	0.8	0.6	0.8	0.4	0.2	—	0.4
11. Forced you to sit on his or her lap, and rubbed against you to reach sexual satisfaction.	0.5	0.8	—	0.3	0.5	—	0.5	0.3	0.8
12. Tried to have sex with you against your will.	0.6	1.0	—	0.3	0.3	0.4	0.2	0.3	—
13. Had sex with you, and used force.	0.3	0.3	0.4	0.5	0.3	0.8	0.3	—	0.8

304

The Patriarchy comes up a lot in discussions about the challenges women face in the world today. What they call the Patriarchy in the first world pales compared to actual Patriarchies in various Arab countries, including Palestine. And yes, women are looked down upon and seen as a source of evil in some sects of religions. What many overlook is the expectation of males to appear strong, dominant, authoritative, aggressive, and not effeminate. So should a boy be sexually abused, they are looked upon as being weak, unable to defend themselves, and of course, effeminate.[305]

Sexually abused males in a patriarchal society are harmed in their masculinity, and a public incident can tarnish a family's honor. This incentivizes males not to report abuse to protect themselves and their families. This also means that perpetrators know males are less likely to report their abuse, so they have a level of safety in their attacks. Not to take away from females who face more dangerous outcomes of their sexual abuse. However, just because females might face death doesn't mean that males are any less of a victim of patriarchal cultures.[306]

From the previous page, at age 12-16, boys are more often the victim of being exposed to family members' genitals, being forced to expose themselves, being forced to touch genitals, and having their genitals touched. Boys and girls were in near parity in being kissed all over their bodies across the ages.[306]

Sexual abuse of female and male students by a relative: rates at three periods of age (at least once, in percentages) ($N = 652$)

Age and gender / Acts of sexual abuse	Sexual abuse at age:								
	Under the age of 12			12–16 years old			Over the age of 16		
	Total	F	M	Total	F	M	Total	F	M
1. Touched you against your will.	16.7	19.0	13.1	8.0	9.5	5.6	4.8	6.8	1.6
2. Tried to kiss or hug you in a disturbing way, against your will.	13.1	13.9	12.0	6.2	6.5	5.6	4.6	6.0	2.4
3. Kissed or hugged you in an upsetting way, against your will.	7.5	8.7	5.7	4.0	4.5	3.2	3.5	4.5	2.0
4. Kissed various parts of your body (not just your face) against your will.	3.4	3.8	2.8	2.3	2.8	1.6	2.0	2.3	1.6
5. Exposed his or her genitals.	10.8	5.3	19.6	5.5	2.3	10.8	4.5	3.3	6.3
6. Tried to force you to expose your genitals.	5.1	4.0	6.8	2.3	1.3	4.0	1.2	1.0	1.6
7. Tried to force you to touch his or her genitals.	4.5	4.0	5.2	2.3	2.3	2.4	2.1	2.3	2
8. Touched your genitals against your will.	8.8	7.0	11.6	4.9	3.0	8.0	5.1	4.5	6.0
9. Forced you to touch his or her genitals.	3.4	3.3	3.6	2.5	1.8	3.6	2.0	1.5	2.8
10. Forced you to sit on his or her lap to fondle you.	5.5	6.3	4.4	1.8	1.8	2.0	0.8	1.0	0.4
11. Forced you to sit on his or her lap, and rubbed against you to reach sexual satisfaction.	3.1	3.0	3.2	1.4	1.5	1.2	1.4	1.3	1.6
12. Tried to have sex with you against your will.	2.6	2.0	3.6	2.5	2.5	2.4	2.1	2.3	2.0
13. Had sex with you, and used force.	0.8	0.8	0.8	0.5	1.0	0.4	0.9	0.8	1.2

307

Looking at sexual abuse by relatives across all ages, boys are exposed to relatives' genitals, forced to expose their genitals, their genitals touched, and forced to touch their genitals. In nearly equal numbers across the ages were boys and girls forced to sit on a lap and be rubbed against. When looking at being fondled on a relative's lap, 12 – 16 boys and girls were more affected. Attempted rape and actual rape seem to be relatively close as well.[307]

Sexual abuse of female and male students by a stranger: rates at three periods of age (at least once, in percentages) ($N = 652$)

Age and gender / Acts of sexual abuse	Sexual abuse at age:								
	Under the age of 12			12–16 years old			Over the age of 16		
	Total	F	M	Total	F	M	Total	F	M
1. Touched you against your will.	16.7	16.6	17.0	9.1	9.8	7.9	10.6	14.9	4.0
2. Tried to kiss or hug you in a disturbing way, against your will.	11.2	11.8	10.3	5.8	6.3	4.8	6.9	9.3	3.2
3. Kissed or hugged you in an upsetting way, against your will.	7.8	7.9	6.5	2.8	3.3	1.6	4.0	4.5	3.2
4. Kissed various parts of your body (not just your face) against your will.	2.8	3.0	2.4	2.2	1.8	2.4	2.2	1.8	2.8
5. Exposed his or her genitals.	15.7	13.1	19.5	8.3	5.5	12.3	9.8	9.0	11.1
6. Tried to force you to expose your genitals.	6.2	4.0	6.8	2.8	2.0	4.0	3.4	3.0	4.0
7. Tried to force you to touch his or her genitals.	5.6	4.0	8.0	2.9	1.8	4.7	4.8	5.0	4.3
8. Touched your genitals against your will.	10.2	7.3	14.7	6.3	2.5	11.9	10	8.3	12.7
9. Forced you to touch his or her genitals.	3.8	2.5	4.8	2.9	2.0	3.2	3.1	2.8	3.6
10. Forced you to sit on his or her lap to fondle you.	4.5	4.1	4.8	2.3	2.3	2.4	2.3	3.0	1.2
11. Forced you to sit on his or her lap, and rubbed against you to reach sexual satisfaction.	3.3	2.3	4.8	1.8	1.5	2.0	2.7	2.8	2.4
12. Tried to have sex with you against your will.	6.3	3.8	10.3	3.5	1.8	5.9	4.0	4.3	3.6
13. Had sex with you, and used force.	0.6	0.3	1.2	0.5	0.5	0.4	0.5	0.3	0.8

308

For strangers, we see boys again being exposed to genitals, forced to show their genitals, forced to touch genitals, and have their own genitals touched. They also get kissed all over their body at 12 – 18, up to 16 to sit on a lap for the perpetrator's sexual gratification, attempted sex by a stranger up to 16, and are more likely to be raped than girls.[308]

Looking at these charts, we see a pattern for boys' abuse. While girls have it worse in many categories, boys are more often exposed to seeing genitals and having their genitals exposed and touched. In some instances, boys are raped more than girls.

Unsurprisingly, we don't hear about rape and abuse in Arab countries. Boys lose their manhood; girls' family loses social standing to trade off her virginity for marriage. Of course, the latter sounds worse than the loss of masculinity, but in a society that requires men to be the ultimate authority, losing manhood is that of abject poverty and lost opportunity in life. I will not say neither boys nor girls have it worse, as each faces distinct challenges that should be recognized.

India

When it comes to India, I could write an entire book about the challenges men face. When we look at the devastating men's issues all over the globe, nowhere is as bad as India. India can be seen as what may come for the rest of the world if we do not intervene and address gender inequalities.

In 2007, the Ministry of Women and Child Development surveyed 12,447 children, with boys being the majority of victims of CSA.[309] As high as the prevalence of BSA, you will undoubtedly notice no Ministry of Men and Child Development. You might state the Ministry of Women and Child Development covers the concerns of boys in India; after all, they conducted

Gender-wise percentage of children reporting sexual abuse		
States	% Boys	% Girls
Andhra Pradesh	54.21	45.79
Assam	53.48	46.52
Bihar	52.96	47.04
Delhi	65.64	34.36
Goa	52.27	47.73
Gujarat	36.59	63.41
Kerala	55.04	44.96
Madhya Pradesh	42.54	57.46
Maharashtra	49.43	50.57
Mizoram	59.96	40.04
Rajasthan	52.50	47.50
Uttar Pradesh	55.73	44.27
West Bengal	43.71	56.29
Total	52.94	47.06

[310]

this survey. A friend of mine, Anil, who coordinates the Men's Movement in India, informs me that while technically they're supposed to help boys, they often fail to give equal representation to boys' needs and over-represent girls' needs.

When it comes to child abuse, especially CSA, it is regarded as a taboo subject... as something that doesn't happen and only occurs in the West. It is a cultural conspiracy of silence. This is because of traditional conservative family values that regard sex as a taboo subject. Parents do not speak to their children about sexuality, the safety of sex, or physical and emotional changes to expect. This results in unreported incidence of CSA as children don't know that it is wrong, don't know how to handle it, or fear the disappointment of their parents. Even more so, respondents of surveys didn't realize their experience was abusive until researchers asked them about it.[311]

Of all the children, 53% reported at least one form of sexual abuse, with 53% of that being boys.[312] When we break this across the states (on the previous page), we find that 9 out of 13 states, boys were more of a victim than girls.[313]

Of all the children, 21% reported some form of severe sexual abuse, including sexual assault, fondling the perpetrator's private parts, flashing their genitals, and being photographed in the nude. Boys were a majority of severe sexual abuse at 57%.[311] Sexual assault in this study was defined as penetration of the anus and vagina and included oral sex. Sexual assault accounts for 5.69% of total victims. Of that, 54% were boys.[314]

Percentage of boys and girls facing one or more severe forms of sexual abuse											
	Boys-NO	Boys- YES				% of boys facing abuse of one or more forms	Girls -NO	Girls- YES				% of girls facing abuse of one or more forms
States												
		Situations						Situations				
		One	Two	Three	Four			One	Two	Three	Four	
Andhra Pradesh	70.8	14.00	10.00	5.2	-	29.2	61.48	17.96	10.78	7.98	1.80	38.52
Assam	37.45	21.35	27.53	12.73	0.94	62.55	48.81	18.79	21.38	9.29	1.73	51.19
Bihar	64.11	16.51	9.98	8.64	0.77	35.89	69.60	13.63	7.13	9.43	0.21	30.40
Delhi	45.34	23.55	16.34	13.53	1.23	54.66	77.46	10.80	7.04	3.99	0.70	22.54
Goa	97.45	1.82	0.36		0.36	2.55	97.83	1.74	0.43	-		2.17
Gujarat	95.47	2.67	1.44	0.41	-	4.53	89.96	6.69	2.56	0.39	0.39	10.04
Kerala	78.78	11.85	3.82	4.02	1.53	21.22	86.16	6.29	2.94	4.19	0.42	13.84
Madhya Pradesh	92.59	4.56	2.09	0.57	0.19	7.41	87.42	6.71	4.19	1.68	-	12.58
Maharashtra	91.67	6.55	0.99	0.79	-	8.33	88.73	8.25	2.21	0.80	-	11.27
Mizoram	79.72	17.47	2.21	0.60	-	20.28	88.24	8.28	2.40	1.09	-	11.76
Rajasthan	88.89	6.04	2.34	1.36	1.36	11.11	89.48	6.39	2.47	1.03	0.62	10.52
Uttar Pradesh	91.60	3.40	1.20	2.40	1.40	8.40	96.43	1.98	0.99	0.60	-	3.57
West Bengal	82.21	8.32	6.00	2.32	1.16	17.79	83.44	8.81	4.61	3.14	-	16.56
Total	76.94	11.12	6.90	4.33	0.71	23.06	81.42	9.20	5.45	3.46	0.47	18.58

315

Addressing being fondled or forced to touch the perpetrator's genitals (or other body parts), 14.5% of all children reported incidence. Once again, boys were the majority of victims at 58%[316]. Additionally, when being forced to show body parts, 12.6% of total children reported this occurring, with 60% of victims being male.[317] When being shown perpetrator's body parts, this affected 17% of children, with 55% being male victims.[318]

Beyond severe forms of sexual abuse, boys were the slight majority of cases of other forms of sexual abuse.[316] Other forms of abuse included forcible kissing, sexual advances made during travel, and exposure to pornographic materials. Then there is being photographed in the nude. Nearly 5% of children reported being photographed in this way. Boys and girls both suffered from this problem, with boys at 52%.[319]

As we see, many of these types of sexual abuse seem to affect boys more than girls. One of the few exceptions is being forcibly kissed, which 21% of children reported this form of abuse, with the majority being girls at 55%.[320] Of the combined types of abuse, both severe and other, 53% of children reported experiencing both, with boys being the slight majority at 53%.[321]

Abuse of children in India can start as young as 5 but can gain momentum at age 10 and peak at 12 – 15. As the years go on, the rate of abuse declines.[321]

Myths

Women and girls face several myths concerning rape, such as she is lying, asking for it, or deserves rape because of behavior or clothes she was wearing.[322] Feminists state that the reason more women don't report rape is due to not being believed and that all women should automatically be believed.[323]

The challenge with BSA is the myths surrounding male sexuality. As males, we're believed to always want sex, and if we get sex, then there is something wrong with us if we complain about it. The moment we hit puberty, we are overly hormonal maniacs who will do anything to have sex and then brag about it to our friends.

I was once a boy, and I understand. When I was 8 years old, I was raped by an older teenage female. It only happened once, despite my wish to do it again. I don't know why it didn't happen again. It took me a long time to understand how much damage it caused. It took me a long time to recognize it as rape. As I hit puberty, I would have done anything for another chance to have sex. And yes, even as a teen, I had sexual fantasies involving adult celebrities and even my teachers. Just because I daydreamed about adult women doesn't mean it is OK for adult women to sleep with boys. What happened to me at such a young age made me a victim. It wasn't until I was nearly 19 that I had my first act of consensual sex.

This section will look at the following myths:

- A boy who has sex with an adult female is lucky
- A boy controls when he has sex; he could have stopped it at any time.
- It's not rape because all boys want sex.
- Boys can never be victims of rape.
- Boys who had sex at a young age will grow up into men who rape girls.

Allowing myths to prevail makes boys invisible victims and excuses offenders. It sends a clear message that offenders can get away with the evil because society doesn't consider them bad people. These myths explain why most female perpetrators are given light sentencing to no prison time... essentially giving them a slap on the wrist. Furthermore, it leaves victims feeling there is little point in reporting their abuser.[322]

Lucky Boy

In the season ten episode of South Park titled "Miss Teacher Bangs a Boy", Kyle learns that his younger brother is being molested by a schoolteacher. Kyle goes to the police. At first, the police are enraged until they learn the teacher is a hot woman and call the victim lucky.[324]

When a boy has sex with a woman, the boy is deemed lucky. Many other males will cite that they wish an adult seduced them at that age. "Lucky Boy" is society's way of saying a boy wasn't raped. Instead, a boy having sex with a woman is perceived as a learning experience.[325] It can also be viewed as status enhancement, that they can brag about the accomplishment and be awarded admiration from their peers. Because of what is seen as an immediate benefit, it is believed there are no psychological harms related to boys having sex with women.[326]

Ultimately, this can confuse males suffering CSA. If he reports it and is told he was lucky for his encounter, he may feel ashamed for both reporting it and not enjoying it. If he believes society will admonish him if he reports it, he may allow the abuse to continue without receiving the help he needs, resulting in later life complications.[327]

This idea of boys wanting sex and being lucky also takes away from girls, as it implies only boys desire sex prior to the age of consent. I recall growing up hearing girls brag about having sex, pregnancies, and abortions. While I think much of it was false, it demonstrates that, like boys, girls think about sex, too.

Note, I am not saying it is right for any child or teen to have sex before the age of consent. The point I'm making is that if you consider a boy lucky to have sex with an adult, you should consider the same thing for a girl. Likewise, if a girl is a victim of an adult perpetrator no matter what, so too is a boy a victim... no matter what.

He Could Have Stopped It

Another reason boys are Invisible Victims of rape is the perceived notion that rape is an abuse of power. In the dichotomy of Oppressor/Oppressed proposed by Feminism, men oppress women because men have all the power, and by extension, so do boys. Those with power cannot be victims.[328]

Regarding human dynamics and sexuality, males are expected to be the initiator, always assertive and aggressive in pursuing sex. Never is there a reason to consider a male doesn't want sex; if a boy had sex, he wanted it. Having sex is an achievement, adding a notch on his bedpost and the ultimate in bragging rights.[329]

Males can stop sex at any time. So if they complain, they are viewed as less masculine, as they didn't prevent the abuse. This is not unlike a female bullying a male: if a girl beats up a boy, he's a wimp, but if a boy defends himself against a girl, he's a monster; a female bully is never held responsible for her actions. Like the female bully, an adult female is not responsible for the abuse, as the boy is the one with the power. So either he's lucky for the sex or lacking masculinity for letting something happen he didn't want.[330]

If boys truly had power, then why did something happen to them that they didn't want? What power did they actually have in their situation? Are they somehow less of a male because they couldn't stop it? The power that is claimed males have is nothing more than a victim-blaming tactic to take attention away from male victims.

He Wanted It

In the late 90's, Bill Maher hosted the show "Politically Incorrect", which is similar to his current show, "Real Time with Bill Maher". On March 20th, 1998, Bill spoke about Mary Kay Letourneau. Bill expressed it was wrong for her to be locked up and that our society was sick. Her crime was that she was in love. Fortunately, the four guests (Henry Rollins, Celeste Greig,

Cedric the Entertainer, and Kennedy) were against Bill's position, saying it was rape. Bill retorted that an erection is required for sex, and how does one fake an erection?[331]

As society says... all boys want sex. If he got an erection, he wanted sex. So he's not really a victim because he got enjoyment from it. After all, getting a flaccid penis in a vagina is difficult. Crazy enough, Feminists complain that this argument is used against women who are raped, that an orgasm means she enjoyed it. This faulty reasoning leads to mental issues, as males feel guilt and shame for arousal and ejaculation, which can confirm that they must have enjoyed it; thus, they weren't raped.[332]

I consent with my mind, not my penis.

There are various reasons males get an erection, and not all of them are sexual. Males can get an erection for no reason. Doing work or watching TV, and suddenly... it's there. Even for sexual stimulation, males, like females, can get aroused and have an orgasm, even if the encounter is traumatic and painful. This can be used by perpetrators and society to say that if an erection happened, you wanted and liked it. Erections do not equal consent. Put another way, I can actively plead with someone to stop raping me and still get an erection.[332]

And this isn't just a small, hateful fringe that believes this; we're talking about a way of thinking that permeates all aspects of society, even in academia and the court system. A double standard exists within the legal system that judges don't believe any harm comes to male victims of a female perpetrator... that it was desired.[333] Judges are supposed to be neutral arbiters of the law. So if we can't convince a judge this is wrong, imagine what challenges we face for the rest of society.

Can't Be Victims

If you look at this group of men who identify themselves as a rape victims raped by women... their shame is not similar to women, their level of injury is not similar to women, their level of injury is not similar to women and their penetration experience is not similar to what women are reporting.

— Mary P. Koss[334]

Society speaks loud and clear: boys and men can never be victims. This affects males because they are less likely to report they are victims. An example of this belief is that most studies barely recognize when boys suffer

101

abuse. The study may then focus exclusively on girls, or state boys are the vast minority, measure rates of boys and girls, and then combine their results and list them as children.

So a researcher says a vast minority of victims are boys, then lists children who suffer abuse rather than how males and females are individually affected... what conclusion would you draw? Probably that the vast majority of victims are female. Oh, but it gets better. Because that research is cited as a source of another research, and those papers are cited in other papers, all with the conclusion that males are a vast minority of victims (also known as the Woozle Effect).[335] It's the perfect crime.[336] Therefore, researchers believe males can't be victims because the academic community says so in previous research. It's a vicious domino effect that leaves most people believing it to be an absolute truth.

Another example of Invisible Victims is Child Welfare Agencies. A study in Scotland found that 80% of boys who were victims of CSA were not reported as victims. This represents a twofold problem. First, the methodology to identify CSA is female-focused. While there are similar symptoms of sexual abuse between boys and girls, there are other factors that boys exhibit that girls may not, and thus are overlooked. Second, characteristics that girls exhibit as signs of sexual abuse are easily overlooked in boys because of the bias that boys can't be victims.[270]

While this was conducted in Scotland, we see the Child Welfare System around the world overlooks boys because there is a lack of awareness about boys' issues. The service meant to help them... ignores them.

Victim-to-Victimizer

A great fear amongst men that suffered BSA is that one day they will abuse children. That is what society says. As a result, men are reluctant to reveal their CSA past. However, there is a grain of truth to this myth.

A study of male sex offenders found that 58% of those who sexually abused their family, 53% who offended outside their family, and 73% of those who abused in and out of their family were themselves sexually abused as children.[337] Another study looked at 224 victims of BSA and found 26 (12%) had committed sexual offenses.[338]

While many child molesters were molested as children, the majority of molested children don't become molesters, despite the commonly held belief that male victim of CSA are destined to become adult sexual abuser.[339] This falsehood echoed throughout society prevents many men from having children for the fear they will become a monster.[340]

Females Can't be Perpetrators

The next part of this chapter will go into perpetrators. Studies show that adolescent boys' sexual abuse is perpetrated by men and women in nearly equal numbers. Yet, many people believe women cannot rape. The only exception is if a man forces her to do it.

People don't believe women can do such evil, so if a woman does, she is an outlier. Part of this is the under-reporting of male victims, and another part is the political agenda that categorizes rape as a male-only trait.[341] After all, rape is about power, and who has power in a Patriarchy? Men. So by extension, rape is a male trait. And in a Patriarchy, women have no power, and thus, they cannot possess the rape trait. So if a woman commits rape, it is either an aberrant case, the result of male coercion, or she was sexually abused in her past by the hands of a man. All exceptions used to minimize her involvement in the rape and to instead highlight her victimization. Or rather, find the nearest man to blame instead.[342]

Perpetrators

In a conversation about rape percentages, I presented that men and women are raped in nearly equal numbers. I was mocked for saying such a thing. They asked for proof. I provided the Time magazine article by Cathy Young[260], demonstrating that men and women get raped in nearly equal numbers. The response I got was, "So men also rape men as much as they rape women?"

One of the challenges in our society is that we don't hold women to the same level of accountability as men.

When it comes to violence and rape, society looks at this as a male-perpetrated problem. When you suggest males can be victims, people cannot even comprehend that women can be responsible. Should they try, it will inevitably lead to making excuses for women:

"a man made them do it"
"it's not the same as when a man does it"
"males want it"

An investigation into adults' sexual interest in children asked men and women if they had child sex fantasies, masturbated to thoughts of children, or had a sexual attraction to children. Additionally, they were asked if they would have sex with children if they could get away with it, and how likely they would look at child pornography. Overall, 9.8% of the men said yes to at least one question, with the vast majority admitting to looking at child porn. Only 4.2% of females answered yes to at least one question, with the majority stating they look at child porn.[343]

The researchers concluded that this proves that sexual interest of children is more common in men than women... but let's not ignore the fact that 30% of those with a sexual interest in children are women. This might be consistent with society, or further research might reveal a higher rate among women. This certainly goes against the idea that women are nurturers and thus unable to commit criminal actions against children.

Perpetrators of CSA are likely to have backgrounds of maltreatment and/or sexual abuse. Not all who suffer terrible childhoods become rapists, but most rapists have horrible childhoods.[344] Not to excuse perpetrators of CSA, as they are unhappy in life and require sexual and emotional fulfillment to fill the void their abuse caused. Reasons to fill the void are likely because of self-esteem issues, sexual potency issues, alcoholism, deviant sexual arousal, and a lack of empathy.[345]

Perpetrators can also lack social skills, have intimate relationship issues, and be lonely. What trauma they suffered in childhood likely interfered with their natural development. Outside of sexual abuse, perpetrators probably had problems with parents who were too strict or abusive. This is not to put all blame on parents, but parents can have a profound impact on our lives, resulting in disrespecting authority, fear of forming close bonds, having few close friendships, and not taking part in group activities.[345]

Boys are more likely to be abused by teachers, daycare providers, boy scout leaders, and those in the entertainment industry. We'll look at these perpetrators later in this chapter, but note that teachers and daycare providers are female-dominated occupations. Boys can be raped within their families but are more likely to be raped by someone outside their family.[346]

By contrast, girls are more likely to be abused by family members and less likely by someone outside their family. Boys are more likely than girls to be abused by multiple perpetrators, whether perpetrators are acting together or different people throughout their lives.[347]

Adolescent Offenders

It is believed that only adult men sexually abuse children. However, older children are just as capable of sexually abusing their peers and younger children. Some theorize that, for males, it can be a means of establishing their masculinity. Society often pushes the idea that males can only become men if they have sex. As a result, some teen boys decide they will get sex by any means necessary to prove they are men. Children are ideal as there is less risk of rejection.[254]

Children who grow up in abusive situations, whether neglect, physical, or sexual abuse, may engage in harmful sexual behaviors. This can be a broad subject of what constitutes harmful sexual behaviors, but in teenage child abusers, they are likely repeating the abuse done to them on other children.[348]

Factors that can contribute to young people with sexually harmful behaviors towards children include violence in the home, social isolation, low self-esteem, poor academic performance, bad friends, social isolation, and juvenile delinquency. They may also exhibit behavioral problems such as being neurotic, anxious, attention problems, conduct disorder, and socialized aggression.[348]

It's not just young children targeted by older children; it can also be those close to them in age. This can result from an abusive relationship, friends making cruel dares, or sibling abuse. A UK study examined teen intimate violence relationship victims and found that 31% of girls and 16% of boys experienced sexual violence. Of those boys who reported sexual violence, 55% felt pressured to kiss/touch and 25% to have sex. Additionally, 25% of those boys reported being physically forced to kiss or touch, and 11% physically forced to have sex. Unlike girls, who were more likely to report a single partner who engaged in sexual abuse, boys reported being sexually abused by many different partners more often.[349]

Men

What is most surprising about male perpetrators of BSA is that many males claim to be heterosexual, as they are the ones penetrating, and boys are the ones receiving it. In *ABDUCTIONS*, I discussed men who engage in sex with hijras, which is the same mentality mentioned here; it's not homosexual because the men are penetrating.[350]

Male perpetrators are found to have histories of childhood sexual abuse, dysfunctional family backgrounds, and cognitive disorders. They also have social deficits, including a lack of social skills, problems with intimate relationships, and loneliness. This can be due to feeling betrayed by parents or other authority figures.[351]

Beyond gratification and power, men are believed to rape boys as a means of **Masculine Status Abuse** (MSA). MSA is about destroying a boy's status as a man, generally as a symbolic measure (though it can cause physical damage), and then used as a weapon against them. Males won't admit to others if they fear being looked at as less than a man, so this is used to silence them. MSA is often found within male hierarchies, including schools, universities, religious institutions, orphanages, prisons, and group activities. In many of these places, sexual abuse is often kept secret from others, so the destroyed status abuse is known only to the perpetrator and victim.[352]

Women

Many scholars and criminologists have painted rape as simply a trait of masculinity. When crossing into the realm of rape and femininity, experts maintain masculine principles. They avoid the possibility that femininity is as capable of a heinous act as. Women, after all, are naturally caring, nurturing, sexually passive, non-aggressive, and always innocent. This means for women to do such a bad thing, it must be one of three possibilities: aberrant case, the case of male coercion, or previous victimization from a male. In the end, a woman's misdeeds are ultimately the responsibility of a man.[353]

I call bullshit.

Rape and CSA are not gendered issues, as all genders are capable of both actions. Painting males as the only perpetrator does more harm than good, as it prevents us from having an honest conversation about women being as capable of evil actions.

So, let us have an honest conversation.

Invisible Perpetrators

For a very long time, women have been ignored as perpetrators of sexual crimes, deemed by society incapable of this action. This wasn't just men viewing women as unable, but women viewing women as incapable. When it became noticed that women could commit such atrocities, everyone tried to find some excuse for her actions, assigning some level of virtue or mitigating circumstance. Effectively denying women full agency and preventing females from facing the consequences to instead saying a man was responsible while stating women can do anything a man can do and doesn't need a man.

The research is out there. Yet most people are unaware thanks to the powers that be who's hidden and ignore this problem. And ignoring it has made the situation so much worse. The world needs to wake up to what is really happening. No longer can the global society stick its heads in the sand. It's a vicious cycle that when women rape boys, boys grow up to rape girls, who then grow up to rape boys. Yes, not all who get raped become rapists, but rapists were quite often raped as children. If society ever has a chance to progress, two simple truths must be known:

1. Females can rape
2. Males can be raped.

In the 70s and 80s, female sexual offenders were viewed as so rare that it was considered insignificant. This had the everlasting, unfortunate outcome of being the paradigm when discussing CSA. Studies should have looked deeper into the complete picture of rape rather than abide by society's assumption.[354]

The few studies that look at female offenders of CSA state they are poorly educated and of lower socio-economic status. Female offenders tend to be from chaotic homes, poor living conditions, and a lack of mental health services.[355] Other studies suggest female offenders may share the psychological traits and disorders of male offenders, including low self-esteem, poor coping skills, impulsivity, impaired emotional self-regulation, substance abuse, emotional immaturity, intimacy problems, social isolation, repressed anger, sexual dysfunction, and inappropriate person boundaries.[356]

The study above really drives home the point that only the worst of the worst females are capable of CSA. While there is an element of truth to it, female perpetrators can be of any age, social class, marital status, and any type of employment. In fact, female perpetrators may have chosen roles as teachers or caretakers to give them easier access to children. Women can behave seductively and sadistically towards their victims,[357] more likely to use verbal coercion than physical force. Females are likely to engage in vaginal intercourse, oral sex, fondling, group sex, mutual masturbation, anal sex, showing child pornography, and playing sexual games.[358]

A 2020 US study reported that females were 12% of sexual perpetrators for victims of 6 and under, 6% of 6 – 12, and 3% of 12 – 17. However, female perpetrators represented only 1% of adults arrested for rape and 6% of other sex crimes. Researchers were skeptical of these results as research into female offenders used small and convenient sample sizes, and since incidences happen in private, this revealed to them a clear indication of underreporting.[359]

<u>Types</u>

While women remain invisible perpetrators to most criminologists, research has been conducted by sociologists and psychiatrists that allows us to have a better understanding of female perpetrators. Criminologists who acknowledge female perpetrators' existences often lack a sense of their motivations, either attempting to justify her actions or using male motives as a starting point. To understand why females abuse children, we need to explore the motives specific to women and not rely on the motives of men.[360]

There are four basic types of female perpetrators[359]:

- Teacher/Lover
- Intergenerational Offender
- Coerced by Male
- Predators

It is believed most female sexual abusers are Teacher/Lover and Predators, specifically teachers and babysitters.[359]

Teacher/Lover

Teacher/Lover perpetrators are women who view their relationship with a child as romantic and reciprocal. There is no malice towards the victim unless there is a feeling of betrayal, like a breakup. Teachers are likely to engage in a romantic relationship if they are lonely or lack intimacy from dating/marriage, turning to a child to fill the void.[361] Her hope is that the boy will love her the way she loves him. Her "love" is an act of kindness in her mind, an expression of intimacy.[357]

While the Teacher/Lover wants to be submissive to the "man of the relationship", she often exerts control to ensure they don't get caught. She understands the relationship is illegal and insists on secrecy. It is often the act of keeping it hidden from peers and parents that can cause boys the most harm.

Intergenerational Offender

Intergenerational Offender refers to female family members who abuse boys, primarily mothers sexually abusing sons. Sometimes the abuse is blatant, while at other times, it is concealed. Intergenerational Offenders are good at masking the abuse, making it appear as an extension of their motherly duties. Due to this, abuse can go unnoticed for a very long time.[362]

Likely, the mother was sexually abused by family members in adolescents and possibly ongoing in adulthood. She has difficulty discerning normal sexual behavior and family, easily blurring the lines due to ignorance of proper family dynamics. Certainly not an excuse for her behavior, just a likelihood of where her misconduct originated.[361]

Some women in this category may very well be in love with the child they abuse. And not Parent/Child love necessarily; it may also be romantic. Though she may also distance her feelings for her child, seeing them as more of a means to an end for her desires. Her behavior may also escalate into sexual sadism as children become older, for the victim to serve as a revenge proxy to any males who abused her.[361]

Male Coercion

Male Coercion, as the name states, is a woman who is forced to (or fears her partner's temper) commit sexual abuse by a male against his kids, her own kids, or other children.[363]

While Male Coercion is an actual thing that happens to women, I've seen it used as an excuse by women who engage in sexual abuse, such as Karla Leanne Homolka. Homolka got a plea deal for the rape and murder of three females (one of which was her own sister) by testifying against her partner that she was coerced. She was sentenced to 12 years in prison. A few years later, a video was discovered showing her as an active participant in the rape and murders, which reversed the plea agreement. Strangely, she got an early release from prison.[364]

Prior to Male Coercion, a woman is likely to suffer substance abuse problems and be a victim of domestic violence. Her biggest fear is her partner leaving her; thus, she will acquiesce to the abuse of children, prioritizing his love over a child's wellbeing. Some research has revealed that women may still engage in CSA if the male partner leaves or is arrested.[361]

Predators

While this may be present in the other three types to some extent, female **Predators** simply want sex with boys. They don't need special justifications; they just do it. While the other female perpetrator types are more likely to use verbal coercion, female predators are more likely to use physical intimidation and violence. They are often compared to men, as they desire power and control over their victims. They may crave sexual gratification but more likely gain the most pleasure from the harm they cause.[365]

Teen babysitters are another example of Predators, as they may experiment with the children they look after, often due to lacking sexual experience. Ironic when you think about it... people fear male babysitters to be molesters and put a lot of trust in females watching their kids. Very often, **Babysitter Predators** are not themselves sexually or physically abused victims, nor do they have any emotional or phycological damage. What makes for a Babysitter Predator is having the opportunity and means to get away with it.[361]

It's entirely possible they didn't become a predator until after being a babysitter; that the thought of the crime beforehand disgusted them. Very likely, the abuse discontinues when they stop babysitting. However, it may reemerge later when they become mothers, i.e., Intergenerational Offenders. Or, they go into a profession that allows them access to children, i.e., Teacher/Lover.

I caution that not all babysitters are evil. Most babysitters, in fact, won't become predators (and that includes male babysitters). That said, take precautions such as nanny cams and have a sitter give references.

Another example is **Hypersexual Predators**. Hypersexuality is different from sex addiction, though a hypersexual can eventually become a sex addict. I stress that not all abused females become abusers, nor do all hypersexuals become abusers, but some abused females can become hypersexual and then a predator.

Hypersexual predators have a greater need for sex and gains more gratification by abusing children. Likely, their need for sex is to fill a void. Unfortunately for them, there is no such thing as enough sex. They likely abuse children, more often boys, to recreate the abuse done to them. Hypersexual predators are chameleons that, while emotionally disturbed, are quite sociable and functional in everyday life. Many would be surprised they are abusers, often well-loved by friends and family.[361]

Grooming

Like grooming for girls, grooming for boys often starts as a positive experience; activities may be normal for all children, but for an adult predator, their intention is for the activity to lead to something sexual.

Roughhousing

For boys, often, the abuse started as roughhousing, such as wrestling and tickling. Likely it was a family member or an adult they admired. When it went from fun to abuse, it was often roughhousing that led to inappropriate touching or fondling. This would lead to confusion on the boys' part, as they struggled to determine if this was normal, some mistake, or inappropriate. Eventually, the "accidental" occurrence would lead to more fondling, genital contact, and anal penetration.[366]

I will point out here that roughhousing is necessary for child development, especially between fathers and his children. Roughhousing is proven highly beneficial to children in the long term. I recommend reading the "Boys Crisis" by Warren Farrell[367] for more explanation of why roughhousing is necessary.[368]

Roughhousing is one example of grooming, as there are other forms of grooming that still involve proximity to the child, which can lead to "accident" incidence. Like so many things in life, someone can always pervert something for selfish gain/pleasure.

Threats

From "accidental" incidents comes coercing a boy to secrecy, primarily through threats. Threats could also include blackmailing boys, such as revealing their activity to others or posting content online. Another threat is the same sexual abuse done to their siblings, "Do this, or I will abuse your brother/sister". Too often, blackmail compliance doesn't prevent abuse of siblings.[366]

Rewarding Secrecy

Not all coercion is so negative. Often times boys are rewarded for their ability to keep a secret, gifts for their silence. Beyond gifts, boys also receive attention and affection. This is a gradual manipulation that will lead a child with a lonely life to convince themselves that sex with their predator is a good thing.[332] Children who lack friends and/or family closeness are the ones who are targeted precisely for this reason, which often translates into their willingness to keep a secret. Perpetrators need to conceal their sexual contact with children, so they need to make sure the boy they prey upon will be one they can control in the form of grooming.[369]

Grooming is not just a method of buying trust but also determining a child's ability to keep a secret. This means that transitioning from an "accidental" touch to full intercourse can be lengthy, with the perpetrator slowly escalating and rewarding the child's participation and secrecy. It desensitizes the child to progressive sexual behaviors while providing information that can be later used against the child if necessary. Through receiving rewards, keeping silent, and "consenting" to the actions, the perpetrator can convince the child they are responsible for all of this as they never said "no" or "stop".[369]

Grooming Victim's Parents

Perpetrators, especially teachers, can actually groom the parents, even if the parents are unaware of the sexual abuse. Giving the child extra attention by helping with homework, learning a musical instrument, practicing lines in a play, helping with a science project, and outdoor activities can double as grooming a child and the parents simultaneously. The parents see a wonderful teacher/mentor and want their child to spend more time with the perpetrator, unaware of what is actually going on.[369]

Not every teacher who dedicates themselves to their students is a pedophile. They may very well be good teachers. However, terrible teachers don't just ruin education for children; it makes it more difficult for excellent teachers to be there for their students.

Love

Once the interaction becomes more intense, the grooming can start to include love. While love is already present in intrafamilial abuse, extrafamilial abuse, such as teachers, will state that they have romantic feelings. Children, especially teens, know that this is something everyone desires and may well be something they crave... especially if they are loners.[370]

Exposure

Social media apps are a relatively new concept. Older online users are often unaware of how they work. Newer generations always seem to better understand new trends than the previous generations. Using social media apps such as Instagram and Snapchat can greatly benefit perpetrators as they can accelerate the grooming process by having more access to children. Before our society's addiction to social media, perpetrators such as teachers' exposure were limited to school hours. With social media, they can now communicate well into the evening, even when the child should be sleeping.[371]

One way social media apps help speed up the process is by perpetrators sending pictures. They can start as "Rated G" and slowly escalate to PG, PG-13, R, and finally XXX. Pictures may not be the perpetrator, but memes or pornographic images of other people. This can also be an exchange, encouraging the child to send pics back.[371]

Awareness

While grooming is understood to occur between perpetrator and child, it is primarily seen as men seducing girls. We need to be more aware of grooming patterns for male victims with male and female perpetrators, especially educators and other positions of authority that often gain automatic trust. Understanding patterns of grooming behavior may well help prevent or detect when grooming is happening.[369]

Boy Scouts of America

So much of what we see with sexual abuse of children is the victims are easily accessible and weaker compared to non-victims. Vulnerable victims make it easier for perpetrators to molest them. No instance of that is bigger than the Boy Scouts of America.

The exact number of victims of Boy Scout leaders sexually abusing boys is unknown, but in 2019, the Scouts reported that over 12,000 victims were abused by 7800 Scout Leaders from 1944 - 2016. That is roughly 170 victims per year.[372]

The Boy Scouts of America was founded in 1910 and has had 110 million American participants, with 1.2 million active members in 2019. The core mission of the Scouts is to *"prepare young people to make ethical and moral choices over their lifetimes by instilling in them the values of the Scout Oath and Law"*. Scouting members range from age 5 – 18, with programs extending to age 21. In 2019, Boy Scouts of America changed its name to Scouts BSA to reflect the inclusion of girls in its organization.[373] I will refer to it as Scouts to avoid confusion with Boys' Sexual Abuse (BSA).

The Scouts comprises 889,000 adult (mostly male) volunteers to help train boys (and now girls) in the core values. This would include regular meetings, camping trips, and gathering events such as Jamborees.[374] I acknowledge that the organization throughout the 20th and 21st centuries has been a positive for the US. Not every volunteer is a rapist. Not only do most boys enjoy their time within the Scouts; they accomplish great things in life because of the Scouts.[375]

Despite the positives, sexual abuse has existed since the Scouts' early history.[376] It's hard to know precisely when boys started being victims of rape or sexual abuse, as it took a long time for people outside the organization to become aware. That being said, the sexual abuse survivors have reported the impact of the abuse they suffered, from suicide attempts, drug and alcohol abuse, difficulty holding down jobs, trouble maintaining relationships, distrust of authority, and years spent in therapy. [377]

In 2010, a jury awarded Kerry Lewis $18.5m in punitive damages. He was abused for two years by an assistant Scoutmaster, Timur Dykes. Dykes had been reported to superiors that he abused boys but remained within the organization. During the trial, it was revealed that the Boy Scouts had 1200 files on potential pedophiles. They did their best to keep it out of the trial, but the jury saw a small fraction of them.[378]

In 2020, the Scouts filed for Chapter 11 bankruptcy to restructure its finances and to create a trust to pay victims.[379] This was done for various reasons, including a 58% reduction of membership over the last decade, the halting of in-person Scouting programs due to COVID-19, and an overall public distrust.[380] Worse was the loss of the Church of Latter-Day Saints, who had partnered with the Scouts for a long time and established their own youth program. This resulted in a loss of about 400,000 members, or one-fourth of the Scouts membership.[381] To top it all off, many states extended the statutes of limitations for reporting rape, which allowed many to file lawsuits against the Scouts.[382]

In the wake of Chapter 11, over 95,000 suits have been filed against the Scouts, making it the largest child sex abuse scandal involving a single organization in the US,[383] more extensive than the Catholic Church in the US. In December 2021, the insurer for the Scouts agreed to pay $800 million in the victim fund.[384]

The LA Times has records of nearly 5,000 cases dating back to 1947. Of those, 1900 can be viewed on their database. Identifying information and victims' names have been redacted. In many of the cases, no criminal charges were filed.[385]

Hollywood

Hollywood is a loaded term for the entertainment industry, from acting to modeling to directing to animation. Like many institutions discussed, quite often those on the inside know there is a problem. The insiders either turn a blind eye to it or are actively a part of it. Thankfully, some whistleblowers are out there, though it comes at great personal cost and career suicide.

I In this section, we'll examine what victims say about their abuse. Understand that I make no proclamation of who is innocent or guilty of these charges; that is for a court to decide. I only report what people have said and public allegations.

Overview

Every year, 20,000 children audition for parts and 95% fail to land a role.[386] To be that 5%, one will do most anything to get a role. Once they have success, they are liable to do anything to keep the success going. To that end, one must be willing to keep their mouth shut and look the other way. Unfortunately, doing the right thing will label an actor a troublemaker no one wants to work with. This can cause an end to a career. Look no further than Johnny Depp, whose career got wrecked based on an accusation alone.[387]

Corey Haim & Corey Feldman

One could say that thanks to the #MeToo movement, we're aware that sexual misconduct happens within Hollywood. However, as a society, we were well aware of BSA for a long time before #MeToo became a thing.

Of the many actors to come forward, two such actors tried to report their abuses to the world, and much of it fell on deaf ears. Both Corey Haim and Corey Feldman grew up in Hollywood as child actors. Corey Feldman started his acting career at age 3, first by starring in commercials and later starring in lead roles in "Gremlins", "The Goonies", "The Lost Boys", and "License to Drive".[388] Corey Haim started acting at age 10, starting in commercials, which led to roles in "Lucas", "The Lost Boys", and "License to Drive".[389]

Feldman reports that his being underage and famous caused him and his friends a loss of innocence and a lost childhood. Many of his troubles he blamed on the various adults surrounding him, from those who looked at him as a profit machine to those who saw him as a sexual object. He claims that at age 3, he didn't want this lifestyle, describing it as being child slavery.[390]

Feldman identifies the number one problem in Hollywood is pedophilia. Something he realized for much of his career is that he was surrounded by pedophiles, but in his younger years, he didn't quite understand what was happening.[388]

By his account, the pedophilia problem in Hollywood is what led to the death Corey Haim. Haim would identify Charlie Sheen as his molester on the set of "Lucas", though Charlie Sheen has denied the allegation.[388] Haim died from a drug overdose in 2010 after taking 500 prescription pills over five days; medications including Valium, Soma, Vicodin, and Xanax.[390] Feldman stated the drugs were a coping mechanism to deal with his demons.[388]

Haim's mother, Judy Haim, has denied that Charlie Sheen raped her son and implicated Dominick (possibly referring to Dominick Brascia). Judy Haim claims it was Feldman who introduced the two.[391]

In Feldman's 2020 documentary, "My Truth: The Rape of 2 Coreys", Feldman blames Judy Haim for not protecting her son, implying that she is trying to cover up the truth.[392]

Feldman's former manager, Chris Snyder, says parents can be the biggest problem for child stars. Parents push their children into pursuing a career, often against a child's wishes, and do things to secure the role. Parents can start with the best intentions, but once the money rolls in, they live through their child's success. Feldman states his parents managed his career until money came between them. At 14, Feldman legally became emancipated when he discovered that out of the $1m ($2.7m in 2022) he should have, he only had $40,000 to his name. That $40k ended up going to his father as payment for time lost from his job, putting Feldman into debt.[388]

Feldman revealed on "Dr. Oz" that Alphy Hoffman was a man who molested him. Hoffman ran the Soda Pop Club from 1985 to 1989, a club for elite under-16 teens in Hollywood. Feldman and Haim were photographed there quite often.[393]

Feldman states that he tried to go to the police in 1993 about his rapes. The authorities at the time didn't seem to care and buried the information.[394]

Both actors starred in a reality TV series, "The Two Coreys". During the show, the two had a very serious conversation about the abuses they suffered. Feldman confessed that a man hired to be his assistant had molested him and introduced him to drugs.[390] On the show, Haim wouldn't identify the man who raped him. Haim would have a drug relapse. This would also lead to a long-standing feud between Feldman and Haim. Feldman was a recovering heroin addict himself and would cut ties as a form of tough love for Haim and self-preservation.[395]

Feldman was on The View promoting his memoir "Coreyography" and spoke about the abuse he suffered. He described powerful, wealthy men passing children around from one pedophile to the next. Walters asked if they were still in the business today, to which Feldman confirmed. Walters would then state: *"You're damaging an entire industry."*[396]

Feldman would apologize to Walters, telling her that wasn't his intention. He wants parents to enter the entertainment industry with both eyes open with their children. Many viewers felt that it was Walters should have apologized instead of Feldman.[396]

In an email statement sent to Newsweek, Feldman stated[396]:

> *The gratuitous display of carelessness and thoughtlessness for the weight and importance for what I was trying to put across, showed a particular callousness to the concept that anyone in Hollywood could be doing something wrong. Even worse, the concept that even if they were I should just endure the personal pain and keep my mouth shut, because that's what is most convenient for others. It's shocking that only a few years ago, this was completely acceptable in the media.*

Anthony Edwards

Anthony Edwards is most notable for his role as Goose in "Top Gun" and Dr. Greene in the hit TV series "ER". He started out as a child actor, citing actor and producer Gary Goddard as a mentor. Goddard best known for directing "Masters of the Universe" and often collaborated with Bryan Singer.[397]

Edwards described a relatively positive relationship with Goddard. He taught the young Edwards about the value of acting, respect for friendship, and the importance of studying. Edwards mentions his emotionally unavailable father left him vulnerable to being exploited and molested by Goddard.[397]

Edwards and his close friends (who were also abused) stayed quiet. He felt deeply responsible for what happened to him. Worse, he feared being ostracized by his abuser, being a mentor and friend, and a surrogate father. Not wanting to lose that, Edwards felt this made it easier to be exploited by Goddard.[397]

Alex Winter

Alex Winter is best known for his role as Bill S. Preston in the comedy "Bill & Ted's Excellent Adventures", spawning two sequels. Prior to this film, he worked as a child actor on Broadway, where he states he was molested by an adult. To this day, he refuses to name who molested him. The experience left scars in the form of severe PTSD.[398]

Winter started doing stage acting at age 10 and was cast in a Broadway revival of "Peter Pan" at age 13. Winter states that year was a hellish experience as he was sexually abused. He wouldn't describe the experience publicly for nearly 40 years. Instead, he ignored it and moved on with his life. This energy would continue until the completion of "Bill and Ted's Bogus Journey" in 1991. At that point, he decided he would walk away from acting and move into directing (though he acted in a few more films).[399]

In recent years, Winter directed the documentary for HBO "Showbiz Kids", which discusses the early life fame of various child actors. The documentary included himself, Henry Thomas (ET), Todd Bridges (Diff'rent Strokes), Wil Wheaton (Stand by Me, Star Trek: The Next Generation), and many others. The show covers sexual abuse but doesn't reveal names.[399]

Anthony Rapp

Anthony Rapp is best known for "Star Trek: Discovery". As a child, he appeared in "Adventures in Babysitting". Anthony publicly accused Kevin Spacey in 2017 of sexual misconduct when Rapp was 14 years old in 1986. He states he waited so long to come forward as he felt for the longest time that Spacey was too powerful and famous and nothing could touch him.[400]

After Rapp reported Spacey, other stories about Spacey came to light. Such as the groping of an 18-year-old high school student and a sexual relationship with a (different) 14-year-old aspiring actor.[400] More accusations have come forward against Spacey, though many dropped the suit against Spacey.[401]

Regarding Anthony Rapp, Spacey remarks on the charge of him trying to have sex with the teen, that he has no recollection of if it happened or not. For other allegations, the actor has denied they happened.[401] The aftermath of Rapp's accusation resulted in the shutting down the "House of Cards" production. The series would continue again with a different actor playing Spacey's part.[402]

Todd Bridges

Todd Bridges starred in the show "Diff'rent Strokes". Todd Bridges played the older brother to co-star Gary Coleman. Bridges reports he was sexually abused by his publicist and mentor at 11.[399]

Like many child stars who suffered CSA, he turned to drugs. This led to his being charged and later acquitted of murdering his drug dealer.[403] In his memoir, "Killing Willis: From Diff'rent Strokes to the Mean Streets to the Life I Always Wanted", the first line reads, *"Suicide by cop. It was my only way out."*[399]

An Open Secret

Along with Showbiz Kids, An Open Secret is a documentary about former child actors who suffered sexual abuse as children. This had a limited theatrical release and became a financial failure. A financier of the film stated that no one in Hollywood wanted to distribute the film.[404]

Pointed out in the film is that not only were the men accused of CSA working closely with children every day as photographers, directors, and managers, but also that many who were convicted of pedophilia found jobs working with children in the entertainment industry.[404]

Religion

The fundamental problem with religions is their belief of a moral authority higher than the law of man. This moral authority leads to their preference that any problem that occurs be dealt with in-house rather than bring an "outsider" in. Handling things in-house is nothing more than a need to save face with the public to remain morally superior by making problems vanish. In doing so, they rarely deal with the problem; they give the problem an opportunity to fester and/or resurface.

I am not saying that all parishioners of a religion condone this action or that the religion excuses the evil, only that members within did. I do put the onus on religions to seek justice for victims and rid themselves of their faith's destructive elements.

Catholics

It's too easy for various sects of Christianity to look at the Catholics and say, "I'm a Baptist" or "I'm a Presbyterian" followed by, "We don't do that" or "They're not actual Christians". It becomes a case of the No True Scotsman fallacy, that if someone does something terrible, then they are not part of your group. It doesn't matter that Catholics identify as Christian, which also goes towards In-Group Bias: those outside of our religion are not like us, and we're nothing like them.

I think all people, religious or atheist, Christian or any other religion, should pay careful attention to the Catholic church on how easy it was for them to get away with such a horrendous act for God knows how long. Money talks. Money makes things disappear. And don't forget, all legally recognized churches get tax-exempt status. They keep all the money they get through donations.

These days, it's hard to discern a religion from a business and a business from a religion. I don't mean to be insulting, but the Catholics were able to use their influence for a very long time to cause a lot of pain and suffering. Be sure what you put your money and faith into are not themselves guilty of crimes against humanity.

Transparency keeps your flock strong.

There really isn't much I can say about Catholic priests that isn't already known. I will quickly discuss priests and then focus on the sexual abuse conducted/condoned by Nuns.

Prevalence

In the 2015 film "Spotlight"[405], Richard Sipe stated that 6% of Catholic priests had sex with children. The actual statistic of the 1,500 priests he interviewed found 4% had a sexual interest in children, and 2% had engaged in sexual activity with children. Another study from 1983 – 1987 found over 200 reports made to the Vatican Embassy for sexual misconduct against children, which averaged about one case per week. Most victims in the study were teenage males. A more recent study in 2012 found that 40% of all clergy abuse victims were males between 11-14.[406]

By 2002, 4,268 victims reported 1,205 abusive priests. Sixteen percent of offenders had abused five or more victims.[406] Another report has similar numbers. Of 4,392 priests, 56% of priests abused a single victim, about a third abusing two or three, 14% from three to nine, and 3.5% ten or more. Just about 4% of priests had abused 26% of total victims, which accounts for about 20 children per priest.[407]

Of the 4,392 priests, the police had contacted 1,021 priests for allegations of abuse, representing 24% of priests. Of those, 384 led to criminal charges, with 252 convicted but only 100 serving prison time. This means that out of the total number of priests identified by the report, only 6% were convicted in a court of law, and 2% received prison sentences.[407]

All of these numbers are believed to be a low estimate of Priest Perpetrators, as victims are less likely to come forward, and there is great secrecy among the clergy.[408]

Locations

Because this was done by a priest, most would assume it happened in a church. A church was the second most common location. The location of abuses happened in the following places[409]:

- Priest's home or parish residence (41%)
- Church (16%)
- Victim's home (12%)
- Vacation home (10%)
- School (10%)
- Car (10%)

Quite often, the abuse occurred during social events (20%), visiting or working at a priest's home (15%), or during travel (18%). The abuse occurred in other settings beyond those listed in less than 10%, such as counseling sessions, during school hours, and at sporting events.[409]

Victims

Males composed 81% of victims. Male victims are often older than female victims, with 40% of all male victims being between 11 – 14. When looking at males and females together, 51% were between 11 – 14, 27% were 15 – 17, 16% were between 8 – 10, and 6% were under seven.[409]

Nuns

The Spotlight team worked on exposing the Catholic Priest CSA scandal, and just as they were about ready to go to print... they were halted due to 9/11. An event so massive for American history that it usurped a case as important as this. I'm not trying to underplay 9/11 and the events that followed; a nation was deeply wounded that day. Ironically, the same thing happened to the reporting of Nun's CSA. Many reports were forming in 2019 and 2020, which seemed to stop due to COVID. I hope when the pandemic ceases to be at the forefront, perhaps investigations into Nuns can pick up where they left off.

In reporting Priests CSA, there were often hints that Nuns knew about the abuses and contributed to them. There's barely any study on this, as it is hard to see boys as victims, women as perpetrators, and clergy as less than holy. This might be the unholy Trinity of BSA and likely lead to no one kicking up too much of a fuss regarding Nuns. The world is more focused on priests raping nuns and nuns raping girls, both of which need to be investigated. Boys being raped by nuns will always be of less interest, making a full investigation more difficult.

One such incident to come forward comes out of Germany. Boys living in boarding houses of the Order of the Sisters of the Divine Redeemer were sold for weeks at a time to priests and businessmen. The nuns were engaging in sex trafficking of boys. Said boys, now men, are suing the Order. They state that many were denied being adopted or sent to foster families because selling them *"lined the sisters' coffers"*. The most prized boys were groomed to be sex slaves. The boys were raped for many years. Even when they aged out and left, the nuns would find them, drug them, and take them to predators to continue to be raped.[410]

A second German lawsuit led to an investigation by the Archdiocese of Cologne which concluded in 2021. The report was deemed so horrific that a confidentiality agreement was demanded by Archbishop Reiner Maria Woelki to any reporters who view it to not report on what they see.[410]

What is the point of a reporter
not reporting on what they see?

Despite the restriction, some details have surfaced, including gangbangs and orgies boys were forced to participate. Upon returning from the rapes to their dorms, the boys would be severely punished by the nuns for wrinkling their clothes or being covered in semen.[410]

Part of the problem with the report is that it fails to blame nuns directly, instead referring to "systematic management errors". This is an effort by the church and other institutions to protect the church and the clergy involved.[410]

The German lawsuits involve 1412 children and teenagers with 654 monks, nuns, and other clergy abusers. 80% of victims were males, though 80% of the abusers are now dead. The rate for nuns vs priests appears relatively small. When looking at 3,500 Catholic religious leaders who committed CSA, only 82 (2%) were nuns.[411] While the rate of abusive Nuns is likely higher than 2%, in 2016, it was reported that there were 47,160 total Nuns in the world. Two percent of that is 943 Nuns who are potentially guilty of sexually abusing children.[412]

Teachers

This section will look at BSA done by teachers and how it affects victims and the education system. While anyone who works within education can abuse children, whether administrators, coaches, counselors, teacher aides, and bus drivers, primarily it is teachers who abuse students. Examples of abuse include[413]:

- Sexual harassment
- Text messaging
- E-mail
- Social media contact
- Showing/producing sexually explicit images
- Sexual touching
- Oral sex
- Penetration

Perpetrators

As discussed in the *Perpetrators* section of this chapter, the Teacher/Lover is the most common form of female perpetration of BSA. The thing that marks an outstanding teacher is often their selflessness to their student's education and putting in the long hard hours. Teachers are often salary, so they don't get overtime for their work, and additional school supplies come from their own pockets. I remember teachers giving us a one time extra credit in elementary school if we brought in a box of Kleenex.

Since so little study has been done on female teacher perpetrators, it is difficult to get a general profile of teachers committing BSA. The teacher may be relatively young or has been teaching for quite some time. She might be single or married with children. If she's single, dating proves to be a daunting task. If a teacher has a family, her spouse and children may not get the full attention they need from their mother. As a result, they may end up lonely and need companionship. Now, this is not an excuse for teachers' behaviors but a bit of an understanding of how one can go down a destructive path.

What we can observe of most female teachers of BSA is that they are often popular amongst staff, parents, and definitely the students. This likeability can transfer into trustworthiness. Teacher perpetrators tend to abuse children as opportunities present themselves. She is more likely to have met the child through one of her classes rather than search for a child outside her classroom.

In order to maintain their "coolness", teachers may be inappropriate with students conversationally. This likely comes from a weak self-image and excitement when talking to an attractive male student. A teacher will justify pursuing the student because society says teenage boys want sex, so she's doing nothing wrong. In fact, she's doing him a favor.[414]

Part of the reason female teachers make for such successful predators is that our society instills in all of us to automatically trust female teachers. We also naturally gravitate towards those who are energetic and attractive. A young, cute teacher full of energy is seen as the most trustworthy person in a school and society. We must remember that predators choose the profession that allows them easy access to their prey. Predators such as female teachers know that the more liked they are, the less suspicious they come off. They can easily choose the weakest of children and manipulate them by lying, isolating them, and making them feel complicit, all in order to gain the sexual contact they desire.[415]

These well-liked predators can actually be well accomplished educators. They are likely to have commendations, awards, and other forms of recognition of their teaching ability, and are well celebrated by the schools and parents. Of course, not all well-accomplished teachers are predators, but it's tough for people to associate anything unfavorable with well-received teachers.

Cases

In my files, I have over 600 female teachers who abused boys. I also have male teachers with female students and female teachers with female students. I would love to one day spend months analyzing all these files to gain insight into female teachers perpetrators. For now, I just want to list a few to help put this section into better context.

- **Briana Altrice**[416]
  - **Age**: 34
  - **Victim**: 3 students between 15 – 17
  - **Crime**: sex with underage children
  - **Sentencing**: 2 to 30 years in prison
  - **Note**: Released after 4.5 years

- **Brooke Wright**[417]
  - **Age**: 40
  - **Victim**: 14-year-old boy
  - **Charge**: 2 counts of sex with teen student
  - **Sentencing**: 4 years in prison

- **Christine McCallum**[418]
  - **Age**: 29
  - **Victim**: 13-year-old boy
  - **Charge**: 12 counts of child rape, one count of drugging a person for sex, one count of providing a minor with alcohol
  - **Sentencing**: 29 months in prison
  - **Note**: Had sex with the child 300 times

- **Haeli Wey**[419]
  - **Age**: 29
  - **Victim**: Two 17-year-old students
  - **Charge**: Inappropriate Sexual Relationships
  - **Sentencing**: 200 hours of community service
  - **Note**: Also doesn't have to be on the registry

- **Debra Lafave**[420]
  - **Age**: 24
  - **Victim**: 14-year-old boy
  - **Charge**: Lewd and lascivious battery against a minor
  - **Sentencing**: 3 years house arrest, 7 years probation
  - **Note**: Lawyers argued she was too pretty for prison, house arrest ended 4 months early, parole was granted early termination

- **Diane Bimble**[421]
  - **Age**: 47
  - **Victim**: 10-year-old boy
  - **Charge**: One act of committing an indecent act with a child under 16
  - **Sentencing**: 200 hours of unpaid community work
  - **Note**: Victims name was tattooed on her chest, wrote the child a love letter

- **Fatinah Hossaid**[422]
  - **Age**: 25
  - **Victim**: 14-year-old boy
  - **Charge**: One count of perverting the course of justice and one count of sexual activity with the boy while in a position of trust.
  - **Sentencing**: 5 years, 4 months
  - **Note**: Used social media to threaten boy and family to drop charges against her

- **Jaimee Marie Cooney**[423]
  - **Age**: 38
  - **Victim**: Two under 16-year-old students
  - **Charge**: Sexual relations with minors, 2 counts of sending indecent material
  - **Sentencing**: 2.5-year prison sentence
  - **Note**: Paroled after serving 10 months

- **Jaena Wesson**[424]
  - **Age**: 48
  - **Victim**: 17-year-old students
  - **Charge**: Inappropriate Relationship
  - **Sentencing**: 10-year sentence deferred

- **Jennifer Fichter**[425]
  - **Age**: 30
  - **Victim**: Three 17-year-old students
  - **Charge**: Sexual Battery
  - **Sentencing**: 22 years in prison
  - **Note**: Got pregnant from student, got an abortion

- **Kandice Barber**[426]
  - **Age**: 35
  - **Victim**: 15-year-old student
  - **Charge**: Inciting child to have sex
  - **Sentencing**: 6 years, 2 months
  - **Note**: Lied to boy about being pregnant, sent topless photos of herself and video of herself masturbating

- **Kate Boozer**[427]
  - **Age**: 28
  - **Victim**: 16-year-old student
  - **Charge**: Inciting child to have sex
  - **Sentencing**: Police refused to press charges
  - **Note**: Would give victim presents, would have sex in the classroom by covering up the windows a hundred times

- **Mary Kay Letourneau**[428]
  - **Age**: 34
  - **Victim**: 12-year-old student
  - **Crime**: 2 counts of Second-degree rape of a child
  - **Sentencing**: Served 6 years
  - **Note**: After released from prison, married her victim. She already had two of his children.

- **Melissa Nosti**[429]
  - **Age**: 23
  - **Victim**: 15-year-old student
  - **Crime**: Sex with a minor
  - **Sentencing**: 1 week of an 18-month sentence
  - **Note**: Was an attendance officer. She became a flight attendant, which was used as why she shouldn't be in prison.

- **Shelley Dufresne & Rachel Respess**[430]
  - **Age**: 32 & 24 (respectively)
  - **Victim**: 16-year-old student
  - **Crime**: Consensual Sexual Intercourse with a Juvenile
  - **Sentencing**: No prison time
  - **Note**: Both women were later charged for the threesome act. No updates have been given.

- **Lisa LaVoie**[431]
  - **Age**: 24
  - **Victim**: 15-year-old student
  - **Crime**: Statutory Rape
  - **Sentencing**: No prison time
  - **Note**: Had attempted to run off with the victim. Judge granted parole. She later re-offended with same the victim. Sentenced to 15 years.

This is just 16 cases out of 600 I presently have. As you can see, I included a variety of sentencing, with the longest being 22 years and the shortest being 1 week. In many cases, women didn't serve any jail time. When we get into the law section of this chapter, we will discuss the sentencing gap between male and female predators. When looking at this list, if a woman rapes a boy, she'll likely get a slap on the wrist.

Prevalence

Many places around the world don't track the gender of the perpetrators or the victims of CSA, which seems crazy until you remember that most believe it is only men who rape.[432] Because of this misconception, the rate of women being perpetrators and boys being victims is very low. This is how society develops a poor foundation of understanding regarding Child Sexual Abuse, thus having minimal sympathy for boys and making excuses for women.

In 2004, it was estimated that 9.6% (1-in-10) of US students between 8 – 11th grade experienced both contact and non-contact CSA, with 7% reporting contact abuse.[432] Another report found that 7% of all middle and high school students were the target of CSA, though if you include verbal abuse, that number becomes 10%.[433] With nearly 50 million school children from pre-K to 12th, that is a probable 5 million children.[434]

It also estimated that between .04% – 5% of educators were guilty of CSA.[432] In 2019, there were 4,492,114 private and public teachers in the US. By gender, 3,337,641 (74.3%) were female.[435] That is an estimate of 1800 – 225,000 teachers that are potentially guilty of CSA.

These are appalling numbers. Nearly 225,000 teachers sexually abusing 5 million children; one wonders why there isn't more outrage. That's an estimate of 22 students abused for every one teacher. Certainly, there is a flaw in my conclusion, as I took two studies and used basic math to come to the figures. I stress that more study needs to be done. But given the statistic in **Catholic** section that 4% of priests had abused 26% of total victims[407] and 16% of priests had abused 5+ victims, here may be 4% - 16% of teachers abusing more than five victims.

Again, more research needs to be done.

Societal Response

The hardest part in dealing with teachers who sexually abuse their students is how society responds to the issue. For the most part, it is treated as a rare occurrence more than anything else, an anomaly. Women simply don't do this, and any women who do are somehow not responsible for her actions.

This mentality is seen clearly in the comment sections for news stories of female teachers sexually abusing students. Below are examples of people excusing the teacher, blaming the victim, or saying that no crime was committed[436]:

"[Offender name] must be epic she looks hot to me I hope they post the vids on the net"

"Why are all these female perverts so good looking?"

"Outside of her being a teacher … who cares. He's 17 and she's 27 and hot … but there's no real victim here (except maybe the husband) its not like he's in danger of being traumatized by the event."

"I don't feel bad the kid polled the hot teacher."

"Where were these hot horny teachers when I was 17?"

"I would have done her when I was 16."

"A 17 year old in college is probably mature enough to decide if he wants to have sex or not."

"I find it ridiculous that a sexually mature 17 year old male was harmed by having sex with this woman. He is not a child!"

"As much as I don't agree with what she did, you can't rape the willing"

"17 year old men … yes men … and they cried over having sex with a teacher? Omg … I would have cheered … something is very, very wrong here,"

"BS, he was willing and old enough … I am sure she did not rape him,"

"the guys LOVED it, I am sure. They are men, they loved gettin some from the older woman."

"the crime isn't the same as a man raping a girl by forcible compulsion. You will not find a case where the boy was not willing"

"Unless she drugged him with Viagra there was no rape involved … 300 times? The male reproductive organ doesn't work even once if it is afraid."

"Have you no conscience or shame? This woman did nothing to you that you didn't ask for … you boys just ruined this woman's life and sent her to jail for four years. How can you sleep at night?"

"… which leads to the possibility that they took advantage of her as she did of them."

"the kids got what they wanted. Claiming depression is just scamming for money. Its all adult consensual"

Not all comments are so negative to the victim.[437]

> *"These boys are young, emotionally and mentally and there is no excuse for an adult to put them in that position, especially an adult with a position of authority ... such as a teacher"*

> *"Predator, monster, pedophile"*

> *"she is a pedophile plain and simple and will re-offend. Just because she is a woman doesn't mean the same rules should apply"*

> *"she is a predator as much as any of these guys out there doing the same thing to girls."*

> *"If women want equality they must have it in full, and so some feminists want women to be sent in their droves to dirty, violent and overcrowded prisons for long periods of time."*

In this review of comments in response to a teacher abusing a child, 90% ignored that any abuse took place, while 10% believed the teacher engaged in non-consensual sex.[438]

To understand the full scope of society's response to teachers is to compare society's response to the Catholic church. When the story broke out about the church, everyone jumped on that bandwagon; everyone wanted to report the epidemic of what Priests did to little boys. Yet, by many estimates, the problem of schoolteachers molesting boys is likely 100 times bigger than priest abuse, yet very few articles are written about teacher molestation. In 2002, there were 2000 stories about sexual abuse in Catholic institutes, but only 4 stories about sexual abuse in public schools.[439]

Reporting

In today's world, female teachers are never seen as capable of wrongdoing. They are a paragon of virtue, a fountain of knowledge, and a second mommy to our children. Perhaps one reason for this public image is teacher unions. Like any union, they negotiate contracts for teachers to get them the best pay and benefits. You can certainly understand a union's advantage in teachers being seen as practical angels in society for contract negotiation. Thus, unions want to maintain this image in any way they can. While I am not here to debate the morals or ethics of unions, I will note that it is often quite difficult to fire a union worker. We, of course, hear about female teachers molesting students, but we only hear about a few cases a year, suggesting there may be cover-ups in play by schools and unions.[440]

An educator's sexual misconduct can be discovered in a few different ways[441]:

- Formal Complaint
- Informal Complaint
- Observed Abuse
- Observed Behavior
- Rumors

Formal and informal complaints are likely to be made by the victims or parents.[441]

It's estimated that only about 6% of all children report sexual abuse by an adult, and the remaining 94% don't tell anyone. Some may choose to inform a friend but bound them to secrecy. Another study found that 71% of victims told someone, with 57% telling more than one person. Of that, 70% told a friend, 32% a parent, 15% a teacher or other school employee, and 45% telling someone else.[441]

A report done in Canada from 1997 – 2017 found 750 cases of sexual offenses against 1,272 children carried out by 714 employees working in the school system.[442]

STUDENT/NON-STUDENT VICTIMS[18]

Total Victims (n=1272)[19]

- 84% Student Victims
- 16% Non-Student Victims

Total Student Victims (n=1009)[20]

- 76% Females
- 24% Males

Total Non-Student Victims (n=140)[21]

- 67% Females
- 33% Males

443

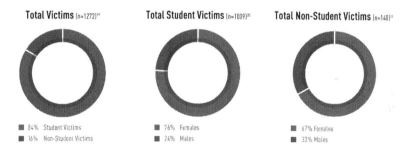

Female Victims Disclosed Their Abuse to (n=86)[42]

- 33% School personnel
- 23% Parents[43]
- 15% Friends
- 14% Police[44]
- 13% Counsellor, therapist, or psychologist
- 2% Other

Male Victims Disclosed Their Abuse to (n=32)

- 25% Friends
- 22% Parents
- 19% School personnel
- 9% Sister
- 9% Girlfriend or partner
- 16% Other

444

Where information about the disclosure or discovery of the child sexual abuse is known (n=253)

■ 53% Victims disclosed abuse[39]

■ 47% Abuse was discovered by a third party[40]

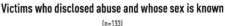
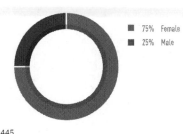

Victims who disclosed abuse and whose sex is known (n=133)

■ 75% Female

■ 25% Male

445

Looking at the graphs, we see that victims who disclose their abuse are overwhelmingly female. Females are more likely to report to school personnel and their parents, whereas males are more likely to disclose to friends and parents. However, out of the 24% of male student victims and 33% of male non-student victims (totaling 289 male victims), only 32 males disclosed their abuse, which is about 11% of male victims who told anyone about their abuse.

When students report, they tend to only report contact sexual abuse, such as touching, kissing, hugging, or intercourse. Verbal and visual abuses are rarely reported. Ninety percent of cases that come to the attention of a superintendent are contact sexual misconduct. However, most complaints are ignored or disbelieved, which can leave a student believing a teacher cannot be stopped or there is no reason to report it; they might as well let the abuse continue.[446]

Sentencing

A study looking at the statistics of female teacher sexual misconduct sentencing was compared to statutory guidelines for sentencing said crimes. It found that female teachers of sex crimes against minors receive a much-reduced prison sentence (if receiving a sentence at all).[447]

In 2003, researchers looked at 606 sexual misconduct discipline proceedings from Texas. Of those, 13% (77) were female. This would indicate that males are more likely to engage in CSA and confirm people's beliefs that rape is primarily a male trait. The key takeaway is that this is what is investigated, not a reflection of the true prevalence of this issue. A few years prior, a study asking students who were victims of CSA identified that 42% of perpetrators were female.[448] So half of perpetrators are female, but only 13% of perpetrators in prison were female. Let that sink in.

In 2017, the US Justice Department found that 10% of all students experience CSA by a school employee sometime between kindergarten and graduation from high school. Their study also found male perpetrators outnumber female perpetrators but that there has been an increase in female educators charged for CSA. It's not believed, however, that there is an increase of female abusers, but rather more female abusers are getting caught.[414]

Below are some examples of the favorable sentencing in favor of female teachers versus what the state's sentencing minimum guidelines.

Ohio

The suggested sentence is one to five years for 3rd Degree Felony of Sexual Battery. Thirty-six-year-old English teacher was indicted on six counts of Felony Sexual Battery against a child. Her plea agreement allowed her to be charged with a single count and serve no jail time. She lost her license and must register as a sex offender.[447]

Colorado

The sentencing guideline suggests up to eight years for Class 4 Felony of Sexual Assault on a Child. A 33-year-old female high school teacher was convicted of coercing a child into participating in sexual activity in a hotel room and had given him alcohol. Her own children were sleeping in the same hotel room. She received a 90-day sentence and had to register as a sex offender.[449]

Another teacher was charged with 13 counts of Class 4 Felony of Sexual Assault on a Child. She served no jail time and was required to attend a sex-offender treatment class.[449]

Maryland

For 3rd-degree sexual offenses, the punishment suggests up to 10 years in prison. A 23-year-old female teacher engaged in sexual contact with a child for 15 months. She was sentenced to 1 year in a detention center and wasn't required to register as a sex offender.[449]

Missouri

The suggested sentencing guidelines for 2nd-degree Statutory Rape and Sodomy are 7 and 10 years, respectively. A 22-year-old teacher was accused of three counts of 2nd-degree Statutory Rape and one count of Sodomy against a Jr. High boy. The teacher was given two years probation.[449]

Oklahoma

For 2nd-degree Rape, the punishment is up to 15-years in prison, and for Indecent Act upon a Child under 16: life. A 33-year-old computer teacher enticed a young boy with cigarettes and alcohol and took him to her home for sex. She was sentenced to 30-days.[450]

New Jersey

The Star-Ledger, a New Jersey newspaper, analyzed 97 cases of CSA. 72 cases are men, and 25 cases are women. While this was a small sampling size and not an official study, it reveals much of what I've spoken about in this book and suggests more study is needed.[451]

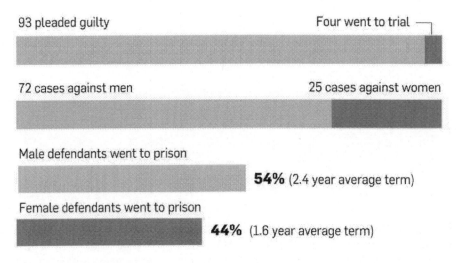

SEX AND TEACHERS

A breakdown of 97 cases in New Jersey from 2003-2013

93 pleaded guilty — Four went to trial

72 cases against men — 25 cases against women

Male defendants went to prison
54% (2.4 year average term)

Female defendants went to prison
44% (1.6 year average term)

451

From this image, we can see that of 97 cases, only four went to trial. Pleading guilty prior to trial is an indication there was a plea agreement. Men were more likely to go to jail through plea agreements than women and served 50% more jail time than women on average.

For Statutory Rape in New Jersey, the crime is punishable by 5 – 10 years in prison. 43-year-old Pamela Diehl-Moore was convicted of having an inappropriate relationship with a 13-year-old boy. She received a sentence of only 5 years probation.[452] The judge stated, *"I really don't see the harm that was done here... and certainly society doesn't need to be worried."* He later stated that the boy was satisfying his sexual needs and didn't see any evidence that the young man had been psychologically damaged by the teacher's actions.[452]

In comparison, James Darden, a 36-year-old teacher, was given 8.5 years with lifelong parole for having sex with a 13-year-old female student. The judge said to Darden, *"You realize what you have done to this child? You made her a woman well before her time, in a very inappropriate way."*[452]

With the similarity of these cases, we know two differences that seem to make all the difference:

1. The gender of the perpetrator
2. The gender of the victim

Female perpetrator, male victim in NJ warrants no jail time. Male perpetrator, female victim warrants 8 years in prison. A male victim is satisfying his needs; a female victim is forever violated.

Problems for Schools

While the impact of CSA is that children may be damaged due to the abuse, another victim of Teacher Misconduct that is easily overlooked... all other children. Whether a teacher is convicted of their crime, the victim's family often sues the school for not protecting children from predators. It's easy to blame the school system since it occurred in a school, as they hired the teacher, but there is only so much a school can do to prevent these tragedies from happening. Maybe more could have been done during the hiring process, but it's not like people put pedophile on their resumes.

Whether you think a school should have the added responsibility or not, they are still taken to court under U.S. Federal law, that victims of Educator Sexual Misconduct can receive monetary damages for sexual harassment under Title IX. Like all laws, this is a complicated issue.

In 2014, the Los Angeles Unified School District agreed to pay more than $139m to the families of 81 children sexually abused by a male elementary school teacher. More than $10m was paid to the victims of wrestling coach Josuah Carrier in Colorado Springs School District 11. Redlands Unified school district in California paid $6m for victims of a female teacher.[453]

In the paragraph above, that is $155m. Just 3 cases of payoffs. Think about this: how might that money have been otherwise used? Hire more teachers? Fix schools? More programs? Raises for teachers? There are many ways for that money to be used for education; instead, it went to pay victims of sexual misconduct by teachers. This is just the tip of the iceberg, as the amount of payoffs for all schools combined is in the billions.[454]

Billions upon billions of dollars not used on children's education because of Sexual Misconduct by Teachers.

I often hear schools saying they are under-funded. Having to pay for the actions of terrible teachers is one reason schools lack money. There are other reasons than that, but we are talking billions of dollars that could have been put toward children's education. And I don't blame the victim's family for suing the school. By right, they should. Losing a lawsuit should force schools to change how they do things, yet it doesn't seem to. In part because dealing with unions makes change extremely difficult. This is a problem that is here today, and very few are raising a fuss about it. And if for nothing else, this issue is having a detrimental effect on all our children and their futures.[453]

Prevention

How do we prevent teachers from sexually abusing children?

First off, there need to be real consequences for female teachers. As it stands, if I am a female teacher and I want to have sex with a male student, odds are I won't get caught. If I get caught, the school or my union will try to cover it up. If it can't be covered up, the odds are good I won't face jail time. If I face jail time, chances are good it will be a short sentence. And to top it all off, my life is not ruined; while I will lose my teaching license and be a registered sex offender (maybe), society will forgive me. As a female teacher, society has taught me that I can get a slap on the wrist for my misconduct, so I should go right ahead and molest my students.

If I'm a male teacher, I will probably be caught having sex with a student, all of society will hate me, I am more likely to go to prison, and life will be extremely difficult as very few will hire a man on the registry.

There have been proposed standards that could help protect students and reduce school liability. They are[455]:

(1) More Screening and Better Selections of Staff
(2) Implementing Formal Codes of Conduct
(3) Ensuring Safe Environments
(4) Policy on Staff-Student Communications Including Electronic/Social Media Use
(5) Educating Staff, Parents, and Students About CSA
(6) Monitoring All Staff
(7) Better Reporting Options for Victims

Mind you, no system is foolproof. While I think the school system should make more efforts to screen teachers and staff for potential problems, it's not like a teacher will advertise a sexual attraction to children. However, this is more about schools covering their ass in hopes of reducing the problem. Victims can't sue a school if the school did everything it could to prevent the problem. And the money that would go to pay the victims for the school's incompetence can instead enrich the education of all students.

Better Recruitment and Screening

Better recruitment and screening processing is a step in the right direction. While it is CYA for schools, it can also ensure they get the best staff to work with children. It can also keep out unfit individuals who may have had a criminal past or had some sort of plea deal. Not everyone who goes to court is bad for children, but it needs to be identified as a potential problem that needs to be investigated.

You might ask, don't schools already do this? You would think so, but not all schools do. Public schools require criminal background checks, but private schools are legally exempt. Public schools can check for disciplinary actions against an educator, but private schools don't record disciplinary actions or misconduct of teachers. Moreover, a school may forego reporting misconduct if it can make their school look bad, that it is better to cover up than to admit fault.[455]

The US Government Accountability Office (GAO) surveyed schools in the US. Of that, 46 states require background checks for public school jobs. Thirty-six states use state and federal sources for criminal data, while other states

137

only check for state violations. If an adult wishes to volunteer with a school to work with children, only 17 states require background checks.[456]

This might be appalling to you, but remember that the only thing a criminal background will determine is if someone has been convicted. Numbers show that this is a widespread problem, with upwards of a hundred thousand teachers committing sexual abuse, yet so few get caught, and even fewer get prosecuted. Only a fraction would be found through a background check. Few victims, parents, and schools report CSA to law enforcement agencies.

Safer Environment

There are steps schools can take to provide a safer environment. However, there is no such thing as 100% safety, and if an enterprising predator wishes to do wrong, they will find a way to make it happen. The goal then isn't 100% prevention... the goal is deterring it from happening, making it nearly impossible to do.

Of course, so many would claim any steps to make the environment safer would be totalitarian, but some things can be done that won't be so *Orwellian*:

- No staff should meet alone with students[457]
- No staff should meet with a student behind closed doors and/or covered windows[457]
- Staff should limit contact with children to school-sanctioned activities and programs only[458]
- Staff and volunteers need to be monitored, supervised, and evaluated through documented performance reviews[459]

CSA Prevention Training

All staff should be given awareness and prevention training for CSA. Teach for signs and encourage reporting of suspicious actions. Teach what boundaries teachers have and what ways to avoid violating boundaries.[460]

According to the GAO, only 18 states require schools to provide awareness and prevention training on sexual abuse or misconduct by school personnel. Furthermore, only 10 states required training of coaches. Where training was conducted, the focus was more on reporting incidents and less on identifying inappropriate boundaries. If child maltreatment was discussed, it rarely examined teachers abusing students.[460]

Law

The strictest law sometimes becomes the severest injustice.
– Benjamin Franklin

One challenge we will see in the legal system is that many laws were initially made to protect women and girls. When laws started to apply to men and boys, the same laws almost seemed non-existent. When everyone seems to push for an egalitarian society, very few seem to mind when laws overwhelmingly favor women and disenfranchise men.

To truly understand the depths of BSA, we need to understand laws in their entirety and how the system has failed men and boys. Laws are as much of a cultural element as any other aspect of society, and they can shape people's views. So if laws such as the Violence Against Women Act exist, people are likely to believe that an overwhelming number of domestic violence victims are women. If, say, a reform changed it to the Violence Against People Act or Violence Against Males and Females Act; people might understand that domestic violence is not a gendered problem but affects men and women in nearly equal numbers. Or at least beg the question, why make a law for men and women unless it is a problem that affects both?

There are laws that are specific to children or persons under the legal age of consent, but every country has its own laws. Thus, it is difficult to cover all the laws in the world to a sufficient means. Instead, this chapter will focus primarily on examples of double standards, the sentencing gap, and child support within the US court system.

The System Should be on Trial

"We're all raised in a culture that says boys are always supposed to initiate and enjoy a sexual experience and males are never supposed to see themselves or be seen as victims. The easiest default is to blame the victim, to say 'he wanted it, he must have chosen that.'"
-Peter Pollard, Co-Founder of 1in6

The problem with the court system is that sentencing and how the law is presented comes down to the personal interpretation of a judge. A judge can make many decisions affecting how the case is presented, influence the jury directly and indirectly, and even determine what sentencing should be despite the law's mandate. And while there are processes one can undertake to overrule a judgment, it proves exceedingly difficult to undo the actions of a judge. Unfortunately, I don't have a recommendation for a better system; all I can do is point out a big problem affecting men and boys that our society ignores.

Perhaps the biggest problem is the Old Guard Judges and the Social Justice Judges. In many ways, they seem antagonistic to one another because they come from different times. For instance, when a boy has been raped by a female, the Old Guard Judge will see the female as having made a mistake and will be given next to no sentencing. The Social Justice Judge will see a woman who is a victim of the Patriarchy, which her actions resulted from; thus, she is not at all responsible and serves no jail time. Both types would let a guilty woman go free for entirely different reasons. And when it comes to males who might be guilty, they will throw the book at them.

Then there are the True Judges. The law is the law. If you violate the law, you suffer consequences. Your gender is irrelevant. This judge, unlike the other two, is a relatively uncommon type. Feel lucky if you get one.

Of course, these are my personal observations. You are free to make your own conclusions, and you are welcome to prove me wrong. However, one study I found seems to support my observations. In the study, it was argued many judges and prosecutors don't believe males can be raped because all males want sex or because they had an erection. Judges and prosecutors are so far removed from society that they are "shrouded by misconceptions and ignorance". Thus, no harm is done to males, and any ruling by a court is based on that founding, allowing female perpetrators to feel the light touch of the law. These are beliefs echoed beyond the courtroom and found within many homes across the world.[461]

Maybe judges and prosecutors are not entirely at fault, but I still put a lot of responsibility on them. While there is so much about protecting women from harmful men, no one stops to think about how boys need the same protection from women.[461]

After all, we only know what we are taught:

- 90% of rape victims are female[257]
- 1 in 4 women will be sexually abused in their lifetimes[262]
- All males want sex[332]
- It is a good thing when males have sex[325]

I can't really blame people for the conclusions they draw on their lack of information. However, I hold people responsible for lack of critical thinking, for not going out there and finding the truth, the truth I found in writing this book series. And it's not like I'm making shit up; I went out and found the sources. More intelligent people than me should have done their homework, and this book shouldn't need to be made because it would already be common knowledge. Instead, I have to write this book hoping to educate the world that men and boys can be raped, and women and girls can be perpetrators, and all the other things I state in my books.

Facing this world, why should any boy report to their school, to the police, or go to trial when dealing with a female predator? We see so many examples of women getting a slap on the wrist; all it does is make boys feel ashamed of their actions. In other places in the world, a boy will face the reality that they are less of a man for letting it happen. Until recently, reporting your pastor or scout leader proved ineffective. These institutions, along with schools and Hollywood, would rather cover it up and pretend it didn't happen rather than force the perpetrators to face legal ramifications and prevent it from happening again.

Perhaps one of the biggest challenges boys face is even law enforcement agencies don't recognize them as victims. In 2011, the FBI announced changing their definition of rape from "the carnal knowledge of a female, forcibly and against her will", which only identifies female victims, to the standard today "penetration, no matter how slight, of the vagina or anus with any body part or object, or oral penetration by a sex organ of another person, without the consent of the victim."[462] This allows males to be recognized, but only if the perpetrator penetrates the boy. Lacking that, it's not rape. This is an example of laws protecting women and girls and disenfranchising boys and men.[266]

You might say:

> That's just the FBI; they don't really deal with rapists except under special circumstances. The rest of the US and their respective court systems deal with these issues, and they are fairer; they are for protecting boys and girls, men and women.

It would be great if that were true.

Michael M. v. Superior Court of Sonoma County

In Michael M. v. Superior Court of Sonoma County (1981)[463], Michael was charged with Statutory Rape and argued that the law was unconstitutional regarding the Equal Protection Clause of the 14th amendment as it precludes protection and assumes guilt for males. At the time, the California law stated: "*an act of sexual intercourse accomplished with a female not the wife of the perpetrator, where the female is under the age of 18 years.*"

The California Supreme Court found that the statute did discriminate based on gender but decided the law was not unconstitutional because of the physiological differences between males and females, primarily that females can get pregnant. Justice Richardson wrote[464]:

> *...the law challenged herein is supported not by mere social convention but by the immutable physiological fact that it is the female exclusively who can become pregnant. This changeless physical law, coupled with the tragic human costs of illegitimate teenage pregnancies, generates a compelling and demonstrable state interests in minimizing both the number of such pregnancies and their disastrous consequences.*

This case was brought to the Supreme Court of the United States. They ruled states could make laws specific to gender to address the unique challenges girls face. These challenges for this case were[464]:

1. Girls alone face the risk of "illegitimate pregnancy"
2. Girls face the added burden of being susceptible to sexually transmitted diseases
3. Girls are susceptible to both psychological and physical coercion to engage in sexual relationships
4. The state alone should not shoulder the burden associated with the costs of teenage pregnancy

Another reasoning adopted for this kind of discriminatory law is the belief boys were incapable of being harmed by sex, unlike girls.[464] Another argument made during this law challenge was by the ACLU in 1979[465]:

> *The trouble with the majority's justification of the disparate treatment is that it disregards the fact that minor males can and do suffer from sexual intercourse harm as grave as, albeit different from, that suffered by minor females... minor males are assumed to be able to "take care of themselves." For them, early sexual experience is supposed to be a welcome and pleasant initiation creating no appreciable risk of psychological harm.*

This was rejected by the state of California because there was no evidence that an "older minor" girl or adult woman was likely to be the aggressor or initiator of sexual contact with boys or men. This would render males as invisible victims as they could not be recognized as ever being victims, so thus they gained no legal protection.[465] Later, the state of California would change the law to be gender neutral that any sex with a person under the age of 18 is unlawful, even if the perpetrator is also under the age of 18.[466]

Michael's case is one such example of a more significant issue that will be explored more in **Child Support** later in this section. Primarily, there are two very different standards for female and male victims of statutory rape. Female victims are provided with legal protections, whereas male victims are not and therefore are not deserving of any protection.[466]

While the California law has changed, the mindset remains unchanged. Equal under the law, but women are more equal than men. Feels like I'm reading "Animal Farm". Even today, the idea that a woman can be a rapist like a man is just too impossible for people to handle. Yet women possess the same emotional and psychological desires as men, which makes women just as capable of doing immoral acts such as statutory rape of boys.[466]

The upside is that laws have been changed to be gender-neutral regarding CSA. However, you cannot change people's perceptions, whether the Old Guard Judges who see women as incapable of being evil like men or the Social Justice Judges who see women as victims even when they are perpetrators. No matter how much laws changes, judges, prosecutors, and society cannot see young males fall victim to female sexual predators.[467]

Sentencing Gap

When we analyze judges' rulings on women molesting adolescent boys, we can conclude that boys are seen as adult men. Whereas, with the genders flipped, an underage girl can never consent to sex, and a man is always guilty even if said girl lied about her age. Boys are assumed to know the risk involved with sex, and girls can never understand the risk. A girl can make the same decision as a boy, and the law will provide her safe harbor and protection.[468]

This calls for judges and the world itself to be educated on the effects that an adult woman can have on a boy, from easily being coerced to long-term damages. From my observations, no one really wants to charge a female with a crime, from the police not taking it seriously to judges reducing the otherwise mandatory (or strongly suggested) sentencing. Because of this, the criminal justice system will always make excuses that show women they can get away with the crime.[468]

The Sentencing Gap refers to the discrimination in sentencing between two demographics. Reports show men on average have up to 31% longer sentences than women. One likely explanation for this is **stereotypical femininity**. The more a perpetrator displays stereotypical feminine traits, such as being a mother, the more likely she is to receive a reduced sentence (or no sentence at all). Lacking feminine characteristics, they are likely to get a harsher punishment.[469]

A survey of 487 media reports from Australia and the UK on female sex offenders from 2000 – 2010 found that women who offended against boys (compared to all other female crimes) were the most likely to receive lighter sentences, including suspension. In one high-profile case in Australia in 2004, a 37-year-old teacher was found guilty on 6 counts of sexual penetration with a child and was given a 3-year suspended sentence of twenty-two months. The judge felt she was not a predator.[352]

We see stories of women getting a light sentence, but we can say those are just the exception. After all, I identified a woman who got 21 years in prison, proving women receive harsh sentences. However, when looking at the prison population in the US by sex crimes, only 4% in 2008 were women. We know a large population of women engage in CSA and is comparable to men, yet only represent a small percentage actually in prison.[470] Texas estimates up to 20% of all molesters are female, yet only 221 women serve time for sex offenses compared to 12,215 men. That is roughly 2% of all prisoners for sex offenses. And that was at a 5-year high in 2008.[471]

A small sample size of judges (23 males, 3 females) were asked about their considerations for female offenders. A third stated they would protect the female offender from incarceration. Most judges stated the offender's children would influence their decision toward leniency, especially if they were the primary caretakers. They also stated males would receive the same leniency if they were the primary caretakers of their children.[472]

Judges' methodology toward sentencing decisions relies on three dimensions:

- Offender Dangerousness
- Blameworthiness
- Practical constraints of the court

When looking at these three items, it makes sense that judges are lenient on females, as men are consistently portrayed as the more dangerous offender. It's only when a judge perceives a female offender to break gender stereotypes will they consider giving a harsher sentence.[473]

With stereotypes, males are perceived as the only predator, and the same bias that goes easy on female predators often means judges go harsher on male predators. Males are perceived as more dangerous and threatening to communities and are more likely to re-offend. Women are more trustworthy and less likely to re-offend when they are on probation and monitored by the system. Women can still add to their community once they receive counseling or work through the system to be responsible citizens once more.[474]

An excellent example of women getting a lighter sentence and the book thrown at men can be seen in three cases[475]:

- Former Baltimore Ravens cheerleader Molly Shattuck was sentenced to 48 weekends at a work detention facility—spread out over the next two years—for performing oral sex on a boy.

- A 32-year-old man was found guilty of sexually abusing a girl for years, starting when she was 6. He was sentenced to 366 years to life in prison.

- A 25-year-old woman pleaded guilty to the attempted rape of a boy. She previously had been indicted for the first-degree rape of another boy. In a plea deal, she got 5 years probation.

- Miranda Smith, 30, pleaded no contest to having her 2-year-old son use a toy on her vagina, recorded it, then sent the video to her boyfriend. Initially sentenced to 10 years to life, she was later released from prison, as her attorney argued the strict definition of rape (penetration) didn't apply to her.[253]

Of course, raping a little girl for years seems much worse than trying to have sex with a boy or even sucking off a little boy or having him use a sex toy, but 366 years in prison... doesn't that seem extreme? And if that is OK in your book, shouldn't the women have gotten a longer sentence? And if the women's sentences are OK, then shouldn't his sentence be more reasonable? Or does it come down to that damage to a girl is far greater than the damage done to a boy? Or that a woman is not truly a predator at all? While you think about it, consider these other cases[475]:

- Utah man charged 15 to life for pleading guilty to 8 charges of rape and abuse against a 14-year-old boy

- Indiana man sentenced to 200 years in prison for abusing a boy

- Maryland man sentenced to life in prison plus 215 years for abusing a boy

The book was still thrown at men when both the perpetrator and the victim were male. So I guess it's not so much what gender the victim is; all that seems to matter is the perpetrator. Being male is the worst crime of all, especially regarding rape. Perhaps the reason sentencing is such a double standard is due to perceived power. Men are perceived to desire power and control others, and women can never have power. Men are perceived to want sex for physical gratification, while women want sex for emotional reasons and never for gratification.

When a man is perceived to have power over another, his actions are exploitative. In the case of sexual assault, a man's actions must be judged more harshly as he exploited his victim. Women only desire an emotional bond, and their intentions are more noble, and their victims can only really enjoy the sexual gratification she is giving them. Women, even in a position of authority, really have no power.[476]

You might find this insulting... I know I do. Yet, this is the perception of society.

Child Support

It seems unfair that he was taken advantage of, and then he gets prosecuted for child support. He's considered a victim on one hand and a perpetrator on the other.

–Mary Ann Mason

What's most shocking in cases involving BSA is not that women get a lighter sentence or the view boys are not seen as victims. That's how society has been all my life; so it really comes as no surprise for me in my research. No no, the most shocking thing I discovered in my research for this book is the pregnancy that results from the sexual assault that puts boys on the hook for child support.

One argument why it is so much worse for a man to rape a girl versus a woman to have sex with a boy is that a girl is forever altered; she becomes a woman before she is ready. Yet, this is not ascribed to boys, that the sexual act by women forces boys to grow up before they're ready. Especially since she has a baby, he is now financially responsible for paying for a child when he's incapable of caring for himself.

How is this possible? After all, a woman lost her livelihood and possibly faced criminal justice because of her actions. Shouldn't that preclude him from any responsibility for her misconduct when legally he can't consent to sex? You'd think so.

This becomes possible because her punishment results from Criminal Court, but for a boy to be financially responsible for a baby results from Family Court. As we will discuss in a future book about divorce and child custody, there is a difference between Criminal Court and Family Court, and the outcome of one doesn't affect the other.

In this section, we will look at cases that required boys to become men and pay for a child they couldn't consent to. Keep in mind that the state doesn't want to shoulder the burden of a child's welfare and will find some man to be responsible for the welfare of a child (with interest) no matter what the circumstances are, and they get away with it.

Hermesmann v. Seyer

Colleen Hermesmann was a babysitter for Shane Seyer in 1987. The 16-year-old began a sexual relationship with the 12-year-old boy. Two years later, their daughter was born. She was charged with **Engaging in the Act of Sexual Intercourse with a Child Under Sixteen**. She became a Juvenile Offender to **Contributing to a Child's Misconduct**, which is not a sexual crime.[477]

When Seyer was 16, the Kansas Department of Social and Rehabilitation Services took Seyer to court, seeking child support. Since this was a civil court case, the criminality of how the baby was born was not addressed. Kansas Department was awarded $7000 USD ($13,800 in 2021).[477] Understand that the Kansas Department of Social and Rehabilitation is being awarded this money from the minor from the moment the baby was born. Meaning, Seyer was supposed to pay for the welfare of the child, even though he was 14 when the child was born.

In 1993, the Kansas Supreme Court rejected an appeal by Seyer. Even though by criminal court standards Seyer wasn't able to consent, the Kansas Supreme Court stated by civil court standards, since he did not lodge a complaint to a parent or other authority figure, he had indeed consented to sex and thus responsible for the child.[477]

Additionally, the mother's culpability under criminal statutes was of no relevance in determining a father's child support liability in a civil case.[477] The court stated[478]:

> This State's interest in requiring minor parents to support their children overrides the State's competing interest in protecting juveniles from improvident acts, even when such acts may include criminal activity on the part of the other parent.

> Considering the three persons directly involved, [the mother, the father, and the child,] the interests of [the child] are superior, as a matter of public policy, to those of either or both of her parents.

> This minor child, the only truly innocent party, is entitled to support from both her parents, regardless of their ages.

Effectively, their only focus is on the baby in a civil court matter. No matter how that child was conceived, their well-being outweighed deterring statutory rape.

Stringer v. Department of Human Services

Justin Stringer was 15 years old when he had sex with 19-year-old Larena Baker. At the end of 1988, KB was born. Shortly after, Baker sued Stringer in Texas to establish paternity and an order for him to pay child support. Stringer was found to be the father via DNA testing; however, the district court dismissed Baker's child support action.[478]

Twelve years later, Baker reopened the case in Oklahoma. Upon receiving notice from the Oklahoma DHS Office of Administrative Hearings for Child Support, Stringer filed a petition to relinquish his parental right. The court in McCurtain County took the case. The court ordered Justin Stringer to pay future and past-due child support.[478]

Stringer took the case to the Court of Civil Appeals of the State of Oklahoma. The court identified that while Baker's action was rape under Oklahoma criminal law, Stringer never filed a rape charge against Baker. Instead, Stringer acknowledged he consented to the sex even though, by Texas and Oklahoma criminal law, he couldn't have consented.[478]

Stringer didn't dispute consent or the fact the child was his. His dispute was that he was liable for child support, given he was too young by criminal law to consent. He argued Baker should not be permitted to profit from her criminal acts through an award of child support.[478]

The Appeals court ruled that child support is for the benefit of the child, not the parent. The guidelines for child support focus on parental status, not marital. Since Stringer has been found to be the father through testing, he is, therefore, liable for the child. Furthermore, Stringer voluntarily engaged in sex with Baker, which resulted in the conception of KB. They stated parental support of children outweighs any policy of protecting minors from their willing participation in sexual misconduct with adults. Stringer's status as a minor at the time does not absolve him of his responsibility.[478]

Once again, this is a case of what is best for the child. Now perhaps Stringer is trying to use the law to escape his responsibility for child support, but he is required to pay not only when he was an adult capable of earning an income but also when he was still underage.

I also dislike Oklahoma made Sayer pay for this despite being dismissed in Texas. Oklahoma likely didn't want to be financially responsible for the child and pursued Stringer to be economically accountable rather than honor the judgment of the Texas court.

In re Paternity of JLH,

Fifteen-year-old JJG lived in a home for children in La Crosse. In 1981, he ran away and met a girl named LH. She was 18. He went with her to her father's house, where he stayed for fourteen days and had sex with her on four separate occasions. She had initiated sexual intercourse with him and had taught him how to have sex since he was a virgin. This union results in a pregnancy.[479]

LH gets the court to prove JJG is the father, and the court orders him to pay child support equal to 17% of his gross income. JJG took this to the Court of Appeals in Wisconsin. He argues that because he was sexually assaulted and unable to consent under sexual assault law, he shouldn't be required to pay child support, which would be a profit to LH for her crime. The court ruling violated his constitutional rights of substantive due process and equal protection. JJG asserts that he suffered psychological damages because of the sexual assault, and he cannot support himself, much less support a child.[479]

The Appeals Court rejected the assertion that at 15, he was incapable of consent. They also reject that because the action was illegal should preclude him from paying child support, as statutory rape is a criminal justice issue and child support is a civil proceedings issue. In addition, they don't believe the sex with LH was forced upon him or occurred without consent. The kissing and petting prior to intercourse can be seen as evidence of his willing and consensual participation. Because the court determined the sex was consensual, then the resulting parenthood was also voluntary.[479]

The Appeals Court also stated his paying child support to LH was not a benefit for her crime, but the child's benefit. LH receives support payments but only in trust to be used for the child's welfare.[479]

JJG's father states in an affidavit that he is a practicing clinical psychologist, and his son has been hospitalized for severe psychiatric problems on five occasions in a single year. JJG is incapable of holding a permanent job and will likely never be able to have a permanent full-time job. The father's position is that the sexual assault is partly to blame for his son's psychiatric problems. With the "voluntary parenthood" the Court claims he consented to, his psychological state doesn't affect the fairness of his parental responsibility and is only relevant to the amount of child support he must pay.[479]

JJG also argues existing law discriminates against males as female assault victims can end their pregnancy, but males cannot terminate their parental responsibility. The Court of Appeals saw no evidence JJG attempted to compel LH to have an abortion, so they considered this a non-issue.[479]

The court's final ruling was to uphold the lower court's decision.[479]

County of San Luis Obispo v. Nathaniel J.

In 1995, 34-year-old Ricci Jones gave birth to a daughter. The father, Nathaniel J., was 15 years old when the child was conceived. Nathaniel told police the sexual intercourse was a mutually agreeable act. Jones was convicted of **Unlawful Sexual Intercourse with a Minor.**[480]

Nathaniel appeals the decision to the Superior Court of San Luis Obispo County. He argues that extracting child support from a victim of statutory rape violates public policy. He also contends he was denied due process of the law. The public policy protects him from the effect of sexual exploitation by an adult, which the reserved child support order is the kind of exploitation the Legislature intended to prevent as it inflicts an economic loss on a crime victim.[480]

Nathaniel appeals the decision to the Superior Court of San Luis Obispo County. He argues that extracting child support from a victim of statutory rape violates public policy. He also contends he was denied due process of the law. The public policy protects him from the effect of sexual exploitation by an adult, to which the reserved child support order is the kind of exploitation the Legislature intended to prevent as it inflicts an economic loss on a crime victim.[480]

The Court states that by California law, every child has a right to receive support from both parents, and they share equal responsibility. Moreover, since Nathaniel consented to the sex, he was not a victim from a civil standpoint. He was a willing participant, so he was not a typical crime victim. As a result, the higher Court affirmed the original decision of the lower court.[480]

Nick Olivas

Nick Olivas was 14 years old when he had sex with a 20-year-old woman. The victim feels this woman took advantage of a lonely kid with a rough childhood. Arizona Law states that a child younger than 15 cannot consent to sex with an adult. Nick didn't press charges, nor was he aware he could. He graduated high school, went to college, and became a medical assistant.[481]

When Nick turned 21, the Arizona Department of Economic Services (DES) told Nick not only must he pay child support, but he also owed $15,000 USD in back payments, medical bills, and interest. This letter is how Nick learned he was a father. The state has seized money from his bank account and is garnishing his wages at $380/month.[481]

Nick wants to do right by his daughter and is willing to pay child support. He feels, however, that it is not right for the state to charge him for when he was still a child himself nor knew the girl existed. DES disagrees as it is about the care of the child, who had no control over the situation.[481]

Nick wants to do right by his daughter and is willing to pay child support. He feels, however, that it is not right for the state to charge him for when he was still a child himself, nor knew the girl existed. DES disagrees as it is about the care of the child, who had no control over the situation.[481]

Like Nick had any control over the situation!? He woke up one day and opened a letter telling him he had a 6-year-old girl. The child had no control, but the other child, Nick, seems to have complete control, according to DES.

Mel Feit, director of National Center for Men, felt the basic legal premise of rape is that the victim can't be held responsible. And with statutory rape, even if the victim was willing, they still cannot be held accountable as they couldn't knowingly consent.[481]

> *"The idea that a woman would have to send money to a man who raped her is absolutely off-the-charts ridiculous. It wouldn't be tolerated, and it shouldn't be tolerated."*
>
> *"We're not going to hold him responsible for the sex act, so to then turn around and say we're going to hold him responsible for the child that resulted from that act is off-the-charts ridiculous. It makes no sense."*
>
> **-Mel Feit, director of National Center for Men**[481]

Arizona (as with many other states) has no exemption for a child born to a child. However, DES cannot get child support against a non-custodial parent until they are legally an adult. It also doesn't matter whether a parent knows of the child, as child support is a separate legal issue from custody. DES can also garnish wages up to 50% of income, take tax returns, put a lien on a home or vehicle, suspend driver's licenses, and revoke passports. It can also take money directly out of a bank account.[481]

Discussion

When looking at BSA and Child Support, it's like this is Schrodinger's Cat: a boy is simultaneously a victim and a victimizer. He can be a victim of statutory rape and a deadbeat dad for not paying child support when he was incapable of caring for himself. In criminal court, he's a child who can't consent, but in civil court, he's an adult. Worse, the civil court can decide he did consent, even with laws today such as Affirmative Consent that a person can remove their consent at any time, and any resulting action is deemed rape unless the court is trying to find someone to pay the bills.

I love how the law states that a child has a right to two parents, yet the mother can decide if the father has any right to see the child. Custody and child support are considered two different legal issues.

In all fairness, when it comes to the state paying child support, the money has to come from somewhere. Taxpayers are the primary source to help families in need. In order to recoup the high costs, the state needs to collect money back from parents who aren't contributing, so they go after the father for lack of financial involvement. It makes sense, though a later book will show the injustice of child support.

Going after boys who were sexually abused makes little sense, and it is far from fair. There is a reason age of consent laws exist, as a child/teen is incapable of making an adult decision regarding something that affects the rest of their lives. Yet, when the Civil and Family court judges say that a victim has responsibilities, they hurt boys a second time. The system forever alters boys' lives. In the eyes of the court, there is an even greater victim; the child born of the criminal action. This creates a financial hardship that can affect boys' lives even before it starts. *The best interest of the child* only doesn't cover the child that got raped... what about his best interests?[482]

Financial Abortion

Another thing that irks me is that the civil court system says women who rape boys who then are taken to court for child custody payments are not rewarded, that the money goes to the child. As will be discussed in a future book, the problem with this is the lack of oversight in how women spend the money. Mothers can spend the money however they want. They don't need to show receipts for what they purchased, so there is no way to know if the money spent was truly for the baby or something else. Sure, we'd like to believe the mothers would use the money responsibly, but we'd also like to believe women don't rape boys. So yes, the boys in these appeals were right; these women are rewarded for committing a crime.

What's my solution? **Financial Abortion.**

Financial abortion is a controversial concept for reproductive rights. Women and girls are allowed many options for her reproductive rights, from keeping the baby, excluding the father from child's life, giving up the baby for adoption, safe haven baby dumping, and abortion. The only rights males have is pay for the baby, pay for the baby, and pay for the baby. In situations such as sexual assault of a minor, since the father was not capable under criminal law to consent, he should be able to remove himself from the baby's life and financial responsibility.

Perhaps if the family and civil courts recognize a male can be a victim of a female perpetrator and give him a chance to opt out financially, then perhaps boys would be more willing to come forward to report their rapes and abuses. Boys will see that their reporting will mean actual consequences for the perpetrator.

Reporting & Disclosures

As we discussed in ABUSE, most boys don't report their abuse. This is doubly so when it comes to sexual abuse. Why? It's unsafe to do so. Those who disclosed are disbelieved and mocked. They face hostile responses from their peers and community. They are left unprotected, as society will more likely rally behind the female perpetrator and excuse their actions as being virtuous. Why would a boy put themselves in harm's way when staying compliant, no matter how damaging, is the safer of two options?[483]

To Whom

Most boys don't report their abuse. If they do, it's most often to a friend they swear to secrecy. The next likely person they would tell is their mother or a teacher. A boy may be reluctant to tell an authority figure for fear that they will get the police involved, though they may find out by other means and will call the police.[350]

Of all child victims, only about 60% report the abuse to a third party. By gender, that is 42% boys and 72% girls. Fifty-four percent of all children told a friend, and 23% informed a family member. Up to 5% of victims will disclose to school services, medical professionals, or the police.[484] When it comes to intrafamilial abuse, children found it easier to disclose their father's abuse than their mother.[355]

As mentioned, parents are often the ones that come forward when a boy is being sexually abused. And a lot of times, the boy is not happy about it. Boys see this as a positive experience and don't want to lose the status of having a girlfriend or even having sex, even if both are done so in secret.[327]

Length of Time

A Northern Ireland study of 2,079 adults who had been sexually abused as children found that 44% of boys had reported their abuse within 48 hours of its first occurrence. Beyond the first 48 hours, only 17% of boys reported their abuse at all during childhood. The remaining 39% didn't report their sexual abuse until adulthood.[485]

On average, men who waited until adulthood to report their sexual abuse waited two decades before feeling capable of divulging it. Generally, men will tell their closest friend rather than their parents or authority figure. Peers may lack awareness of what resources or support are available as most believe rape of boys is very rare.[485]

Unknown Abuse

One reason boys may not initially report sexual abuse is they are unaware their experience is abuse. Our society projects the images to boys that they're basically walking penises and they want sex, so when they receive it, boys believe this is what they're supposed to want. Moreover, if they think they're supposed to want this, that their abuser is giving them something special, then the last thing a boy wants to do is get their abuser in trouble.[486]

Threats

Another likely reason a boy may not report their abuser is if their abuser has used threats of harm to the victim and/or the victim's family. Included with verbal threats is physical abuse, that the perpetrator might be physically harming them.[486]

Disbelieved

Perhaps the biggest reason for not reporting is that the perpetrator is an authority figure. As we've discussed in this chapter, they may be a scout leader, a big name in Hollywood, a religious leader, a teacher, or other figures that are considered important and/or a community leader. Because of their influence and likeability, a boy may feel they won't be believed. Why would such an important person do something so wrong? Quite often, a person of such influence engages in CSA because no one would suspect them.[486]

Societal Rejection

In many ways, it is worse now for boys than ever before. Boys are taught that they are responsible for all the problems in the world, that their need to express masculinity is toxic, and they will grow up to be rapists. It is their privilege that prevents women from succeeding.[487]

On top of that, boys are told their issues are in no way comparable to girls'. Instead, boys are quickly put on medications to curb their behavior and are more likely to get in trouble and drop out of school. Those in a position of power have no qualms about destroying a boy's life. And destroy they will, as we now live in a society where if you're not in the top 20% of males, the likelihood that you will date or have sex drops significantly, with vastly more males remaining virgins past the age of 18 than ever before.[488]

Even in yesteryear, when males had more of a chance to be married with children, males had to be dominant, independent, powerful, and aggressive. Anything less, and you weren't considered a man. Males had to prove their worth through competition and the suppression of emotions. They weren't allowed to feel helpless or vulnerable. They also had to be experts at sex, that any female they were with they could completely satisfy her and not expect any form of reciprocation.[489]

For a male to admit that a sexual experience with a female, especially an adult female, was a negative experience is likely to render his masculinity obsolete. Furthermore, he faces the fear that he might not be respected with a loss of his masculinity, whether this is in the first world or third world.[489]

And I hear the argument now, *"That's the Patriarchy. The Patriarchy hurts men by putting them into strict gender roles"*. The Patriarchy, the system designed by men for men, that hurts men. That's what Feminism fights against, to undo the system of oppression so everyone, men and women alike, can be free to express themselves.

The Feminist solution to the Patriarchy was to discourage stereotypical (in their viewpoint) masculinity and say that it is OK for men to have feelings. Yet it was also Feminists who talked about "Drinking Male Tears" as a response to men discussing the challenges or difficulties they have in life.[490] It was also Feminists who pulled fire alarms at Men's Rights conferences and yelled at them.[491] Again, it was also Feminists that stated it was OK to joke about hating men.[492]

The Feminist solution to the Patriarchy was to attack any male who attempted to take any attention away from females in any shape or form, even though these men were technically attempting to fight the supposed Patriarchy. And even if you want to say, **Not All Feminists Are Like That**

(NAFALT), that it wasn't all feminists who committed misandry... where was the National Organization of Women (NOW) condemning these actions?

How can a male believe he can have emotions or report his abuse if society makes fun of his abuse or says that his pain is nothing? The Societal Rejection of a male and his masculinity is easy to believe that it is other males rejecting him, when in fact, it is also females who will reject him for not being man enough for their needs, even within the Feminist mindset.

Criminality

Whether a boy has voluntarily committed a crime or is forced to, they may fear that coming forward to report sexual abuse will land them in jail. This can include victims of sex trafficking, and their abusers may lie to them that they can't go to the police because they would be as guilty as their abusers. And it is easy to believe this, as they lack education or are sheltered.

Sex Trafficking will be discussed in the next chapter.

Professionals

Schools

Professionals such as teachers or counselors who interact with children daily may overlook warning signs in boys that they will often see in girls. Once again, this is due to the misinformation that boys are a vast minority of victims; professionals are not looking for problematic symptoms in boys. Possibly, if told that boys are just as likely as girls to be victims of sexual abuse, then professions might pay more attention to boys. Studies have found that girls are six times more likely to be identified as suffering sexual abuse than boys. Even worse, boys are more likely to be blamed for their own victimization than girls are, that most often they're seen as wanting the sex, so they aren't really victims.

Mental Health Professions

Other professionals that might overlook BSA are in the mental health field. While they are trained to look for signs of sexual abuse in females, they easily overlook males because the literature and education state that males are rarely affected by sexual abuse. They only know what they're taught, though I argue that all their years in the field should indicate to them that what they were taught does not conform to reality based on talking to their patients.

British clinical psychologists, psychiatrists, and nurses (within the mental health field) were given identical male and female case vignettes that demonstrated they were sexually abused. They were given a questionnaire that asked about patients with a history of sexual abuse, if they ask their patients about their history, what they do when learning of such a history, and how much training they have in helping patients with a sexually abused past.[493]

Of 179 questionnaires sent out to a group of professionals, only 111 responded. They were 45 nurses, 25 psychiatrists, and 41 psychologists. It was found that the nurses were more likely to identify males to have a history of sexual abuse, albeit not to a great degree.[493]

1. Do professionals ask male patients about a history of CSA? Should they be asked? Why don't you ask?

A third of the staff stated they never ask males about CSA. About 50% say they ask about a third of the time, and 18% say they ask half the time. Psychiatrists seemed more likely to ask to some degree, followed by nurses, and then psychologists were the least likely to ask.[493] We see this pattern repeat for if males should be asked, as 29% of nurses believe men should always be asked compared to the 11.3% of the other two professions combined.[494]

Of the 20% who don't ask male patients about a history of sexual abuse, the reason given were[495]:

- Asking can be too intrusive for patients and prevent engagement
- It is inappropriate to ask patients whose presenting problems are "irrelevant to sexual abuse," for example, simple phobias or psychosis
- If the patient is too distressed or actively psychotic
- The patient could become angry or violent
- It is uncomfortable asking
- It could worsen a patient's condition
- One could implant false memories
- There may be more pertinent issues to assess in the time given
- They may not be the resources to deal with the consequences of disclosure

Looking at this list, one can see that mental health professionals don't want the responsibility of a male's sexual history. Instead, they make up excuses to conform to the idea that males continue to be the minority of victims.

2. How do you find out about sexual abuse history? What do you do when you find out? Does it affect your approach to care?

The most common way mental health professionals learn about a man's CSA is if the patient brings it up. About a third bring it up when it comes to the mental health professional's mind, and the last common way is through a questionnaire.[495]

Psychologists were more likely to deal with the issue upon hearing it than less than half of the psychiatrists and nurses were. Psychiatrists and nurses were more likely to refer them to other professionals. About a quarter of psychiatrists report they would do nothing upon learning of a BSA past.[496]

Does learning of abuse change the standard of care professionals provide? Sixty-five percent said that it would change it somewhat. Eighteen percent said it wouldn't change their standard of care (most of which were nurses), and 17% said it would drastically change their level of care.[496]

3. What amount of training have your received on male CSA? Do you feel you've had sufficient training?

Two-thirds of staff state they've received no training for male CSA. Of the 30% who received training, it was reported to be a 2-day workshop or as part of their schooling. Psychologists were the ones to report the highest rate of training.[496]

Only a third reported feeling they had adequate training to deal with BSA. Nineteen percent of nurses and 26% of psychologists felt they had sufficient training. Psychiatrists might be overconfident at 61%, given only a third stated they received any training at all.[497]

Caretakers

Fortunately, professionals such as caretakers or medical staff (doctors and nurses) are more likely to report BSA. Often this requires closer inspection that might be unnoticeable in other situations. Boys of sexual abuse can exhibit infections, genital injury, abdominal pain, constipation, and behavior problems. Caretakers such as babysitters or nannies might also see changes in verbal and physical movement, so they might spot sudden differences in behavior and personalities.[267]

There is a note of caution... signs most commonly associated with sexual abuse can also indicate several other things, such as a stressed-out child. One shouldn't immediately jump to sexual abuse as the culprit.[498]

Later Effects

This chapter is really a continuation of ***ABUSE*** and its section ***Later Effects***. From there, we gain a good foundation for how sexual abuse might affect a boy. However, sexual abuse takes its toll on males differently than physical abuse and neglect. While there are similarities in the later effects of all types of abuse, there are differences concerning sexual abuse.

One of the challenges in understanding the later effects of BSA beyond the lack of recognition is that so many boys and young men feel their experience was positive. Because of this, many researchers think that there are no lasting effects. Thus, there is little research on the subject.

It should be noted that not all who suffer CSA develop problems later in life, whether male or female. Some do, however. BSA victimization can be pretty devastating to boys and have long-lasting effects. As was discussed in the ***Later Effects*** in ***ABUSE*** chapter, correlation does not equal causation, but when taking Telomeres into consideration, it puts the list into better context. The way Boys' Sexual Abuse likely impacts victims:

- 5x more likely to suffer sexual problems in adulthood[499]
- 4x more likely to suffer depression[499]
- 2x more likely to have behavioral problems[499]
- 10x more likely to be diagnosed with mental disorders[500]
- 10x more likely to threaten suicide[501]
- 15x more likely to attempt suicide[501]

Other issues males may experience are conduct disorder, PTSD, aggressiveness, dissociation, eating disorders, incontinence, difficulty in self-regulation, depression, self-blame, low self-esteem, anger, and anxiety.[498] Boys may also be diagnosed with ADHD, though this is likely a misdiagnosis.[500]

Sexual Abuse left untreated into adulthood makes males more likely to have substance abuse issues, criminal justice issues, further victimization, and difficulties with identity.[502] They are likely to distrust others, seeing people as dishonest, malevolent, and undependable. They become avoidant or frighted of emotional connection and isolate themselves.[339] They are more at risk for sexually transmitted diseases, respiratory conditions, asthma, heart disease, and diabetes.[503]

Interesting how many of the later effects of BSA are associated with Toxic Masculinity.

Sexual Problems

Men may get into toxic or abusive relationships, confusing abuse with love and affection. They may lack the awareness of being in abusive relationships and being manipulated. Lacking a relationship, these men are likely to have compulsive sexual encounters. Sex for them is not about enjoyment but more as a coping mechanism to get it out of their system. They become hypersexual or a sex addict, constantly needing a fix. It's not that they don't desire love, most men do, even those surviving BSA, but they have difficulty reconciling sex and intimacy, as sex makes them feel empty and lonely. They know that having random sex is unhealthy, but it becomes a compulsion.

Some men may avoid sex altogether, as the memory of their abuse may be triggered during the act.[504] Instead, they may rely on pornography, with their sexual gratification reliant on masturbation only.

Suicide

While many media sources like to exclaim that suicide rates for girls are climbing faster than for boys (13% for girls, 6% for boys[505]), boys commit suicide at a rate of 3 to 4 times more than girls.[208] Sexually abused boys have a suicide at a rate of 1.5 times more than non-abused boys. These boys have feelings of hopelessness, helplessness, futility, and worthlessness. They are likely to be alcoholics and suffer mental disorders such as depression.[506]

Over 2100 teenagers were sampled from 93 schools in Sweden, with nearly 500 who had dropped out. The study found that a third of boys who had been sexually abused had attempted suicide and exhibited self-destructive behavior. A US study of 7970 men and 9367 women found that 25% of women and 16% of men were victims of CSA and that suicide attempts were twice as common among men compared to women.[504]

Of men who desired suicide, what stopped them was often revealing to others what had happened to them. They had reached that rock bottom stage and were ready to do it and finally told someone about it, which made choosing life a bit easier. Until this point, men had remained silent because of the myth that males can't be victims. Their silence was also the fear that if people knew they had suffered child abuse, then people would believe them to be pedophiles.[507]

Coping Strategies

Boys can develop a coping strategy to deal with their trauma, from passive victim, angry avenger, the rescuer, daredevil, conformist, and the prostitute.

The **Passive Victim** believes it was fate of what happened to them; condoning themselves to embrace the abuse without reporting it or trying to escape.[508] Passive victim likely won't ever report it.

The **Angry Avenger** believes someone has to pay for his misery, desiring revenge against the world and will abuse others. He becomes the very thing that abused him to get a sense of power and control. He grows up going after children that are unlike him now or like what he would have become if he wasn't abused.[508]

The **Rescuer** seeks a relationship with someone of the age of their abuser who will love him properly. In a way, he wants to undo the abuse he suffers by recreating the situation and changing the outcome.[508]

The **Conformist** is a boy who feels he was denied a "normal" life and attempts to cover his insecurities, vulnerability, mistrust, and self-doubts with a mask of normalcy. He effectively is playing a character, and to accomplish this, he forces himself to block out memories, fears, and insecurities associated with the abuse.[508]

The **Prostitute** as the name suggests will turn towards sex work. This will be touched on in the next chapter.

Preventions

Simply put, our society needs to wake up and understand that this is an actual problem with serious repercussions. society needs to wake up and understand that this is an actual problem with serious repercussions. CSA is a vicious cycle of women raping boys and boys growing up raping girls, with girls growing up to rape boys. While not all victims of CSA grow up to be an abuser, and not all CSA abusers were abused as children, enough of them do for it to be a continued problem. However, our society only focuses on female victims, and the cycle continues as we only look at half the problem.

First, we need to expand mental health services for boys and men and encourage them to use it. The problem with this is many psychologists went to schools and universities that are Feminist focus which subscribes to Patriarchy theory. Psychologists' basic university education will be of little help in treating boys and men if they're told that male privilege is the problem or their female attackers are not perpetrators.

On the one hand, I don't blame psychologists for using a "female-centered-only" model because they're taught that male victims are rare, if they exist at all. Men who engage in this kind of counseling from professionals feel that their experiences and issues are dismissed and dehumanized. As a result, males abandon therapy as they feel it is not for them, which leaves a lot of issues unresolved.[509]

Just like any profession, most of what we learn comes after schooling. Any time spent with men should inform mental health professionals that what they were taught does not conform to reality. Many psychologists, therapists, and even counselors I have spoken to have told me they adjusted how they deal with men upon realizing what they were taught incorrectly. So just because one has a gynocentric mental health foundation doesn't mean they can't undo their professional biases to truly help men.

We need more studies on male victims of sexual abuse. As stated, academic studies often mention boys in passing but then conceal how they are affected or use a small sample size. We might uncover preventive measures if we can better understand victims, the long-term effects, and the perpetrators. More importantly, in discovering that there are male victims, it can be used as a guide to educate the public about this very real issue that is otherwise ignored or joked about.[510]

We need more severe punishments for female perpetrators. While criminal prosecutions are not a significant deterrent to preventing crime, they can be a slight hindrance. If female caretakers, mothers, and teachers understand that there is substantial risk in engaging sexually with a boy, they may opt not to risk it. As it stands, women have an excellent chance of not facing prison for sexually abusing boys. While treating women like men when it comes to sentencing won't stop all women, it should stop some of them, and some are better than none.

Next, civil law needs to be affected by the age of consent laws. When it comes to child support, if the legal system recognizes a male as a victim, that needs to prevent him from being financially responsible for another child. If a boy cannot financially support themselves before the age of majority, then it makes no sense for them to be responsible for another life.

Women may make different decisions if they know they will be more financially responsible for their children. The state may even put more effort into preventative education so they can reduce their costs. Boys shouldn't be in financial hardship before starting their adult life.

How to Help

It's not as simple as treating the symptoms of BSA, even though that needs to be addressed. The worldwide culture needs to first recognize that males can be victims too. This section looks at what I believe are necessary steps to take to help improve the quality of care for boys who are sexually abused and quite possibly prevent it from happening.

Support Systems

As mentioned, most don't recognize that a female can rape a male or that a male can be raped, and victims seeking help may experience adverse reactions. An intimate partner violence survey out of Portugal found that men feel that support services (victim support service, police, and the justice system) are unhelpful. These facts are largely unknown to the world as many believe the more mainstream research that males simply are a minority of victims. Policies are derived from research data, and policies create guidelines. This ignorance of male victims leads to support services geared only towards female victims, which is inadequate to help male victims.[511]

The first step towards any level of treatment is for the support systems in place to realize there is a problem. Not just that there is sexual abuse of men and boys, but that those who can help generally don't. A study in 2017 found that many police still view male rape as "unimportant" or "not serious", holding the assumption that "men can't be raped". This leaves men with the label "undeserving of a victim status" or "undeserving of justice".[511]

Research

More research must be done on male victims. From prevalence rates to long-term effects, we need research that when it looks at all children, there is no gender bias, but equally, we need analysis that looks at boys specifically. In many ways, we need to start from scratch and not look at any earlier research,[511] even that which supports boys.

As great as that sounds, research needs funding, and funding is often political. From government to Feminist-led academia, this creates a vicious cycle of funding research based on a conclusion to prove their already established ideology to continue to mandate policies and laws that take away from where the resources are truly needed. It would be great if we could find third parties to fund research, but the private sector is generally only interested in research that leads to them making more money.[511]

Politicians

What's the solution to research funding then? As I said in my 2020 International Conference for Men's Issues video[512], we need to get the conversation out there. Others want to go to the top, such as Warren Farrell wanting to create a Council of Boys and Men[513], which I 100% support. Others are petitioning for laws to change, which I also support.

My solution is that we need to get the everyday people talking, which I hope this book does. Politicians do their best to listen to the people. If the conversation is about the inadequacy of men's rights, then politicians will run on that platform. And they want to stay in office, so eventually, they have to make good on their promises. Those promises will lead to better research, which will lead to better policies and laws. It is a long and slow process, but it is my belief that, along with what others are doing, is the path to make a change.

That, of course, is the US. How other countries will do it is beyond me. I know there are people who are doing good work to make those in power more aware of boys' and men's issues, from the UK to Australia to India.

Education

Whether we get policies and laws in place, we need to push schools to provide an education that sexual abuse affects girls and boys and should be reported. If you have children, sons or daughters, you must talk to them about sexual abuse. Not just that it is bad, but why it is bad. This will help boys and men get the recognition they need and recognize the abuse they suffer in the long run.[514]

Treatment

Although prevalence for boys and girls is near parity, treatment for sexual abuse is targeted at females, which can be hit or miss if it helps males. For instance, sexual assault referrals/care centers are often located in gynecological or maternity wards. Since there is no center/ward equivalent for males, this may be a barrier for men seeking help. Many hospitals are not prepared to collect evidence from male victims as they would with female victims, such as a rape kit.[511]

Immediate

Perhaps the most critical action is when a boy has suffered to get him help... Immediately. Boys don't always show their abuse right away, and it can take time to process it or affect them. Unfortunately, when a boy seems OK after the abuse, it's presumed that it didn't affect them. Given that many men can wait twenty years to report their abuse and how it has affected them... believe me when I say not to assume a boy is all right because he doesn't seem bothered by an adult having sex with him. There's a chance he can let it go and move on, and there's a chance he cannot, and it will affect the rest of his life.

Like Robin Williams' character tells Matt Damon's character in "Good Will Hunting", *It's not your fault*. It must be established to a boy who has been sexually abused that it wasn't his fault. Society will blame him, his abuser will blame him, and he will blame himself. He needs to know it wasn't his fault.[514] And yes, Will Hunting was not sexually abused, but the result of abuse, whether physical or sexual, still weighs heavily on boys.

Children will often experience Post-Traumatic Stress Disorder, though it is more of a matter of how much time before it manifests. There is a suggestion that **Eye Movement Desensitization and Reprocessing** (EMDR) and **Cognitive Behavioral Therapy** (CBT) can be helpful. EMDR requires patients to recall traumatic memories while experiencing a bilateral sensory input. CBT is a talking therapy designed to deal with the present effects of experiences. I will stress to speak to a professional about this and not take my advice.[515]

Regarding boys and men, it might be best to avoid group therapy. Boys can be overwhelmed by talking in a group as they can be reluctant to share their feeling. Men can have difficulty viewing themselves as a victim. To reach males, having a one-on-one meeting can be helpful. There is some suggestion that gamification can also help boys to use the principles of gaming to aid in their recovery.[515]

Boys should receive treatment as early as possible because the longer they wait, the harder it becomes. And not just that. There are more resources for boys than there are for men, so early treatment for boys has the greatest chance for them to grow into healthy adults than for adult men to become whole.

Regrettably, the behaviors of males suffering the horror of sexual abuse in childhood will be more seen as toxic masculinity than that of a vulnerable male in need of help.

Delayed

Due to societal viewpoints on BSA, boys may wait until adulthood to reveal their abuse, and even then, they wait too many years. Meaning that any treatment they receive is delayed and may make it more difficult to properly treat a man who has lived a life of a shameful sexual past.

When boys are sexually abused, their psychosocial development is likely affected, impacting short-term and long-term emotional, social, and psychological functioning. Untreated, it can cause distrust. They will either avoid or be unable to express personal needs and/or vulnerabilities. Instead, they will shut down and isolate themselves to avoid dealing with problems they have to feel safe. This, in turn, prevents them from developing long-term relationships in adulthood and having trouble with physical and emotional intimacy.[516]

To engage a man with a history of BSA in therapy is to engage in a relationship. For the success of a damaged male in any dynamic, whether friendship, love, or counseling, the damaged man needs a caring partner willing to take on the extra responsibility of their psyche. They do not want to trust, and it is easier to push away than to accept help.

In order for a man to open up, they need someone to really be there for them and not phone it in. Males need to learn how to communicate, have a healthy sense of self, be open to change, and be willing to be emotionally intimate. As a defense mechanism, boys of sexual abuse will disable the things to protect themselves from further harm, leading to being underdeveloped as they mature. Undeveloped maturity will hinder males in adulthood.[517]

A relationship with an attentive friend or professional is likely the best therapy for a male with delayed treatment, as they can relearn what it means to be human, be part of a partnership, and join a community. To be human is to engage with others. This is known as "relational recovery". It's not even that they are cynical of long-term commitments and fatherhood, as most men perceive them as positive experiences. Relational Recovery can guide men to look at the abuse they suffered as a meaningful yet tragic experience. They just don't know how to go from a broken man to one who eventually gains self-actualization.[517]

TRAFFICKING

The male victim... looks nothing like the sympathetic, traumatized and vulnerable victim that the public recognizes but may instead appear aggressive, violent, masterful, commanding and threatening.

– Fran Sepler

We often hear about human tracking and how it affects women and girls. Yet, global statistics show that men and boys represent nearly half of the victims.[518] However, as a lot of focus is put on females, there is inadequate care for male victims. As a result, men and boys go unidentified and remain within the trafficking system longer. Male Sex Trafficking is a hidden and under-reported problem due to many believing that boys cannot be victims.[519]

This also ties into the chapter **CHILD LABOR**, as many work sectors make use of forced labor by children that were smuggled to perform a task. Industries engaged in child trafficking include mining, forestry, onstruction, health care, factories, hospitality, and agriculture.[519] While there is more focus on sex tracking in this chapter, it will also look at trafficking in concerns to labor.

Invisible Victims

The commercial exploitation of children has existed for pretty much all of history, from child prostitutes to laborers to CHILD SOLDIERS. In the US, public awareness came about with enacting the Trafficking Victims Protection Act of 2000 (TVPA). With its enactment, state and local governments, law enforcement, and service providers put attention to the sexual exploitation of girls. Thankfully, in recent years, there has been an awareness of the sexual exploitation of boys. However, most with the power and resource to help exploited children either miss boys altogether or view them as too few to be seen as an immediate problem. Instead, men and boys are seen exclusively as exploiters, pimps, buyers of sex, or volunteer prostitutes.[520]

What is Trafficking

Despite traffic within the word, travel is not necessary for someone to commit trafficking with a minor. Most people think trafficking is where you take a young girl from one country and transport her to another country for sex. The US legal definition of sex tracking is "recruitment, harboring, transportation, provision, obtaining, patronizing, or soliciting of a person for the purpose of commercial sex act." The commercial aspect of sex must be "induced by force, fraud, or coercion", as further defined as "any sex act on account of which anything of value is given to or received by a person". Age is not technically a component of sex tracking, but anyone under 18 involved in commercial sex is automatically considered a victim of sex trafficking under the law, even if said child was a "willing" participant.[521]

A few other things to keep in mind as we discuss male victimization. First, you'll notice that the language is gender-neutral about who can be victims. Second, the laws do not require a third party's involvement, like a pimp. The significance of this is that a buyer can become a trafficker if they knew, or recklessly disregarded, that the victim was trafficked and observed the victim's age. The last part is tricky, as not knowing the age of the victim, say a 16-year-old looking 20, is an invalid excuse for your actions.[521]

Ignorance of the law
doesn't exempt you from justice.

Research

Research into forced prostitution and trafficking have either denied males being victims or acknowledged it at such a low rate that they were not investigated further. There are studies that look into male victims, but as mentioned in **SEXUAL ABUSE**, the few studies out there tend to use a small sample size to indicate a problem but not enough to be definitive in convincing people.

Looking at 166 published Articles in social science journals, researchers noted that 84% discussed females with no mention of male sex workers.[522] The few to discuss male sex workers indicated that male workers could leave at any time and likely chose the profession. In contrast, females are forced into prostitution, and leaving tends to require outside intervention. The only danger facing males was HIV, whereas females faced violence. Males were questioned on their sexuality, whereas females were always assumed to be heterosexual.[523]

Table 7: Trafficked Population Discussed inJournal Articles

Women	173
Men	14
Girls	6
Boys	1
Children (No distinction)	42
Unknown	20

*Totals presented in this table exceed the actual number of journal articles due to multiple categorizations (i.e. a single journal article could be categorized under both "Women" and "Girls").

[524]

Another study looked at Reports (429 total) and Journals (218 total) relating to human trafficking. Of the reports, 34% discussed women, and 28% discussed girls. Only 10% discussed men, and 20% discussed boys. As many reports can discuss multiple genders, we can sort of see that up to ~60% discussed females while ~30% discussed males.[525]

As we see, 79% of journal articles discussed women, whereas only 6% discussed men. Twenty percent of the articles addressed children but made no distinction between their genders.

As discussed in **SEXUAL ABUSE**, researchers may hide the rate of male victims to give the idea that there are more female victims. I'm willing to bet that these studies had the line somewhere: "Men and boys can be victims as well, but not nearly as much as women and girls." Of the research that was gender specific (accounting for 3% of the studies), girls were represented 6 times more than boys.[525]

Male Resiliency

I am like a small bird that has been flying a great distance
for a long time. I'm tired and have no food to eat, so I take
a rest on one of the branches of a tree and I feel like I have
been shot by someone... I fall down and nearly die.

–(unknown) 15-year-old sexually exploitated male[526]

Patriarchy theory states that the Patriarchy is a society created by men for men. Yet, when issues such as these are brought up, Feminists are quick to point out that Patriarchy also hurts men by putting them into narrowly defined gender roles. However, academic research is largely Feminist and has precluded males from their research over the years, even though recent research has revealed a high prevalence rate.

Academic research into human trafficking assumes that most victims are female and most perpetrators are males. Worse, males are seen as wanting sex[527], so they can never truly be victims of exploitation and rape. Additionally, males are viewed as being stronger and can defend themselves (unlike females), so they are more resistant to being trafficked and need fewer resources than females.[528]

Males who are trafficked are seen as having more agency than females. That somehow, males are able to make the choice to leave, and because they stay, that must mean they make the choice to stay. Females lack agency and are forced to stay and thus need more help than males.[523]

The hyper-agency that males are given results in a less vigilant world, with cases of abuse being less likely to be reported and perpetrators being less likely to get caught. This places males at greater risk of abuse and exploitation. As discussed in **ABUSE**, males are less resilient to trauma than females are. Yet, society believes that males and invulnerable and that nothing can affect them, and that females are hyper-vulnerable.[529]

Researchers often cite the myth about female vulnerability and male resiliency, even though no evidence corroborates this. A study into the streets of Manilla found that 70% of street-involved youth were male. Teresita Silva quoted this statistic, citing that 30% of street children are girls, "girls face a more harrowing situation than boys, which makes them more vulnerable". And to twist the knife, she stated boys are better able to protect themselves.[522]

Ignore boys, because we all know they can't be hurt.
What proof do we have of that? None.
But everyone knows it to be true.

Runaways & Street Children

While no one situation leads all boys to be sexually exploited, running away or being kicked out often puts boys in a vulnerable spot. When boys become desperate for survival, they do almost anything for food and a warm place to sleep. This desperation can lead them to be manipulated and groomed, leading them to cross a line they might not have done otherwise.[530]

Sometimes the exchange is more direct, that a perpetrator tells a boy upfront that sex is involved, and the boy might initially think he is consenting to the proposition. After all, if society has thrown him away, why should he be bound by the laws? Without realizing it, they are being trafficked, and the requirements escalate to where a boy feels trapped to go along with it, understanding that even an escape means a return to the life that led him to this hostile situation.[530]

The majority of US research on the sexual exploitation of boys focused entirely on runaways and homeless youth. This is of note for various reasons, as not all sexually exploited boys are runaways or homeless. And not all runaway or homeless boys are sexually exploited. Many boys that run away from home or are homeless can often be due to their sexuality and their families kicking them out.[531]

Sexual Identity

Much of the research into sexually exploited boys in the US has been on runaway children. Whether these children left their homes or were forced out, most identify as gay, bisexual, or transexual. This led researchers to the conclusion that boys who are exploited sexually are not heterosexual. Yet, while this seems to be a common belief, other research has found the majority of boys who are sexually exploited are, in fact, heterosexual.[532]

Heterosexuality

Studies have found that most boys who are exploited are straight and forced to be with men, not unlike females. Unlike females, males may also be forced to be with women.[533]

As a method to protect their sexuality, many boys would define themselves as escorts rather than prostitutes to help keep a clear division of what services they offer to clients. For instance, 95% of commercial sex acts with boys are oral sex, but boys will mostly refuse anal intercourse. Likely because it causes pain and doing so is seen as an act of homosexuality.[534]

Note that I'm not saying straight men can't enjoy anal stimulation; rather, many boys within sex trafficking or perpetrators who molest boys may view anal intercourse as homosexual.

Gays, Bisexual, and Transexuals

While there is a belief that most sexually exploited boys are gay, bisexual, or transexual, many males belonging to the LGBT are hesitant about reporting their sexuality.

Why would an LGBT male victim hide their sexuality?

Because in cultures around the world, including the US, gay, bisexual, or transexual males who are abused and exploited sexually are believed to have wanted it; therefore, no harm is done. Males have a hard enough time being seen as victims due to their gender, but gay, bisexual, or transexual males face an even great fear of discrimination, retribution, and blame. Gay, bisexual, or transexual males fear that their sexuality will be seen as the reason they got into the situation they're in, and this is why many males refuse to share their sexuality.[521]

All Are Victims

Gay, bisexual, or transexual boys fear their sexuality will be seen as the cause of their exploitation. In contrast, heterosexual boys fear that their activities due to their exploitation will give people the impression they're gay. This needs a lot more research, and while understanding sexuality is important, we must remember that sexually exploited gays, bisexuals, transexuals, and heterosexuals **ARE ALL TRAFFICKED BOYS**. And trafficked boys are not getting the help they need.

Something to keep in mind is that while most homeless youths are LGBT, not all who are sexually exploited come from the streets. If you only focus on homeless youth, then you will find a significant representation of gay, bisexual, or transexual boys who are sexually exploited. If you instead shift focus on all of those who are sexually exploited, then you will find a large number of heterosexual males.[532]

It is estimated that 26% of LGBT youth end up running away from home due to family not accepting them, peers harassing them, and their community ostracizing them. It is further estimated that 200,000 LGBT youths are homeless (no estimate of how many are boys). Another study found that 40% of homeless youth are LGBT, which then means that 60% are heterosexual. When looking at sexually exploited boys, only 25% - 35% identified as gay, bisexual, or transexual, again signifying that upwards of 75% are heterosexual.[535]

I'm not trying to take away from the LGBT and put heterosexuals on the victim pedestal. The problem I am trying to identify is that people tend to see boys who are sexually exploited as gay, bisexual, or transexual only, even though these studies show they represent a minority of victims. It's because of this that many heterosexuals don't come forward because while LGBT can find pride in their sexuality, so too do heterosexuals find pride in it, and neither would want to be automatically assumed to be something they're not.

All boys need help, and their sexuality shouldn't be a point of contention. Yet, society wants to push this as an LGBT problem, as gay, bisexual, or transexual boys should elicit more sympathy because they are considered a protected minority. As a result, the same society wants heterosexual males to be forgotten due to "their privilege" of being straight and male.

Prevalence

It's extremely tough to identify how prevalent trafficking and exploitation of boys truly is. As has been discussed, most of the focus for trafficking is on girls, and boys are rarely considered for being victims. Some boys come forward to report their abuse, but many experts agree boys are under-reported.[536]

Many academic papers do their best to downplay the prevalence rate of boys in favor of girls[537], suggesting girls are the majority of victims. For example, one paper reported that out of every four sexually abused children, three are girls.[538] Even if that is true, 25% of victims are still boys.

In the US, John Jay College and the Center for Court Innovation released The Commercial Sexual Exploitation of Children in New York City study in 2008. It was reported that boys represented 50% of commercially sexually exploited children.[518] In 2016, the DOJ estimated that 36% of children forced into the sex industry in the US were boys.[539]

Looking at 9,042 cases of commercial exploitation in 28 services in England, Northern Ireland, and Scotland, 33% (2,986) of cases were male. It is noted in this study that there are fewer services available to males than females, and believed that this doesn't truly reflect the overall rate of sexually exploited males.[536]

In 2009, the UK started the National Referral Mechanism, a national system to monitor trafficking. In 2012, it identified 549 potential trafficking victims, with 208 (40%) being boys. It found that 28% of children were sexually exploited, and 24% were for criminal exploitation. No information was revealed on gender and exploitation type.[540]

Law Enforcement

Understand, first and foremost, that I have a love for our men and women in blue. However, for issues such as this, I do make criticism in hopes of reform.

Boys are rarely seen as victims of human trafficking, especially in law enforcement. Law Enforcement generally believes in the stereotypical characteristic that to be sexually exploited requires a third party, such as a pimp. It is further believed that pimps are males and only pimp out females; boys don't have pimps. So boys are not victims of sexual exploitation. Because of this, Law Enforcement typically does not refer boys to agencies as they would a girl who is a victim of sexual exploitation. Their understanding of the problem means they are only looking for the stereotypical signs and are unaware of who else can be a victim.[541]

This extends to the juvenile justice system. You would think a division of the law that works with minors would be more aware of potential problems in sexual exploitation. After all, when they encounter exploited girls, they give girls referrals to the agencies they need. Not boys. Once again, they are not seen as victims, so thus not seen as needing help.[542]

Resources

As has been said many times, people believe males cannot be raped, males cannot be victims, and even if we want to acknowledge they can be victims, it is nowhere near what females endure. This misconception impacts males in a big way when it comes to services offered to victims or the allocation of resources. Females are given top priority, and males are lucky to receive anything.

Programs and Services

In 2009, the DOJ disseminated funding for programs combatting domestic and international trafficking. Of the 222 institutions and programs receiving US funding, only two were for combatting the trafficking of men and boys, representing <1% of total funding. Fifteen institutions and programs were aimed at women and girls, receiving 4% of the total funds.[543]

In 2018, the US Government Activities to Combat Trafficking in Persons awarded funding to 150 organizations in the US that were serving survivors of human trafficking. Of those, 119 addressed sex tracking and forced labor, with only one with a program dedicated to helping male victims. Of that initial 150 organizations, only 21 addressed sex trafficking only, none of which addressed male victims.[521]

Of 40 youth agencies and other services to help sexually exploited children, 37 agencies provide trafficking-specific services. Fifteen of those 37 stated they are willing and able to serve boys for labor trafficking, and 10 said they already offer services to boys for labor trafficking. When looking at sexual exploitation, of the 25 agencies for this category, only 6 serve boys.[542]

Why so Little for Boys

This is a Catch-22.

Services are not available for male victims, but if male victims don't come forward to show they need help, no funding will be given to help male victims. But why should male victims come forward if they know they won't receive support? If seeking support gains them nothing, they will remain vulnerable to sex and labor trafficking, as at least the traffickers can provide something, even if the cost is so high.

Why are services designed to help children underservicing boys? The reasons (or excuses) are[542]:
- All available spots for a program are filled by girls already
- Boys are not referred by law enforcement or other social services
- Services feel they lack proper training to handle sexually exploited boys' needs
- Males don't self-identify as needing help

The last one is fascinating. If males know a location only service girls, why would they seek help from there? If they know society won't recognize them as victims, why would they identify as victims?

Distrust of Help

There can also be distrust from male victims for those offering help. The kinds of people who purchase children for sex are quite often professionals. Social workers and law enforcement often come off as professionals. Boys (girls too) will quickly associate professional attire with a bad person. Thus, a professional offering help is likely someone they won't trust. Fortunately, girls may be more willing to trust a female offering help as most of the perpetrators that abuse them are male. Boys encounter men, but also encounter women.[544]

Short-Term Solutions

A male can get help and stay in a shelter, but shelters are short-term solutions. When their stay is up, they will probably return to the streets. While resources are stretched thin for all victims of sex trafficking, less is given to males. With very few shelters, no education opportunities, and a lack of mental health services, there is a very good chance that a male will return to trafficking to fulfill their needs for food, shelter, money, and their drug addiction.[544]

Beyond shelters, another fear boys may have is being put into the welfare system and placed in a foster home. Many boys end up leaving a foster home due to abuse they suffer and fear that if they seek help, they will be placed back into that situation.[544]

Lack of Training

It would be too easy to paint shelters, programs, and NGO's as being evil for not helping boys and only focusing on girls, but it is not that simple. In fact, many who work in abuse shelters and fight against trafficking acknowledge a lack of training and ability to help boys. More importantly, many want to do more for boys.

The problem starts with social workers. They are in the trenches; they see firsthand what is going on, and their reports are used to map out children's issues. For whatever reason, social workers ignore that boys are at risk for exploitation. I hope in the future to give more study to the Child Welfare system and how it affects boys.[542]

Because of a lack of specialists reporting on this issue, there is a general ignorance of its prevalence. What little information is out there (much of which I had to really scour the internet to find) is often not communicated to those working with youth victims. This also translates into organizations with stated goals based on this ignorance to only help female victims, giving a distinct impression that only females suffer this problem.[545]

Thankfully, some organizations are attempting to give aid to boys, but that is met with frustration and helplessness as they lack a complete under-standing of boys' needs. Most others, when looking to help boys, lack the insight into seeing them as victims in their own right, instead being seen as defective girls.[545]

Boys are viewed as defective girls, especially in the case of sexual abuse and sexual exploitation, because treatment of sexual abuse has been centered on female rape victims. When "professionals" encounter a boy needing help, their training inappropriately transfers to males, which can often do more harm than good. **Victim Advocacy** developed from the Feminist movement and focused on all perpetrators being males and all victims being females. So a male being a victim would likely be seen as a perpetrator or be given help that only applies to females. This is referred to as the **Feminization of Victimization**.[546]

What Do Boys Want

Boys in Cambodia who are sexually exploited were asked what kind of help they wish they could receive[545]:

- Physical and Emotional Safety
- Confidentiality
- To be Accepted and not Judged
- Receive Empathy and Respect
- Protection
- Affection and Love
- Sense of Belonging
- Help with Education and Work Placement

When asked what message they wished to send out to the world, the key theme was to be believed, that boys need to be protected, to stop mocking them, and that boys can have pain and be vulnerable and be affected by sexual abuse.[545]

Vulnerability

Boys are like gold.
Girls are like white cloth.
If boys fall in the mud, it can easily be washed off.
If girls do, the stain remains.
– Cambodian saying[547]

Talking about the vulnerability of males is a taboo topic in nearly all societies. Males are not associated with vulnerability. Males are perceived as lacking emotions and having the strength to defend themselves. So boys being vulnerable means that they can never become men, be respected for their masculinity, and be looked down upon by society. This is the harmful behavior we need to correct... and no, it's not the Patriarchy that created this; this has been around since civilization started so that men could willingly sacrifice themselves for back-breaking work and die in war.

Basic Needs

We all have the same basic needs, and most of us have those needs met. When our most basic needs are met, we can obtain higher needs, such as socialization, relationships, and self-esteem. When we lack access to basic

needs, we forgo higher needs and do whatever we can to get the bare ne-
cessities. Boys, either on the streets or from a background of abuse, may
turn to the sex trade to gain money, shelter, food, drugs, clothing, and even
love. To which their needs are used against them, and that is how boys are
exploited.[531]

Drugs don't seem to be a basic need of life. Most of us do well without it. For
children in the sex trade industry, drugs are a basic need. Drugs help boys
to escape the horrors that life offers. Drugs can give temporary happiness,
and temporary happiness is better than no happiness at all.[532]

This is not an endorsement for drugs.

Ironically, children choose prostitution as a means of survival. Yet, to make
sure they remain slaves in the sex trade, perpetrators deprive victims of
their basic needs of shelter and food, all to keep them hungry and exhausted. Being hungry and exhausted keeps one more compliant and too weak to
fight back. Perpetrators are also likely to get victims addicted to drugs and
alcohol and then deprive them of both to have them suffer withdrawal as
further means of control.[548]

Family

There are two types of street children in the Philippines: children 'on' the
street and children 'of' the street. The former refers to children who have a
home and spend time on the streets to earn money, whereas the latter lives
on the streets with no contact with their families. In fact, street-involved
boys are more likely to have less contact with family than street-involved
girls.[549]

Children who do have a home but engage in prostitution are more often
from a single-parent home that has a mother for a primary caretaker who
is unemployed.[549]

Family dynamics often indicate why boys turn to the streets or to prostitution. Such as[550]:

- Exposure to Poverty
- Separation/Divorce
- Death of a Parent or Sibling
- Domestic Violence
- Substance Abuse

This doesn't paint a complete picture of all boys who become sexually exploited, as children of all backgrounds and situations can end up sexually exploited, from poor to high society. This just demonstrates one aspect of what leads boys to sexual exploitation, either prostituting themselves to help the family or to escape family violence.

Held Captive

Another reason males don't come forward is they may not see themselves as victims. After all, this is the only life they have ever known, and they often lack exposure to the outside world. They are kept in captivity. Perpetrators will often move locations, stay ahead of law enforcement, and keep victims clueless about their location. Boys will often be given new names. How can a male fight back if they don't know where they are, who they are, or have any way of contacting someone who can help them?[548]

Economics

Action Pour Les Enfants, a French-based program, rescues children of sexual exploitation. It also investigates and prosecutes child sex offenders. Unfortunately, there are few shelters and services to which they can send the boys, but boys often refuse counseling. Primarily because of the economics of places like Cambodia, that the average boy earns $1 USD a day, while a boy who prostitutes himself to men can earn $10 - $50 USD a day.[547] In other places of the world, boys can earn up to $1000 USD a month as a sex worker, more than government employees.[533]

While being sexually exploited and trafficked has long-lasting effects, being poor can also have long-lasting effects. Often times people choose that which has the greatest monetary rewards as it is better than having no money.

Recruitment

So how does a child get into the sex trafficking industry? It's not like one can find a pimp and volunteer to be abused. In fact, most reports say that boys don't have pimps. Instead, they are called "market facilitators", someone the child may initially trust that will later facilitate their exploitation. Someone they find who they trade sex with for basic needs that will eventually escalate into servicing customers.[532]

Boys are most often recruited from[532]:

- Streets
- Internet
- Bars or other hangouts
- Truck Stops or Bus Stations
- Conventions

Online

Perpetrators will use Grindr, Kik, and Instagram to connect with underage boys by posing as a child or propositioning them for sex. They can then use a cash app to show their seriousness and set a location. Once again, not all forms of trafficking involve the underworld and moving locations. Any act of knowingly engaging sexually with a child is trafficking.[521]

Pre-existing Relationships

Pre-existing relationships are people who hold some sort of trust with a child, whether they are doctors, religious leaders, teachers, parents, family members, or other people close to them in their life. They can abuse their trust and protection, often exchanging money or items of value for their silence. They can also give drugs to make them more compliant. This can quickly escalate into sex with others or be used to recruit their friends.[521]

False Promises

Other ways of sexual recruitment are under the false promise that they are going to a different country to have a good job.[548] They can also be promised to join a football (soccer) club with a lucrative contract. Many of these con men can be a part of sports organizations, but rather than giving them the promise of their dreams, they instead are exploited for sex or labor.[551]

Peers

Peers can refer to friends, but not all of your peers are people you know. Often, hanging out with a stranger around your age is better than being alone, which can be a way of building rapport. Unbeknownst to the boy, this new "friend" is recruiting them into the trafficking industry.[552]

Peers lurk around homeless shelters, bus stations, and anywhere else they can find vulnerable children. Peers may even provide basic needs like an adult, which can escalate into the homeless male now being a victim of sexual exploitation.[552]

Women

Once again, females are thought to be the only victims of sex trafficking. It's hard for society to imagine that boys can be victims of rape and trafficking, including that about half of those who have sex with boys are women. Even more difficult than that is that women can recruit boys in the sex trade industry. In the UK, women make up 40% of recruiters.[553]

Perpetrators

Because boys are barely recognized (if at all) as victims of trafficking, those who perpetrate sexual exploitation of boys become even more difficult to prosecute. It's assumed that perpetrators of trafficking are only men, and while boys are abused by men, they can also be sexually exploited by women.[532] It's believed there is a 60/40 split of men and women (respectively) who sexually exploit boys[554], though another report has found it to be 80/20.[538]

Pornography

Boys are attractive victims for sexual exploitation. As more focus is put on protecting girls, fewer people are on the lookout for male victims. As a result, whole trafficking networks specialize in obtaining young boys for sex and child pornography.[555]

According to the FBI, more than half of victims featured in child pornography are boys. Boys in these films are subject to various forms of sadism, bondage, rape, and torture.[556]

Escaping

Many victims of sexual exploitation develop Learned Helplessness, that an opportunity to leave is within their grasp, and they choose to stay. They often can't imagine their life without the abuse, but for boys, it can also be because they fear going to prison. As bad as their life is now, they can only imagine prison being much worse.[557]

Why would sexually exploited males fear prison if they escape? Because boys are not recognized as victims, if they encounter law enforcement, they are more likely to be charged for crossing a border illegally or be arrested for crimes committed as a result of their sexual exploitation, even if they were forced to commit the crimes.[557]

Commercial Media

In 2010, Larry King Live aired the segment "Worldwide Crisis: Human Trafficking". Larry King described trafficking as "women and children, kidnapped, bought, [and] sold into bondage". The show made 25 references to women and girls as victims of men's enslavement.[558] Despite many reports being available by this time to show a prevalence of males who are trafficked, not once did the show mention boys. Larry King is not the only commercial media personality with such a glaring omission, as many celebrities are guilty of it.[559]

In recent years we have seen how powerful commercial media is and what kind of influence it can have. Still, unbeknownst to many, the media can even influence criminal justice in the US, including the enforcement of anti-trafficking measures. Law enforcement serves the public, and they are responsive to public perception.[560]

Reporting

Growing up, I believed in the power of the press. Journalism was a powerful tool to help keep the government in check, as they didn't control the media. Writing this book, I see how naïve I was in believing that propaganda. The media and the government are in bed with each other. The media doesn't care about reporting the truth; they care about getting ratings, so people see the advertising and buy products. Don't get me wrong, I use the media, even for this book, but I don't mistake their motive as a service to the people; I know their motives are for lining their pockets.

Studies show that coverage of crimes increases the public perception that a crime is a serious problem. Likewise, if a crime isn't covered, it must not be that serious or is non-existent. Thus, the media shapes public perception, which shapes law enforcement indirectly.[560] This problem is especially bad because the news organization doesn't challenge statistics supporting liberal politics, despite how easy to discredit them. If women and girls are victims, then it must be true, and no need to investigate further.[561]

Happy Trafficker

One of the great sins of commercial media is their attempt to downplay female perpetrators. One way they do that is to call former female traffickers who grow up to become traffickers themselves "happy traffickers". This way, female traffickers are not criminals... they're victims. And their impact on children is minimal compared to men. Whatever their motives may be, whether to avoid being perceived as misogynistic or losing ratings, this need to make female criminals look good does great harm to society as people are not on the lookout for female predators and male victims.[562]

But what about males who were trafficked and grew up to be traffickers and are a byproduct of a system that failed them and became the only thing they could do to survive... are they called happy traffickers? Nope. Because anything a man does, no matter the reason, is always worse simply because he's a man.[563]

Later Effects

This is not about comparing who has it worst. Every single survivor—man, woman, male, female, boy, girl, straight, gay, other—every single survivor has a unique story... It's not a zero-sum game. It's not like, if I give more to men, I'm taking away from women. The more we can address the issue holistically, the better able we're going to be to reduce it.

—Christopher M. Anderson[521]

Like many other chapters describing later effects, sex trafficking affects boys' physical, psychological, and social well-being. They can turn into addicts, develop eating disorders, suffer anxiety, become depressed, and have a volatile personality.[564] There is a feeling of shame and loss of honor, fear of repercussions of disclosing or being discovered, confusion related to sexuality and gender, self-blame, feelings of isolation, nightmares, thoughts of suicide, and need of drugs to dull the pain.[550]

These issues become exasperated when not reporting their exploitation as boys have the socially imposed pressure to be self-reliant and desire sex. Should a boy report what happened to them, they face severe stigmatization from family, peers, and society, leading to psychosocial problems.[564]

It's not always easy for boys to escape. Sometimes they can... but fear keeps them captive. Moreover, boys fear the consequences of their escape. Not just from their abductors but from a society that will look down on them. This may very well result in a conscious choice to stay. Boys feel powerless as victims, but they may regain some control in choosing to stay. This can lead to repeating the cycle of violence as they eventually become a perpetrator themselves and do unto others as what was done to them.

Recommendations

Boys are being trafficked and exploited for sex and labor, which our society ignores. The narrative states that females are the only victims and males are the only perpetrators. So the solution is to wake up the world that males and females can be victims and males and females can be perpetrators.

Education

It all starts with education. The world needs to be educated on what is happening with boys in the sex trade and forced labor industries (along with everything else mentioned in this book). My book proves there is information out there, and I hope that my book can educate the world about the issues boys are facing.

Besides more education, more research into these issues needs to be done. In order to educate, we need to understand the problem; we need to understand who the victims are and how it affects them, who the perpetrators are, and understand how women can do harm as men can.[565]

Laws

Laws are only as good as those enforcing them, and enforcement is only as good as the education, training, and funding that is allocated.
—Irma M. Barron & Colleen Frost[553]

US sex and labor trafficking laws are written in gender-neutral terms, but rarely is it enforced for boys, focusing instead on girls. We need a push for laws to be enforced for all victims.

Prosecutions

As seen in **SEXUAL ABUSE**, when women face charges of sexual abuse, the law gives females little to no sentencing at all. This gives the impression to other women that even if what they do is wrong, it is acceptable conduct, or rather, there are no real consequences to women's actions. The same is true for sexual exploitation; if there are little to no prosecutions of boys' sexual exploitation perpetrators, it gives the impression that there is an indirect invitation to commit the act. There needs to be a balance that any illegal action committed against a child will get the same level of prosecution in a court of law.[566]

Law Enforcement

We need to educate all levels of law enforcement. They need to truly understand who a male victim is and that they can't just easily run away. We especially need Law Enforcement to be more aware of the problems and warning signs. They are the first responders; they see more of what is happening. Lacking education on male victims means they will miss evidence of human trafficking.[567]

Don't let myths override service to the public.

Screening

When runaway or homeless boys enter social service agencies or are arrested, there needs to be a screening done to determine if they are victims of sexual exploitation. Of course, this isn't a topic that males want to talk about, so sensitivity training of personnel needs to be done to help a male open up about his abuse.[565]

Screening of boys and their abuse can help get them into programs that can assist them rather than being treated as a criminal and learning that it is better to be sexually exploited than trying to get help.

Agencies

Put simply, we need agencies helping male victims of sexual exploitation. The challenge is that many will see that helping boys takes away support for girls. However, as mentioned earlier in this chapter, girls receive much more than boys. So, to have equality, some resources must be redistributed from girls so boys can get more help. I know saying that will cause a lot of people to be angry with me, but Feminism has been saying the same thing about redistributing resources for males so more women can get support.

What we really need for boys is more donors, government funding, and the expansion of NGOs working with females to now work with males. We also need collaboration between organizations to maximize efforts. If we can get existing services to expand to help boys, then there is less chance of them cutting back. For that to happen, we also need more added to the existing resources.[568]

Collaboration of agencies is about making new networks between victims and people in a position to help. This requires raising awareness within broader communities. This also means funding research to gain a better insight into how big this problem is.[568]

And there needs to be agencies that are boy-specific in their treatments. Some understand how to help boys directly, but most practitioners approach healing from a female-centric methodology. Boys need safety, protection, empathy, empowerment, acceptance, respect, and community participation. However, boys aren't girls. Treating boys as defective girls won't help boys and make their recovery all that more difficult.[568]

Final Thoughts

This book started as a rough idea in 2013, and nearly a decade later, I finished it. The actual writing of this book began in 2019, but the years prior were spent on my YouTube channel discussing news stories and articles related to men's issues. That proved invaluable, as I learned so much about what is going on in this world. I hesitated for so long about whether I should write this book, as I feared my career as a writer (something I had desired all my life) would be tarnished. But as any writer will tell you, when you have something in your heart that wants to be written, the worst thing you can do is ignore it. This needed to be written, and I am glad to say that it is finally done.

My journey in the actual writing process began with the idea of a quick introduction to critical issues from childhood, education, dating, marriage, and dealing with the family court. Yet, when my fingers touched the keyboard and words appeared on the screen, that wasn't what I wrote. I kept adding more and more about issues concerning boys. I realized we must have a solid foundation to understand any problem I may discuss. And where better to start than boys throughout the world?

In completing this book, I wonder what might have happened had I listened to Hannah. She encouraged me to write this back in 2013. I felt the Karen Straughan or Warren Farrell of the world should write this. Being on the other side of this project, I now know that I was always destined for this book. However, as one part of me wishes I had done it all those years, another part is glad I waited.

During the three years, I watched several movies repeatedly. They included, "Antwone Fisher", "Spotlight", and "Way Way Back". I watch lots of movies, but these stuck out for me as they reminded me why I was writing this book.

"Spotlight" is of particular note, as it is one that I've quoted a few times in this book. This movie is about the Boston Herald breaking the Catholic sexual abuse case, priests raping boys and girls, primarily boys. This movie speaks to me at a greater level than that. Spotlight discovered a scary truth that people in powerful positions didn't want out there. I feel that is a metaphor for this book: I conjured nothing... the information is out there. All I did was connect the dots.

There's a scene in the movie where Robby and Mike are arguing, as Mike found proof that Cardinal Law knew about the abuse and ignored it and wanted to run the story, but Robby wanted to go deeper. Mike's pleading with Robby really hits me hard,

> *"It's time, Robby! It's time! They knew and they let it happen! To KIDS! Okay? It could have been you, it could have been me, it could have been any of us. We gotta nail these scumbags! We gotta show people that nobody can get away with this; Not a priest, or a cardinal or a freaking pope!"*

Academia, Government, Press, Judges, Law Enforcement, NGOs—all know about the issues discussed in this book. Most of my research comes out of Academia. And yet, I see new studies that come out to cite boys are the overwhelming minority of cases of sexual abuse, ignoring the evidence out there. Mind you, I've been working on this project for nine years and have put it together in the last three years, almost four years now.

So many have presented this information, and so many have ignored it because it didn't seem correct. Boys being victims, that just doesn't happen. No, boys can't be victims. Or maybe they can, but only a small selection of them can be victims. No, no, we have to reserve the label of victims only for those we deem worthy of our protection and empathy. Only women and girls can be victims. Not just of actual crimes, but of anything they claim to be victims of, and should they commit a crime against a boy, NO HARM DONE!

I wrote this book because I am sick of the double standards that exist... and to question the status quo labels me a **misogynist**.

Did you know that Rape Culture was a term invented to describe the conditions within prison, that there was an untold amount of rapes among male inmates, rapes that go unreported? The term was usurped by the Feminist movement, and in doing so, excluded prison rape from the discussion. Because if we include prison rape in the rape conversation, then males get raped at a much greater rate than females. Feminists must remove that variable.

But that wasn't enough. They had to manipulate studies to show that 90% of rape victims are female by saying made to penetration is not rape. And the CDC responds that no research exists to show that made-to-penetrate is the same as rape... and why do you think that is? As Cathy Young demonstrated, if we include the variable as rape, then men and women get raped in nearly equal numbers.

Nope, can't have that. No, no, no, no, no. Didn't you see the earlier part? Men and boys can't be victims.

The CDC knew that men and women were raped in nearly equal numbers and buried it. More than the CDC, the UN knew boys were married off at such a young age and ignored it. It wasn't until 2019. Two zero one nine. We got studies of Child Brides from the 80's, and forty years later, someone looks at boys and sees the victimization. Researchers for years saw it and ignored it.

Neglect, the most common form of abuse, primarily happens to boys... Nope!

Physical abuse predominately happens to boys... Nope!

Sexual abuse is the third most common form of abuse, and researchers have manipulated it to look like it is something that predominately happens to girls... Yes!

Borrowing from Mike Rezendes/Mark Ruffalo in the movie "Spotlight":

It is time. The world knew, and let it happen.

To BOYS.
To MEN.

It could have been your fathers, your brothers, your cousins, your uncles, your grandfather, your sons, it could be you and me.

We need to change the world, we need the world to wake up and start having empathy for men and boys.

And we need to enforce the consequences, that crimes against humanity have real punishments, and those who keep their heads in the sand are as guilty as those who hurt men and boys.

This book shouldn't need to have been written. The words I put in here should go into the ether. Because what is said here should already have been known by the world and put into action to correct it so that humanity could be taken into the future as our best selves.

Writing this book has been one of the most challenging tasks I have ever done. I would wonder if this was incoherent nonsense if it wasn't for Janice's words after reading my book (found on the back cover). But I did the work; I read study after study, articles of the worst of what humanity has to offer, and some great people out there fighting what seems to be a hopeless cause.

This book had to be written. I'm proud of what I've done and will do what I can to ensure people read it. If it gets banned from one platform, another will take its place. Sadly, we live in a world where people would rather believe someone else's opinion than investigate for themselves. I am prepared for my book to be hated.

It is vitally important that these facts are at your disposal. I see studies that refer to what research they used, but it's often hard to find that resource, and they don't exactly tell you where to look. Research papers could be two pages to a hundred. I know this is the standard way of doing things in Academia, but at times it feels discouraging to double-check their resources. Or maybe that's just me.

I broke from tradition, primarily because I wasn't trained that way, but because I wanted to know if I got something wrong. I'm far from perfect, so I possibly got something wrong because I overlooked something, misinterpreted the wording, or I'm bad at math. I'd like to think I did my best to make this book happen, but you tell me. I give you where you can find it and what page number. If you really think I did something wrong, let me know. Go to my website (boysmenissues.com), hit contact me and send a message. Let minds come together to get the truth out there.

This book is about changing the world, about making it better. This is a book on troubleshooting, about finding the problems out there so we can fix them. Men and women, boys and girls, all suffer and need help. We can't begin to fix anything by ignoring half of the population in favor of the other half.

If you wish to argue a point with me, I ask you not to say I'm wrong because it goes against everything you were taught to believe. Be prepared to back up your claim, and don't be surprised if I go through any research you present and point out flaws I see. Do your homework and then present your case, as I will probably ignore you otherwise if all you have is your word alone.

With any project I work on, it's important to me not just to identify the issue but to dig in deep to ascertain the how and why. That is why my book transformed into a deep dive into the reality of boys: to really drive home the point, I needed to go bigger. I needed to give all of my effort to show that boys and men are being left behind in this world and that even if you can counter a point I've made, there are 800 more remaining.

Let's make the world genuinely egalitarian, where the issues of men and boys are addressed at the same level as women and girls.

SOURCES

If any link doesn't work, try the Internet Archive.

Check out more resources at Wiki4Men.com

AUTHOR'S NOTE
1 https://www.splcenter.org/fighting-hate/intelligence-report/2012/misogyny-sites
2 https://www.youtube.com/watch?v=FWgslugtDow
3 https://www.campusreform.org/?ID=11006
4 https://www.cbc.ca/radio/outintheopen/i-want-patriarchy-to-fear-women-mona-eltahawy-says-the-time-for-being-civil-peaceful-and-polite-is-over-1.5296597
5 https://www.irishexaminer.com/viewpoints/columnists/louise-oneill/louise-oneill-it-is-impossible-for-women-to-be-sexist-towards-men-440072.html
6 https://www.change.org/p/kate-germano-be-reinstated-as-a-trainer-at-parris-island
7 https://reductress.com/post/the-freshest-male-tears-to-straight-up-bathe-in/
8 https://www.youtube.com/watch?v=NZ4wljj7syY

INTRODUCTION
9 http://theredpillmovie.com/
10 https://www.thoughtco.com/womens-suffrage-victory-3530497
11 https://www.telegraph.co.uk/men/thinking-man/has-everyone-forgotten-male-suffrage/
12 https://www.thesun.co.uk/news/14462491/boys-forced-assembly-apologise-rapes-committed/

ABDUCTIONS
13 https://safeatlast.co/blog/child-abduction-statistics/
14 https://safeatlast.co/blog/kidnapping-statistics/
15 https://www.youtube.com/watch?v=NAQUNkEtDpo
16 https://en.wikipedia.org/wiki/Georgia_Tann
17 https://www.bbc.com/news/education-22938866
18 https://en.wikipedia.org/wiki/Fetal_abduction
19 https://en.wikipedia.org/wiki/Bacha_bazi
20 https://www.youtube.com/watch?v=Ja5Q75hf6QI

21 https://www.nytimes.com/2018/01/23/world/asia/afghanistan-military-abuse.html

22 https://en.wikipedia.org/wiki/Hijra_(South_Asia)

23 http://thingsasian.com/story/eunuchs-indias-third-gender

24 https://www.americanbazaaronline.com/2014/04/16/kidnapped-castrated-boys-men-deformed-genitals-eunuchs-get-legal-acceptance-india/

25 https://www.indiatimes.com/news/lgbtq-the-truth-about-how-hijras-are-made-in-india-because-they-re-not-always-born-that-way-257525.html

26 https://en.wikipedia.org/wiki/Chibok_schoolgirls_kidnapping##BringBackOurGirls_movement_and_protests

27 https://www.huffpost.com/entry/bring-back-our-boys-israel-kidnapping_n_5515945

28 https://www.usatoday.com/story/news/world/2020/12/16/boko-haram-kidnaps-330-boys-nigeria-outcry-uses-bring backourboys/3919404001/

29 https://www.vanityfair.com/news/2017/06/the-shocking-story-of-boko-harams-forgotten-victims

30 https://www.nytimes.com/2017/06/21/magazine/boko-haram-the-boys-from-baga.html

31 https://www.abc.net.au/news/2014-02-26/scores-dead-in-boko-haram-nigeran-school-attack/5284250

32 https://www.usatoday.com/story/news/world/2020/12/16/boko-haram-kidnaps-330-boys-nigeria-outcry-uses-bringbackourboys/3919404001/

33 https://www.dailymail.co.uk/news/article-9054577/Boko-Haram-claims-abduction-hundreds-schoolchildren-Nigeria-Friday.html

34 https://www.albawaba.com/news/why-did-boko-haram-jihadists-kidnap-300-school-kids-1399150

35 https://abcnews.go.com/International/boko-haram-abducted-1000-children-killed-2000-teachers/story?id=54442518

36 https://www.cnn.com/2018/04/13/africa/boko-haram-children-abduction-intl/index.html

37 https://www.aljazeera.com/news/2020/12/15/boko-haram-claims-kidnapping-of-hundreds-of-nigerian-students

38 https://theowp.org/330-students-kidnapped-is-boko-haram-expanding/

39 https://nypost.com/2020/12/15/boko-haram-claims-abduction-of-students-in-northern-nigeria/

40 https://www.dawn.com/news/1595924

41 https://www.youtube.com/watch?v=DE8OD3d9iEk

ABUSE

42 https://youtu.be/apnHp0q1d78?t=716

43 https://apps.who.int/iris/handle/10665/65900

44 https://www.researchgate.net/publication/284513156_Child_abuse_and_neglect_by_parents_and_other_caregivers
45 https://www.acf.hhs.gov/sites/default/files/documents/cb/cm2020.pdf#page=70
46 https://www.researchgate.net/publication/284513156_Child_abuse_and_neglect_by_parents_and_other_caregivers (page 67)
47 https://www.researchgate.net/publication/284513156_Child_abuse_and_neglect_by_parents_and_other_caregivers (page 68)
48 https://www.acf.hhs.gov/sites/default/files/documents/cb/cm2020.pdf#page=39
49 https://www.acf.hhs.gov/sites/default/files/documents/cb/cm2020.pdf#page=38
50 https://www.acf.hhs.gov/sites/default/files/documents/cb/cm2020.pdf#page=59
51 https://www.researchgate.net/publication/269988368_Child_Abuse_in_the_Worldwide_A_Review_Article (page 4)
52 https://americanspcc.org/child-neglect/
53 https://www.drugs.com/cg/child-abuse-neglect.html
54 https://www.vetmed.wsu.edu/docs/librariesprovider16/default-document-library/the-long-shadow-adult-survivors-of-childhood-abuse.pdf?sfvrsn=0#page=3
55 https://www.childwelfare.gov/pubpdfs/long_term_consequences.pdf
56 https://www.researchgate.net/publication/284513156_Child_abuse_and_neglect_by_parents_and_other_caregivers (page 9)
57 https://www.researchgate.net/publication/222580095_Assessing_child_neglect_A_review_of_standardized_measures (page 5)
58 http://www.brown.uk.com/childabuse/legano.pdf#page=17
59 https://en.wikipedia.org/wiki/Collingswood_Boys
60 http://www.brown.uk.com/childabuse/legano.pdf#page=18
61 https://www.sciencedirect.com/science/article/abs/pii/S1359178904000631 (page 7)
62 https://en.wikipedia.org/wiki/Tiger_parenting
63 https://en.wikipedia.org/wiki/Child_abandonment
64 https://americanspcc.org/indicators-of-child-abuse/
65 https://americanspcc.org/physical-child-abuse/
66 https://www.academia.edu/11722246/
67 https://data.unicef.org/wp-content/uploads/2017/10/EVAC-Booklet-FINAL-10_31_17-high-res.pdf#page=47
68 https://www.researchgate.net/publication/284513156_Child_abuse_and_neglect_by_parents_and_other_caregivers#page=61
69 https://en.wikipedia.org/wiki/Psychological_abuse
70 https://www.originsrecovery.com/is-there-a-difference-between-emotional-abuse-and-psychological-abuse/
71 https://southlakecounseling.org/the-differences-between-emotional-and-psychological-abuse-and-why-its-important-for-victims/

72 https://www.vetmed.wsu.edu/docs/librariesprovider16/default-document-library/the-long-shadow-adult-survivors-of-childhood-abuse.pdf?sfvrsn=0#page=4

73 https://www.differencebetween.com/difference-between-mental-and-vs-emotional-abuse/

74 https://www.bbc.com/news/newsbeat-39627969

75 https://www.acf.hhs.gov/sites/default/files/documents/cb/cm2020.pdf#page=62

76 https://www.acf.hhs.gov/sites/default/files/documents/cb/cm2020.pdf#page=13

77 https://www.acf.hhs.gov/sites/default/files/documents/cb/cm2020.pdf#page=72

78 https://www.acf.hhs.gov/sites/default/files/documents/cb/cm2019.pdf#page=70

79 https://www.acf.hhs.gov/sites/default/files/documents/cm99_0.pdf#page=56

80 https://www.acf.hhs.gov/sites/default/files/documents/cb/cm2020.pdf#page=73

81 https://www.researchgate.net/publication/284513156_Child_abuse_and_neglect_by_parents_and_other_caregivers#page=60

82 https://www.unicef.org/media/66916/file/Hidden-in-plain-sight.pdf#page=38

83 https://www.unodc.org/documents/data-and-analysis/gsh/Booklet1.pdf#page=21

84 https://bmjpaedsopen.bmj.com/content/bmjpo/1/1/e000112.full.pdf

85 http://miami.cbslocal.com/2014/01/24/autopsy-released-of-3-year-old-found-dead-in-mothers-home/

86 https://www.breitbart.com/crime/2019/08/04/baltimore-lesbian-couple-charged-with-killing-4-year-old-son-found-dead-in-dumpster/

87 https://pulpitandpen.org/2019/06/12/lesbian-couple-decapitate-dismember-little-boy-after-home-gender-reassignment-went-wrong/

88 https://people.com/crime/lamora-williams-allegedly-killed-children-oven/

89 https://www.amazon.com/Dear-Zachary-Letter-About-Father/dp/B00MF5LH46

90 https://people.com/crime/mom-allegedly-killed-boy-she-didnt-want-and-dad-says-all-she-had-to-do-was-give-him-to-me/

91 https://en.wikipedia.org/wiki/Osaka_child_abandonment_case

92 https://www.acf.hhs.gov/sites/default/files/documents/cb/cm2019.pdf#page=79

93 https://www.researchgate.net/publication/8353520_Borderline_pathology_in_children_and_adolescents (page 2)

94 https://www.psychologytoday.com/us/blog/the-scientific-fundamentalist/201010/girls-are-more-intelligent-boys

95 https://pubmed.ncbi.nlm.nih.gov/28042663 page=4

96 https://pubmed.ncbi.nlm.nih.gov/28042663 page=6

97 https://pubmed.ncbi.nlm.nih.gov/28042663 page=25

98 https://canadiancrc.com/PDFs/The_Invisible_Boy_Report.pdf#page=11

99 https://www.amazon.com/Empathy-Gap-Disadvantages-Mechanisms-Neglect/dp/0957168888 (page 331)

100 https://americanspcc.org/impact-of-child-abuse/

101 https://www.basw.co.uk/system/files/resources/basw_80655-2_2.pdf#page=4

102 https://www.scientificamerican.com/article/childhood-adverse-event-life-expectancy-abuse-mortality/

103 https://www.wales.nhs.uk/sitesplus/documents/888/ACE%20&%20Resilience%20Report%20(Eng_final2).pdf#page=4

104 http://medicineworld.org/cancer/lead/11-2005/physically-abused-boys-more-likely-to-commit-domestic-violence.html

105 https://pubmed.ncbi.nlm.nih.gov/9635069/ (page 6)

106 https://pubmed.ncbi.nlm.nih.gov/9635069/ (page 8)

107 https://pubmed.ncbi.nlm.nih.gov/9635069/ (page 9)

108 http://xnet.kp.org/permanentejournal/winter02/goldtolead.html

109 https://neuro.psychiatryonline.org/doi/10.1176/appi.neuropsych.13100240

110 https://colors-newyork.com/how-long-is-the-cell-cycle/

111 https://pubmed.ncbi.nlm.nih.gov/23258416/

112 https://www.researchgate.net/publication/44646957_Childhood_Adversities_Are_Associated_with_Shorter_Telomere_Length_at_Adult_Age_both_in_Individuals_with_an_Anxiety_Disorder_and_Controls (page 2)

113 https://www.researchgate.net/publication/44646957_Childhood_Adversities_Are_Associated_with_Shorter_Telomere_Length_at_Adult_Age_both_in_Individuals_with_an_Anxiety_Disorder_and_Controls (page 4)

114 https://pubmed.ncbi.nlm.nih.gov/20520771/

115 https://www.youtube.com/watch?v=HqqtFwCg3YM

CHILD LABOR

116 https://www.ilo.org/wcmsp5/groups/public/---ed_norm/---ipec/documents/publication/wcms_653987.pdf#page=7

117 https://www.researchgate.net/publication/237704531_Violence_against_Working_Children_A_report_on_recent_research_relating_to_work_that_is_harmful_to_children (page 21)

118 https://www.ilo.org/wcmsp5/groups/public/---ed_norm/---ipec/documents/publication/wcms_653987.pdf#page=8

119 https://www.ilo.org/wcmsp5/groups/public/---ed_norm/---ipec/documents/publication/wcms_221513.pdf#page=18)

120 https://www.ilo.org/wcmsp5/groups/public/---ed_norm/---ipec/documents/publication/wcms_653987.pdf#page=7

121 https://en.wikipedia.org/wiki/Sadler_report

122 https://en.wikipedia.org/wiki/Child_labor_laws_in_the_United_States#History_of_children's_labor_for_wages

123 https://www.ducksters.com/history/us_1800s/child_labor_industrial_revolution.php

124 https://www.history.com/topics/industrial-revolution/child-labor

125 https://www.history.com/news/child-labor-lewis-hine-photos

126 https://www.ilo.org/wcmsp5/groups/public/---ed_norm/---ipec/documents/publication/wcms_221513.pdf#page=20

127 https://www.dol.gov/sites/dolgov/files/ILAB/child_labor_reports/tda2019/2019_Sweat_And_Toil_Magazine.pdf#page=37

128 https://www.dol.gov/sites/dolgov/files/ILAB/child_labor_reports/tda2019/2019_Sweat_And_Toil_Magazine.pdf#page=32

129 https://www.ilo.org/wcmsp5/groups/public/---ed_norm/---ipec/documents/publication/wcms_653987.pdf#page=23

130 https://www.ilo.org/wcmsp5/groups/public/---ed_norm/---ipec/documents/publication/wcms_653987.pdf#page=43

131 https://www.ilo.org/wcmsp5/groups/public/---ed_norm/---ipec/documents/publication/wcms_653987.pdf#page=44

132 https://core.ac.uk/download/pdf/9552547.pdf#page=10

133 https://www.unicef.nl/media/2535977/child_labour_and_unicef_in_action.pdf#page=8

134 https://www.researchgate.net/publication/237704531_Violence_against_Working_Children_A_report_on_recent_research_relating_to_work_that_is_harmful_to_children (page 15)

135 https://www.academia.edu/15001537/COMBATING_CHILD_LABOUR_ISSUES AND_CHALLENGES (page 10)

136 https://www.researchgate.net/publication/237704531_Violence_against_Working_Children_A_report_on_recent_research_relating_to_work_that_is_harmful_to_children (page 14)

137 https://ecommons.aku.edu/cgi/viewcontent.cgi?article=1008&context=pakistan_fhs_son (page 4)

138 https://papers.ssrn.com/sol3/papers.cfm?abstract_id=2411017 (page 14)

139 https://papers.ssrn.com/sol3/papers.cfm?abstract_id=2411017 (page 17)

140 https://papers.ssrn.com/sol3/papers.cfm?abstract_id=2411017 (page 7)

141 http://sro.sussex.ac.uk/id/eprint/43310/1/Briefing_paper_No_3_-_children_working_in_the_urban_informal_economy.pdf#page=6

142 https://www.researchgate.net/publication/237704531_Violence_against_Working_Children_A_report_on_recent_research_relating_to_work_that_is_harmful_to_children (page 19)

143 https://www.researchgate.net/publication/271673211_Reducing_ child_labour_in_Panama_An_impact_evaluation (page 4)

144 https://www.academia.edu/19641383/CHILD_LABOUR_AND_ ECONOMIC_GROWTH (page 2)

145 https://www.ilo.org/ipec/ChildlabourstatisticsSIMPOC/WCMS_817698/ lang--en/index.htm

146 https://www.ilo.org/wcmsp5/groups/public/---ed_norm/---ipec/ documents/publication/wcms_653987.pdf#page=10

147 https://www.unicef.nl/media/2535977/child_labour_and_unicef_in_ action.pdf#page=5

148 https://www.unicef.nl/media/2535977/child_labour_and_unicef_in_ action.pdf#page=6

149 https://core.ac.uk/download/pdf/9552547.pdf#page=6

150 https://www.academia.edu/19641383/CHILD_LABOUR_AND_ ECONOMIC_GROWTH (page 4)

CHILD SOLDIERS

151 https://www.usip.org/sites/default/files/missing-peace/The%20 psychological%20impact%20of%20child%20soldiering%20-%20Schauer. pdf#page=8

152 https://www.independent.co.uk/voices/comment/ten-facts-about- child-soldiers-everyone-should-know-8427617.html?

153 https://www.cfr.org/backgrounder/child-soldiers-around-world

154 https://ohiostate.pressbooks.pub/humantrafficking/chapter/chapter- 8-child-soldiers/

155 https://www.unric.org/en/latest-un-buzz/29639-4-out-of-10-child- soldiers-are-girls

156 https://www.usip.org/sites/default/files/missing-peace/The%20 psychological%20impact%20of%20child%20soldiering%20-%20Schauer. pdf#page=6

157 https://en.wikipedia.org/wiki/Children_in_the_military

158 https://inkstickmedia.com/a-record-number-of-countries -are-using-child-soldiers/

159 https://www.state.gov/wp-content/uploads/2021/09/TIPR-GPA- upload-07222021.pdf#page=56

160 https://fas.org/sgp/crs/misc/IF10901.pdf#page=1

161 https://www.stimson.org/2020/looking-ahead-child-soldiers/

162 https://cdn.cnn.com/cnnnext/dam/assets/150429151208-child- soldiers-map-1-super-169.jpg

163 https://www.hrw.org/news/2016/01/13/dispatches-education- casualty-war

164 https://www.usip.org/sites/default/files/missing-peace/The%20 psychological%20impact%20of%20child%20soldiering%20-%20Schauer. pdf#page=4

165 https://www.usip.org/sites/default/files/missing-peace/The%20 psychological%20impact%20of%20child%20soldiering%20-%20Schauer. pdf#page=1
166 https://childsoldiercrisis.wordpress.com/physical-impacts/
167 https://tbinternet.ohchr.org/Treaties/CRC/Shared%20Documents/ MMR/INT_CRC_NGO_MMR_59_9683_E.pdf
168 https://childsoldiercrisis.wordpress.com/psychological-impacts/
169 https://www.usip.org/sites/default/files/missing-peace/The%20 psychological%20impact%20of%20child%20soldiering%20-%20Schauer. pdf#page=34
170 https://childsoldiercrisis.wordpress.com/educational-impacts/
171 https://childsoldiercrisis.wordpress.com/for-individuals/
172 https://www.hrw.org/news/2012/02/13/getting-children-battlefield

CHILD GROOMS

173 https://www.tandfonline.com/doi/pdf/10.1080/17450128. 2019.1566584?needAccess=true (page 2)
174 http://www.her-choice.org/wp-content/uploads/2018/11/Child-grooms.pdf#page=13
175 https://theconversation.com/the-forgotten-male-victims-of-honour-based-violence-96041
176 http://www.her-choice.org/wp-content/uploads/2018/11/Child-grooms.pdf
177 https://www.unicef.org/press-releases/115-million-boys-and-men-around-world-married-children-unicef
178 https://www.tandfonline.com/doi/pdf/10.1080/17450128. 2019.1566584?needAccess=true (page 4)
179 https://www.tandfonline.com/doi/pdf/10.1080/17450128. 2019.1566584?needAccess=true (page 5)
180 https://www.freedomunited.org/news/forgotten-male-victims-forced-marriage/
181 https://www.thedailybeast.com/the-sad-hidden-plight-of-child-grooms
182 http://www.her-choice.org/wp-content/uploads/2018/11/Child-grooms.pdf#page=43
183 https://www.latimes.com/world/la-fg-c1-nepal-child-grooms-20150127-story.html
184 https://www.unfpa.org/child-marriage-frequently-asked-questions#what%20is%20child%20marriage
185 http://www.her-choice.org/wp-content/uploads/2018/11/Child-grooms.pdf#page=40
186 http://www.her-choice.org/wp-content/uploads/2018/11/Child-grooms.pdf#page=49
187 http://www.her-choice.org/wp-content/uploads/2018/11/Child-grooms.pdf#page=50

188 http://www.her-choice.org/wp-content/uploads/2018/11/Child-grooms.pdf#page=51
189 https://wfuv.org/content/child-grooms-are-often-overlooked-fight-stop-child-marriage
190 https://www.rferl.org/a/boys-with-brides-afghanistan-untold-dilemma-of-underage-marriages/30106032.html
191 https://legacy.pulitzercenter.org/reporting/grooms-tale
192 https://www.bbc.com/news/10469935
193 https://www.unicef-irc.org/publications/pdf/digest7e.pdf#page=3
194 https://www.spiegel.de/international/germany/overlooked-victims-immigrant-men-are-forced-to-marry-too-a-589130.html
195 http://www.her-choice.org/wp-content/uploads/2018/11/Child-grooms.pdf#page=55
196 http://www.her-choice.org/wp-content/uploads/2018/11/Child-grooms.pdf#page=56
197 http://www.her-choice.org/wp-content/uploads/2018/11/Child-grooms.pdf#pagc=60
198 http://www.her-choice.org/wp-content/uploads/2018/11/Child-grooms.pdf#page=57
199 https://www.tandfonline.com/doi/pdf/10.1080/17450128.2019.1566584?needAccess=true (page 3)
200 http://www.her-choice.org/wp-content/uploads/2018/11/Child-grooms.pdf#page=63
201 http://www.her-choice.org/wp-content/uploads/2018/11/Child-grooms.pdf#page=65
202 https://www.care.org/our-work/health/fighting-gender-based-violence/tipping-point/

BODY IMAGE & EATING DISORDERS

203 https://www.eatingdisorders.org.au/eating-disorders-a-z/eating-disorders-in-men/
204 https://www.academia.edu/6681996/Web_Based_Intervention_for_Adolescent_Males_with_Anorexia_Nervosa page=3
205 https://journals.sagepub.com/doi/10.1177/027243160302 3002002 page 1
206 https://pubmed.ncbi.nlm.nih.gov/25226158/
207 https://pubmed.ncbi.nlm.nih.gov/25226158/ page=3
208 https://www.cdc.gov/mmwr/volumes/66/wr/mm6630a6.htm
209 https://pubmed.ncbi.nlm.nih.gov/29883900/ page=1
210 https://gupea.ub.gu.se/bitstream/2077/19350/1/gupea_2077_19350_1.pdf#page=50
211 https://gupea.ub.gu.se/bitstream/2077/19350/1/gupea_2077_19350_1.pdf#page=51
212 https://en.wikipedia.org/wiki/Anorexia_nervosa

213 https://www.tandfonline.com/doi/abs/10.1080/10640266.2012.71551
5

214 https://www.academia.edu/6681996/Web_Based_Intervention_for_
Adolescent_Males_with_Anorexia_Nervosa (page 2)

215 https://www.tandfonline.com/doi/abs/10.1080/10640266.2013.86489
1 page=2

216 https://www.tandfonline.com/doi/abs/10.1080/10640266.2013.86489
1 page=7

217 https://www.tandfonline.com/doi/abs/10.1080/10640266.2013.86489
1 page=9

218 https://cdn.intechopen.com/pdfs/33137/InTech-Behavioral_and_
psychosocial_factors_in_childhood_obesity.pdf#page=7

219 https://cdn.intechopen.com/pdfs/33137/InTech-Behavioral_and_
psychosocial_factors_in_childhood_obesity.pdf#page=10

220 https://cdn.intechopen.com/pdfs/33137/InTech-Behavioral_and_
psychosocial_factors_in_childhood_obesity.pdf#page=11

221 https://www.tandfonline.com/doi/abs/10.1080/10640266.2012.71551
5 page=4

222 https://www.tandfonline.com/doi/abs/10.1080/10640266.2012.71551
5 page=6

223 http://oaji.net/articles/2015/1264-1431010730.pdf
#page=4

ADHD

224 https://www.arsi.gr/datafiles/file/European%20Child%20and%20
Adolescent%20Psychiatry,%202006.pdf#page=2

225 https://www.cdc.gov/ncbddd/adhd/data.html

226 https://datacenter.kidscount.org/data/tables/102-child-
population-by-gender#detailed/1/any/false/1729,37,871,
870,573,869,36,868,867,133/14,15,65/421,422

227 https://www.addrc.org/dsm-5-criteria-for-adhd/

228 https://www.arsi.gr/datafiles/file/European%20Child%20and%20
Adolescent%20Psychiatry,%202006.pdf#page=7

229 https://www.academia.edu/13478190/Social_skills_training_for_
Attention_Deficit_Hyperactivity_Disorder_ADHD
_in_children_aged_5_to_18_years page=8

230 https://www.arsi.gr/datafiles/file/European%20Child%20and%20
Adolescent%20Psychiatry,%202006.pdf#page=5

231 https://www.arsi.gr/datafiles/file/European%20Child%20and%20
Adolescent%20Psychiatry,%202006.pdf#page=8

232 http://eprints.nottingham.ac.uk/10858/1/Producing_ADHD.
pdf#page=116

233 https://www.jpeds.com/article/S0022-3476(16)00160-8/pdf#page=3

234 http://eprints.nottingham.ac.uk/10858/1/Producing_ADHD.
pdf#page=114

235 https://www.healthline.com/health/adhd/adhd-misdiagnosis#bipolar-disorder
236 https://www.theatlantic.com/health/archive/2014/07/how-childhood-trauma-could-be-mistaken-for-adhd/373328/
237 https://www.spectrumnews.org/news/autisms-sex-ratio-explained/
238 https://www.spectrumnews.org/news/estimate-autisms-sex-ratio-reaches-new-low/
239 https://discovery.ucl.ac.uk/id/eprint/1558343/1/Loomes.pdf#page=12
240 https://www.autismspeaks.org/autism-statistics-asd
241 http://science.psu.edu/news-and-events/2015-news/Girirajan7-2015
242 https://www.foxnews.com/health/study-reveals-why-autism-is-more-common-in-males
243 http://science.psu.edu/news-and-events/2015-news/images/research/bmb/image-related-to-research-by-santhosh-girirajan
244 https://sph.unc.edu/sph-news/genetically-speaking-mammals-are-more-like-their-fathers-study-finds/
245 https://www.pbs.org/newshour/nation/why-the-u-s-ban-on-female-genital-mutilation-was-ruled-unconstitutional
246 https://autismsd.com/autism-and-circumcision/

SEXUAL ABUSE

247 https://www.huffpost.com/entry/rape-study-report-america-us_n_4310765
248 https://www.youtube.com/watch?v=u5NtdgNe-iM
249 https://therandyreport.com/tucker-carlson-teenage-boys-cant-be/
250 https://www.reddit.com/r/insanepeoplefacebook/comments/hcut5c/boys_under_18_cant_be_raped_apparently/

251 https://goodmenproject.com/ethics-values/society-wont-let-boys-men-victims-rape/
252 https://www.researchgate.net/publication/26459340_Diagnosing_Child_Sex_Abuse_A_research_challenge (page 20)
253 https://www.newsweek.com/ohio-supreme-court-narrows-standard-rape-case-involving-2-year-old-1676503
254 https://www.academia.edu/36539221/Child_sexual_abuse_Routledge_International_Handbook_of_Violence_Studies_ (page 7)
255 https://acestoohigh.files.wordpress.com/2013/05/death_survivors_report_1may2013.pdf#page=5
256 https://www.cdc.gov/violenceprevention/intimatepartnerviolence/fastfact.html
257 https://journals.sagepub.com/doi/10.1177/08862609300 8002004 (page 9)
258 https://www.ncbi.nlm.nih.gov/pmc/articles/PMC4692457/pdf/nihms745990.pdf
259 https://www.cdc.gov/mmwr/preview/mmwrhtml/ss6308a1.htm#Table1

260 https://time.com/3393442/cdc-rape-numbers/
261 https://www.reddit.com/r/MensRights/comments/diz4fh
/i_asked_the_cdc_why_they_dont_count_made_to/
262 https://pubmed.ncbi.nlm.nih.gov/15894146/
263 https://pubmed.ncbi.nlm.nih.gov/15894146/ (page 4)
264 https://menaregood.com/boys-raped-more-often-then-girls/
265 https://www.researchgate.net/publication/263895608_It
%27s_a_lonely_journey_A_rapid_evidence_assessment_on_infrafamilial_
child_sexual_abuse (page 16)
266 https://www.tandfonline.com/doi/abs/10.1080/13552600
.2019.1643504?journalCode=tjsa20 (page 4)
267 https://www.academia.edu/36539221/Child_sexual_abuse_
Routledge_International_Handbook_of_Violence_
Studies_
268 https://www.researchgate.net/publication/263895608_It's_a_lonely_
journey_A_rapid_evidence_assessment_on_infrafamilial_child_sexual_
abuse (page 30)
269 https://www.unicef.org/media/84081/file/Preventing-Responding-to-
Child-Sexual-Abuse-Exploitation-Evidence-Review.pdf
270 https://cms.barnardos.org.uk/sites/default/files/2020-10/
Barnardo%27s%20Scotland%20Policy%20Report%20Sexual
%20exploitation%20of%20children%20involved%20in%20the%20
Children%E2%80%99s%20Hearings%20System%20%28PDF%29_0.
pdf#page=9
271 https://canadiancrc.com/PDFs/The_Invisible_Boy_Report.
pdf#page=19
272 https://canadiancrc.com/PDFs/The_Invisible_Boy_Report.
pdf#page=15
273 https://acestoohigh.files.wordpress.com/2013/05/death_survivors_
report_1may2013.pdf#page=32v
274 https://www.unicef.org/northmacedonia/media/4201/file/MK_
ViolenceAgainstChildren_Report_ENG.pdf#page=11
275 https://www.theguardian.com/society/2015/apr/09/reported-child-
sexual-abuse-has-risen-60-in-last-four-years-figures-show
276 https://popcenter.asu.edu/sites/default/files/problems/child_
pornography/PDFs/Smallbone&Wortley_2000.pdf
#page=9
277 https://etheses.whiterose.ac.uk/26956/2/Recovering%20from%20
Childhood%20Sexual%20Abuse%20A%20Salutogenic%20Approach.
pdf#page=81
278 https://popcenter.asu.edu/sites/default/files/problems/child_
pornography/PDFs/Smallbone&Wortley_2000.pdf
#page=13
279 https://popcenter.asu.edu/sites/default/files/problems/child_
pornography/PDFs/Smallbone&Wortley_2000.pdf
#page=15

280 https://popcenter.asu.edu/sites/default/files/problems/child_
pornography/PDFs/Smallbone&Wortley_2000.pdf
#page=57
281 https://www.gov.uk/government/publications/review-of-
sexual-abuse-in-schools-and-colleges/review-of-sexual-abuse
-in-schools-and-colleges
282 https://www.bbc.com/news/uk-28935733
283 https://canadiancrc.com/PDFs/The_Invisible_Boy_Report.
pdf#page=17
284 https://worldpopulationreview.com/countries/canada-population
285 https://www.unicef.org/media/48671/file/Violence_in_the
_lives_of_children_and_adolescents.pdf#page=77
286 https://pubmed.ncbi.nlm.nih.gov/23219443/ (page 4)
287 https://www.cambridge.org/core/services/aop-cambridge-
core/content/view/D0FB762BBFD3BD78736F14B87C3F65D8/
S1749367600004008a.pdf/child_sexual_abuse_and_health_outcomes_in_
the_chinese_context.pdf#page=2
288 https://pubmed.ncbi.nlm.nih.gov/23219443/ (page 3)
289 https://www.statista.com/statistics/251129/population-in-
china-by-gender/
290 https://www.bbc.com/news/world-asia-china-57303592
291 https://www.cambridge.org/core/services/aop-cambridge-
core/content/view/5AA45B0B4E2665D482A520736CBD36DD/
S174936760000401Xa.pdf/child_sexual_abuse_data_from_an
_arabian_gulf_country_revisited.pdf
292 https://www.cambridge.org/core/services/aop-cambridge-
core/content/view/5AA45B0B4E2665D482A520736CBD36D D/
S174936760000401Xa.pdf/child_sexual_abuse_data_from_an_arabian_
gulf_country_revisited.pdf#page=2
293 https://www.statista.com/statistics/645737/kuwait-population-by-
gender/
294 https://resourcecentre.savethechildren.net/pdf/unhcr_
keepitinourhearts.pdf#page=11
295 https://resourcecentre.savethechildren.net/pdf/unhcr_
keepitinourhearts.pdf#page=12
296 https://www.togetherforgirls.org/wp-content/uploads/
2016_Childhood-SV-Against-Boys-A-study-in-3-countries.pdf#page=4
297 https://equityhealthj.biomedcentral.com/track/pdf/
10.1186/1475-9276-7-20.pdf#page=3
298 https://www.togetherforgirls.org/wp-content/uploads/
2016_Childhood-SV-Against-Boys-A-study-in-3-countries.pdf#page=4
299 https://equityhealthj.biomedcentral.com/track/pdf/
10.1186/1475-9276-7-20.pdf#page=5
300 https://www.saferspaces.org.za/resources/entry/sexual-victimisation-
of-children-in-south-africa-final-report (page 11)

301 https://www.saferspaces.org.za/resources/entry/sexual-victimisation-of-children-in-south-africa-final-report (page 36)
302 https://www.saferspaces.org.za/resources/entry/sexual-victimisation-of-children-in-south-africa-final-report (page 35)
303 https://www.saferspaces.org.za/resources/entry/sexual-victimisation-of-children-in-south-africa-final-report (page 48)
304 https://www.researchgate.net/publication/222884781_The_rates_of_child_sexual_abuse_and_its_psychological_consequences_as_revealed_by_a_study_among_Palestinian_University_students (page 8)
305 https://www.researchgate.net/publication/222884781_The_rates_of_child_sexual_abuse_and_its_psychological_consequences_as_revealed_by_a_study_among_Palestinian_University_students (page 2)
306 https://www.researchgate.net/publication/222884781_The_rates_of_child_sexual_abuse_and_its_psychological_consequences_as_revealed_by_a_study_among_Palestinian_University_students (page 3)
307 https://www.researchgate.net/publication/222884781_The_rates_of_child_sexual_abuse_and_its_psychological_consequences_as_revealed_by_a_study_among_Palestinian_University_students (page 9)
308 https://www.researchgate.net/publication/222884781_The_rates_of_child_sexual_abuse_and_its_psychological_consequences_as_revealed_by_a_study_among_Palestinian_University_students (page 10)
309 http://wcd.nic.in/childabuse.pdf#page=49
310 http://wcd.nic.in/childabuse.pdf#page=89
311 http://wcd.nic.in/childabuse.pdf#page=87
312 http://wcd.nic.in/childabuse.pdf#page=88
313 http://wcd.nic.in/childabuse.pdf#page=89
314 http://wcd.nic.in/childabuse.pdf#page=94
315 http://wcd.nic.in/childabuse.pdf#page=91
316 http://wcd.nic.in/childabuse.pdf#page=96
317 http://wcd.nic.in/childabuse.pdf#page=97
318 http://wcd.nic.in/childabuse.pdf#page=105
319 http://wcd.nic.in/childabuse.pdf#page=99
320 http://wcd.nic.in/childabuse.pdf#page=100
321 http://www.wcd.nic.in/childabuse.pdf#page=88
322 https://www.researchgate.net/publication/329208180_Big_Boys_Don't_Cry_A_Critical_Interpretive_Synthesis_of_Male_Sexual_Victimization (page 12)
323 https://www.buzzfeed.com/catesevilla/listen-and-believe
324 https://en.wikipedia.org/wiki/Miss_Teacher_Bangs_a_Boy
325 https://eprints.qut.edu.au/66435/20/66435.pdf#page=25
326 http://johnlang.org/wp-content/uploads/2018/03/Zack-Lang-Dirks-2018.pdf#page=4
327 http://www.regent.edu/acad/schlaw/blogs/docs/femaleoffender.pdf#page=15
328 https://canadiancrc.com/PDFs/The_Invisible_Boy_Report.pdf#page=22

329 https://canadiancrc.com/PDFs/The_Invisible_Boy_Report. pdf#page=22

330 https://www.researchgate.net/publication/350506425_Promoting_ Resilience_in_Children_Who_Have_Been_Sexually_Abused_A_Relational_ Approach (page 13)

331 https://www.youtube.com/watch?v=VXDrmUJvRmE

332 https://1in6.org/get-information/myths/

333 https://www.macleans.ca/news/canada/female-teachers-the-sex- offenders-no-one-suspects/

334 https://soundcloud.com/889-wers/male-rape (7m 20s)

335 https://en.wikipedia.org/wiki/Woozle_effect

336 http://assets.mesmac.co.uk/images/Rapid-evidence-assessment-the- SE-of-BYM.pdf#page=29

337 https://www.researchgate.net/publication/263895608_It's_a_lonely_ journey_A_rapid_evidence_assessment_on_infrafamilial_child_sexual_ abuse (page 39)

338 https://pubmed.ncbi.nlm.nih.gov/23397965/ (page 5)

339 https://www.psychologytoday.com/us/blog/psychoanalysis -30/201101/sexually-abused-boys-and-the-men-they-become

340 https://www.counseling.org/docs/default-source/vistas/ article_28565c21f16116603abcacff0000bee5e7.pdf#page=2

341 https://www.researchgate.net/publication/267329359_Harm_ Responsibility_Age_and_Consent (page 18)

342 https://www.researchgate.net/publication/267329359_Harm_ Responsibility_Age_and_Consent (page 19)

343 https://journals.sagepub.com/doi/abs/10.1177/10790632 13503688 (page 15)

344 https://www.researchgate.net/publication/263895608_It's _a_lonely_journey_A_rapid_evidence_assessment_on_infrafamilial_ child_sexual_abuse (page 38)

345 https://www.researchgate.net/publication/263895608_It's _a_lonely_journey_A_rapid_evidence_assessment_on_infrafamilial_ child_sexual_abuse (page 40)

346 https://canadiancrc.com/PDFs/The_Invisible_Boy_Report. pdf#page=30

347 https://etheses.whiterose.ac.uk/26956/2/Recovering%20from%20 Childhood%20Sexual%20Abuse%20A%20Salutogenic%20Approach. pdf#page=80

348 https://www.researchgate.net/publication/263895608_It's _a_lonely_journey_A_rapid_evidence_assessment_on_infrafamilial_ child_sexual_abuse (page 44)

349 http://assets.mesmac.co.uk/images/Rapid-evidence-assessment-the- SE-of-BYM.pdf#page=19

350 https://www.ijhssnet.com/journals/Vol_5_No_7_1_July_ 2015/3.pdf#page=3

351 https://www.researchgate.net/publication/263895608_It's_a_lonely_journey_A_rapid_evidence_assessment_on_infrafamilial_child_sexual_abuse (page 11)

352 https://www.researchgate.net/publication/320841167_Childhood_sexual_abuse_of_boys_as_gender-based_violence (page 4)

353 https://eprints.qut.edu.au/66435/20/66435.pdf#page=18

354 https://www.researchgate.net/publication/267329359_Harm_Responsibility_Age_and_Consent (page 20)

355 https://www.researchgate.net/publication/263895608_It's_a_lonely_journey_A_rapid_evidence_assessment_on_infrafamilial_child_sexual_abuse (page 42)

356 https://www.researchgate.net/publication/263895608_It's_a_lonely_journey_A_rapid_evidence_assessment_on_infrafamilial_child_sexual_abuse (page 43)

357 http://www.regent.edu/acad/schlaw/blogs/docs/femaleoffender.pdf#page=11

358 https://www.canadiancrc.com/PDFs/The_Invisible_Boy_Report.pdf#page=31

359 https://core.ac.uk/download/pdf/324197946.pdf#page=2

360 https://core.ac.uk/download/pdf/324197946.pdf#page=4

361 https://core.ac.uk/download/pdf/324197946.pdf#page=3

362 http://www.regent.edu/acad/schlaw/blogs/docs/femaleoffender.pdf#page=12

363 http://www.regent.edu/acad/schlaw/blogs/docs/femaleoffender.pdf#page=13

364 https://en.wikipedia.org/wiki/Karla_Homolka

365 http://www.regent.edu/acad/schlaw/blogs/docs/femaleoffender.pdf#page=14

366 https://onlinelibrary.wiley.com/doi/abs/10.1111/j.1744-6171.2005.00005.x (page 3)

367 https://www.amazon.com/Boy-Crisis-Boys-Struggling-About-ebook/dp/B01N4UAA8I

368 https://warrenfarrell.com/father-and-child-reunion-part-ii/

369 https://www2.ed.gov/rschstat/research/pubs/misconductreview/report.pdf#page=40

370 https://www2.ed.gov/rschstat/research/pubs/misconductreview/report.pdf#page=41

371 https://pubmed.ncbi.nlm.nih.gov/30040590/ (page 12)

372 https://time.com/5912452/boy-scouts-sexual-abuse-bankruptcy/

373 https://en.wikipedia.org/wiki/Boy_Scouts_of_America

374 https://en.wikipedia.org/wiki/Boy_Scouts_of_America_sex_abuse_cases

375 https://www.rd.com/list/famous-people-who-were-boy-scouts/

376 https://www.vox.com/first-person/2020/2/21/21147039/bankruptcy-boy-scouts-sexual-abuse-cases

377 https://scoutingabusesurvivors.com/survivors/
378 https://www.nbcnews.com/id/wbna36746861
379 https://www.usatoday.com/in-depth/news/investigations/2020/02/18/boy-scouts-bsa-chapter-11-bankruptcy-sexual-abuse-cases/1301187001/
380 https://en.wikipedia.org/wiki/Boy_Scouts_of_America_membership_controversies#BSA_membership_size
381 https://www.foxbusiness.com/lifestyle/mormons-pull-400000-youths-out-of-struggling-boy-scouts
382 https://www.raiznerlaw.com/blog/boy-scouts-sexual-abuse-statute-of-limitations-changes/
383 https://www.washingtonpost.com/dc-md-va/2020/11/19/boy-scouts-bankruptcy-abuse/
384 https://www.nbcnews.com/news/us-news/boy-scouts-reach-850-million-settlement-tens-thousands-sexual-abuse-n1272955
385 https://documents.latimes.com/boy-scouts-paper-trail-of-abuse-documents/
386 https://nypost.com/2020/07/11/former-child-stars-reveal-sex-abuse-emotional-trauma-of-hollywood/
387 https://www.foxnews.com/entertainment/johnny-depp-dropped-from-pirates-of-the-caribbean-franchise-disney-producer-confirms
388 https://abcnews.go.com/Entertainment/corey-feldman-pedophilia-problem-child-actors-contributed-demise/story?id=14256781
389 https://en.wikipedia.org/wiki/Corey_Haim#Early_life
390 https://people.com/celebrity/corey-feldman-a-timeline-of-the-actors-ups-and-downs/
391 https://www.thewrap.com/corey-haims-mother-identifies-the-man-she-believes-sexually-abused-her-son/
392 https://www.rollingstone.com/culture/culture-news/corey-feldman-documentary-names-revelations-964789/
393 https://movieweb.com/corey-feldman-names-alpha-hoffman-hollywood-pedophile-ring/

394 https://www.foxnews.com/entertainment/corey-feldman-hollywood-sexual-abuse-documentary
395 https://people.com/archive/corey-haim-%e2%80%a2-1971-2010-the-lost-boy-vol-73-no-12/
396 https://www.newsweek.com/barbara-walters-accuses-corey-feldman-damaging-entire-industry-pedophilia-accusations-1525167
397 https://medium.com/@anthonyedwards/yes-mom-there-is-something-wrong-f2bcf56434b9
398 https://www.theguardian.com/film/2020/sep/21/alex-winter-i-had-extreme-ptsd-for-many-many-years-that-will-wreak-havoc
399 https://www.newyorker.com/culture/culture-desk/in-showbiz-kids-alex-winter-weighs-the-costs-of-child-stardom

400 https://www.indiewire.com/2018/10/anthony-rapp-kevin-spacey-sexual-harassment-fallout-1202012943/

401 https://www.the-sun.com/news/2953600/kevin-spacey-accusers-allegations/

402 https://abcnews.go.com/Entertainment/house-cards-shuts-production-amid-kevin-spacey-sexual/story?id=50840251

403 https://www.thedailybeast.com/showbiz-kids-exposes-hollywoods-pedophilia-epidemic

404 https://www.yourtango.com/2017308110/where-hollywood-pedophiles-open-secret-documentary-accused-child-sexual-abuse-now

405 https://www.imdb.com/title/tt1895587/

406 http://assets.mesmac.co.uk/images/Rapid-evidence-assessment-the-SE-of-BYM.pdf#page=17

407 https://www.bishop-accountability.org/reports/2004_02_27_JohnJay_revised/2004_02_27_John_Jay_Main_Report_Optimized.pdf#page=12

408 https://acestoohigh.files.wordpress.com/2013/05/death_survivors_report_1may2013.pdf#page=22

409 https://www.bishop-accountability.org/reports/2004_02_27_JohnJay_revised/2004_02_27_John_Jay_Main_Report_Optimized.pdf#page=13

410 https://www.thedailybeast.com/german-nuns-sold-orphaned-children-to-sexual-predators-says-report

411 https://religiouschildabuse.blogspot.com/2011/06/nuns-among-worst-perpetrators-of.html

412 https://www.cal-catholic.com/number-of-nuns-in-us-is-collapsing/

413 https://pubmed.ncbi.nlm.nih.gov/30040590/ (page 2)

414 https://www.dispatch.com/story/news/crime/2019/06/03/more-female-teachers-caught-having/984743007/

415 https://www2.ed.gov/rschstat/research/pubs/misconductreview/report.pdf#page=39

416 https://www.deseret.com/2013/12/17/20531554/davis-high-teacher-faces-rape-charges#davis-high-teacher-brianne-altice-34-was-charged-tuesday-with-three-counts-of-rape

417 https://knewz.com/ohio-teacher-student-sex/

418 https://www.jdjournal.com/2012/03/30/former-teacher-sentenced-for-sex-with-student/

419 https://www.dailymail.co.uk/news/article-4313204/Texas-teacher-AVOIDS-prison-pleading-guilty-rape.html

420 https://en.wikipedia.org/wiki/Debra_Lafave

421 https://www.theage.com.au/national/victoria/female-teacher-who-sought-sex-with-10yearold-boy-walks-free-20141009-113hlz.html

422 https://www.thesun.co.uk/news/16505476/infatuated-teacher-pregnant-pupil-paid/

423 https://www.stuff.co.nz/national/crime/300155215/untreated-sex-offender-jaimee-cooney-paroled-with-curfew-among-conditions

424 https://www.newsbreak.com/news/2277320774503/former-guyer-high-teacher-pleads-guilty-thursday-after-2019-arrest

425 https://en.wikipedia.org/wiki/Jennifer_Fichter

426 https://www.mirror.co.uk/news/uk-news/breaking-married-teacher-35-who-23612495#ICID=Android_TMNewsApp_AppShare

427 https://www.dailystar.co.uk/news/world-news/teacher-had-sex-student-16-23208450

428 https://en.wikipedia.org/wiki/Mary_Kay_Letourneau

429 https://www.mirror.co.uk/news/world-news/ex-air-flight-attendant-who-22888158

430 https://www.nola.com/news/crime_police/article_0edfe10d-7c67-5c49-96cb-5c63d44ec76a.html

431 https://www.masslive.com/news/2012/05/former_holyoke_teacher_lisa_la_2.html

432 https://pubmed.ncbi.nlm.nih.gov/30040590/ (page 3)

433 https://www.cbsnews.com/news/48-hours-investigates-sex-abuse by women-teachers/

434 https://nces.ed.gov/fastfacts/display.asp?id=372

435 https://www.zippia.com/teacher-jobs/demographics/

436 http://johnlang.org/wp-content/uploads/2018/03/Zack-Lang-Dirks-2018.pdf#page=10

437 http://johnlang.org/wp-content/uploads/2018/03/Zack-Lang-Dirks-2018.pdf#page=12

438 http://johnlang.org/wp-content/uploads/2018/03/Zack-Lang-Dirks-2018.pdf#page=13

439 https://www.cbsnews.com/news/has-media-ignored-sex-abuse-in-school/

440 https://www.investors.com/politics/editorials/media-and-unions-tamp-down-news-of-children-abused-by-teachers/

441 https://www2.ed.gov/rschstat/research/pubs/misconductreview/report.pdf#page=42

442 https://protectchildren.ca/pdfs/C3P_CSAinSchoolsReport_en.pdf#page=11

443 https://protectchildren.ca/pdfs/C3P_CSAinSchoolsReport_en.pdf#page=12

444 https://protectchildren.ca/pdfs/C3P_CSAinSchoolsReport_en.pdf#page=22

445 https://protectchildren.ca/pdfs/C3P_CSAinSchoolsReport_en.pdf#page=21

446 https://www2.ed.gov/rschstat/research/pubs/misconductreview/report.pdf#page=43

447 http://www.regent.edu/acad/schlaw/blogs/docs/femaleoffender.pdf#page=8

448 https://www2.ed.gov/rschstat/research/pubs/misconductreview/report.pdf#page=32

449 https://web.archive.org/web/20110719051004/http://www.regent.edu/acad/schlaw/blogs/docs/femaleoffender.pdf#page=9

450 https://web.archive.org/web/20110719051004/http://www.regent.edu/acad/schlaw/blogs/docs/femaleoffender.pdf#page=10

451 https://web.archive.org/web/20110719051004/http://www.regent.edu/acad/schlaw/blogs/docs/femaleoffender.pdf#page=10

452 https://www.addisonlibrary.org/sites/default/files/The%20Reverse%20Double%20Standard%20in%20Perceptions.pdf#page=2

453 https://pubmed.ncbi.nlm.nih.gov/30040590/ (page 5)

454 https://www.cbc.ca/news/indigenous/iap-final-report-residential-schools-1.5946103

455 https://pubmed.ncbi.nlm.nih.gov/30040590/ (page 7)

456 https://pubmed.ncbi.nlm.nih.gov/30040590/ (page 8)

457 https://pubmed.ncbi.nlm.nih.gov/30040590/ (page 11)

458 https://pubmed.ncbi.nlm.nih.gov/30040590/ (page 12)

459 https://pubmed.ncbi.nlm.nih.gov/30040590/ (page 16)

460 https://pubmed.ncbi.nlm.nih.gov/30040590/ (page 13)

461 https://www.tandfonline.com/doi/abs/10.1080/13552600.2019.1643504?journalCode=tjsa20 (page 3)

462 https://ucr.fbi.gov/crime-in-the-u.s/2017/crime-in-the-u.s.-2017/topic-pages/rape

463 https://en.wikipedia.org/wiki/Michael_M._v._Superior_Court_of_Sonoma_County

464 https://www.tandfonline.com/doi/abs/10.1080/13552600.2019.1643504?journalCode=tjsa20 (page 6)

465 https://www.tandfonline.com/doi/abs/10.1080/13552600.2019.1643504?journalCode=tjsa20 (page 7)

466 https://en.wikipedia.org/wiki/Michael_M._v._Superior_Court_of_Sonoma_County#Later_outcome

467 http://campbelllawobserver.com/hot-for-teacher-gender-bias-in-sentencing-of-teachers-that-have-sex-with-their-students/

468 https://www.tandfonline.com/doi/abs/10.1080/13552600.2019.1643504?journalCode=tjsa20 (page 10)

469 https://core.ac.uk/download/pdf/324197946.pdf#page=5

470 https://web.archive.org/web/20110719051004/http://www.regent.edu/acad/schlaw/blogs/docs/femaleoffender.pdf#page=3

471 https://web.archive.org/web/20110719051004/http://www.regent.edu/acad/schlaw/blogs/docs/femaleoffender.pdf#page=4

472 https://keep.lib.asu.edu/_flysystem/fedora/c7/66249/tmp/package-bzXXXU/Simmon_asu_0010N_12405.pdf#page=13

473 https://link.springer.com/article/10.1007/s10940-019-09416-x (page 6)

474 https://link.springer.com/article/10.1007/s10940-019-09416-x (page 17)

475 https://www.washingtonexaminer.com/gender-matters-more-for-perpetrators-than-victims-in-child-sex-abuse

476 https://www.addisonlibrary.org/sites/default/files/The%20Reverse%20Double%20Standard%20in%20Perceptions.pdf#page=4

477 https://en.wikipedia.org/wiki/Hermesmann_v._Seyer

478 https://www.oscn.net/applications/oscn/DeliverDocument.asp?citeID=441505

479 https://law.justia.com/cases/wisconsin/court-of-appeals/1989/88-1887-6.html

480 https://law.justia.com/cases/california/court-of-appeal/4th/50/842.html

481 https://www.usatoday.com/story/news/nation/2014/09/02/statutory-rape-victim-child-support/14953965/

482 https://ir.law.utk.edu/cgi/viewcontent.cgi?article=1531&context=utklaw_facpubs (page 30)

483 https://www.academia.edu/36539221/Child_sexual_abuse_Routledge_International_Handbook_of_Violence_Studies_ (page 4)

484 https://www.researchgate.net/publication/265739360_Sexual_victimization_of_children_and_adolescents_in_Switzerland (page 9)

485 http://assets.mesmac.co.uk/images/Rapid-evidence-assessment-the-SE-of-BYM.pdf#page=26

486 http://assets.mesmac.co.uk/images/Rapid-evidence-assessment-the-SE-of-BYM.pdf#page=27

487 https://www.newsweek.com/boys-forced-apologize-female-classmates-behalf-gender-1578793

488 https://boingboing.net/2021/03/22/adult-male-virginity-soars.html

489 https://www.researchgate.net/publication/221977317_Theoretical_Perspectives_of_Male_Sexual_Abuse_Conceptualization_of_a_Case_Study (page 3)

490 https://www.dictionary.com/e/slang/male-tears/

491 https://www.youtube.com/watch?v=_a2Umgioia0

492 https://time.com/3101429/misandry-misandrist-feminist-womenagainstfeminism/

493 https://www.researchgate.net/publication/12577367_Mental_health_professionals'_attitudes_and_practices_towards_male_childhood_sexual_abuse (page 4)

494 https://www.researchgate.net/publication/12577367_Mental_health_professionals'_attitudes_and_practices_towards_male_childhood_sexual_abuse (page 5)

495 https://www.researchgate.net/publication/12577367_Mental_health_professionals'_attitudes_and_practices_towards_male_childhood_sexual_abuse (page 6)

496 https://www.researchgate.net/publication/12577367_Mental_health_professionals'_attitudes_and_practices_towards_male_childhood_sexual_abuse (page 7)

497 https://www.researchgate.net/publication/12577367_Mental_health_ professionals'_attitudes_and_practices_towards_male_childhood_sexual_ abuse (page 8)
498 https://www.ijhssnet.com/journals/Vol_5_No_7_1_July _2015/3. pdf#page=5
499 http://assets.mesmac.co.uk/images/Rapid-evidence-assessment-the-SE-of-BYM.pdf#page=25
500 https://www.researchgate.net/publication/223991352_Deep_and_ almost_unbearable_suffering_Consequences_of_childhood_sexual_ abuse_for_men%27s_health_and_well-being (page 2)
501 https://www.researchgate.net/publication/259351987_Consequences_ of_childhood_sexual_abuse_for_health_and_well-being_Gender_ similarities_and_differences (page 2)
502 https://acestoohigh.files.wordpress.com/2013/05/death_survivors_ report_1may2013.pdf#page=6
503 https://www.researchgate.net/publication/223991352_Deep_and_ almost_unbearable_suffering_Consequences_of_childhood_sexual_ abuse_for_men%27s_health_and_well-being (page 3)
504 https://www.researchgate.net/publication/223991352_Deep_and_ almost_unbearable_suffering_Consequences_of_childhood_sexual_ abuse_for_men%27s_health_and_well-being (page 9)
505 https://www.npr.org/sections/health-shots/2019/05/17/ 724299570/ suicide-rate-among-girls-rising-faster-than-for-boys-study-finds
506 https://onlinelibrary.wiley.com/doi/abs/10.1111/j.1744-6171.2005.00005.x (page 5)
507 https://www.researchgate.net/publication/223991352_Deep_and_ almost_unbearable_suffering_Consequences_of_childhood_sexual_ abuse_for_men%27s_health_and_well-being (page 8)
508 https://onlinelibrary.wiley.com/doi/abs/10.1111/j.1744-6171.2005.00005.x (page 4)
509 https://www.canadiancrc.com/PDFs/The_Invisible_Boy_Report. pdf#page=11
510 https://www.tandfonline.com/doi/abs/10.1080/13552600. 2019.1643504?journalCode=tjsa20 (page 5)
511 https://www.researchgate.net/publication/329208180_Big_ Boys_Don't_Cry_A_Critical_Interpretive_Synthesis_of_Male_Sexual_ Victimization
512 https://www.youtube.com/watch?v=ioOxzmuIS0M
513 https://onecirclefoundation.org/the-council
514 https://jimhopper.com/topics/child-abuse/sexual-abuse-of-boys/facts-about-sexual-abuse-of-boys/
515 https://etheses.whiterose.ac.uk/26956/2/Recovering%20from%20 Childhood%20Sexual%20Abuse%20A%20Salutogenic%20Approach. pdf#page=31
516 https://www.counseling.org/docs/default-source/vistas/ article_28565c21f16116603abcacff0000bee5e7.pdf#page=3

517 https://www.counseling.org/docs/default-source/vistas/
article_28565c21f16116603abcacff0000bee5e7.pdf#page=4

TRAFFICKING
518 https://web.archive.org/web/20160305091243/https://www.
d1qkyo3pi1c9bx.cloudfront.net/00028B1B-B0DB-4FCD-
A991-219527535DAB/1b1293ef-1524-4f2c-b148-91db11379
d11.pdf#page=6
519 https://www.state.gov/wp-content/uploads/2019/02/Assisting-Male-
Survivors-of-Human-Trafficking.pdf
520 https://d1qkyo3pi1c9bx.cloudfront.net/00028B1B-B0DB-4FCD-A991-
219527535DAB/1b1293ef-1524-4f2c-b148-91db11379d11.pdf#page=4
521 https://traffickinginstitute.org/the-silenced-minority/
522 http://humantraffickingsearch.org/wp-content/uploads/
2017/06/ManilaStreetWorkingBoys.pdf#page=9
523 https://d1qkyo3pi1c9bx.cloudfront.net/00028B1B-B0DB-4FCD-A991-
219527535DAB/1b1293ef-1524-4f2c-b148-91db11379d11.pdf#page=7
524 https://repository.library.georgetown.edu/bitstream/
handle/10822/551495/Data_research_trafficking.pdf
#page=35
525 https://repository.library.georgetown.edu/bitstream/
handle/10822/551495/Data_research_trafficking.pdf
#page=10
526 https://www.academia.edu/17147312/I_thought_it_could_never_
happen_to_boys (page 89)
527 https://www.d1qkyo3pi1c9bx.cloudfront.net/00028B1B-B0DB-
4FCD-A991-219527535DAB/1b1293ef-1524-4f2c-b148-91db11379d11.
pdf#page=13
528 https://link.springer.com/chapter/10.1007/978-3-319- 73621-1_8
(page 2)
529 http://humantraffickingsearch.org/wp-content/uploads/
2017/06/ManilaStreetWorkingBoys.pdf#page=14
530 https://www.foxnews.com/opinion/geoff-rogers-boys-are-victims-of-
sex-trafficking-too
531 https://www.d1qkyo3pi1c9bx.cloudfront.net/00028B1B-B0DB-4FCD-
A991-219527535DAB/1b1293ef-1524-4f2c-b148
-91db11379d11.pdf#page=8
532 https://web.archive.org/web/20160305091243/https://www.
d1qkyo3pi1c9bx.cloudfront.net/00028B1B-B0DB-4FCD
-A991-219527535DAB/1b1293ef-1524-4f2c-b148-91db1137
9d11.pdf#page=9
533 https://prostitutionresearch.com/wp-content/uploads/ 2016/08/
Download-448-pages.pdf
534 http://assets.mesmac.co.uk/images/Rapid-evidence-assessment-the-
SE-of-BYM.pdf#page=20

535 https://link.springer.com/chapter/10.1007/978-3-319- 73621-1_8 (page 4)

536 https://www.barnardos.org.uk/sites/default/files/2020-12/not-just-a-girl-thing.pdf#page=16

537 https://resourcecentre.savethechildren.net/pdf/trauma_i_ psihoterapija_-_zbornik_radova_eng.pdf/ (page 73)

538 https://resourcecentre.savethechildren.net/pdf/trauma_i_ psihoterapija_-_zbornik_radova_eng.pdf/ (page 171)

539 https://www.foxnews.com/us/boys-are-invisible-victims-in-sex-trafficking

540 http://assets.mesmac.co.uk/images/Rapid-evidence-assessment-the-SE-of-BYM.pdf#page=22

541 https://web.archive.org/web/20160305091243/https://www. d1qkyo3pi1c9bx.cloudfront.net/00028B1B-B0DB-4FCD-A991-219527535DAB/1b1293ef-1524-4f2c-b148-91db11379d11.pdf#page=11

542 https://web.archive.org/web/20160305091243/https://www. d1qkyo3pi1c9bx.cloudfront.net/00028B1B-B0DB-4FCD-A991-219527535DAB/1b1293ef-1524-4f2c-b148-91db11379d11.pdf#page=12

543 https://papers.ssrn.com/sol3/papers.cfm?abstract_id=2411017 (page 25)

544 https://link.springer.com/chapter/10.1007/978-3-319- 73621-1_8 (page 9)

545 https://www.academia.edu/17147312/I_thought_it_could_never_ happen_to_boys (page 12)

546 https://www.academia.edu/17147312/I_thought_it_could _never_happen_to_boys (page 75)

547 http://www.vancouversun.com/news/Part+Four+Boys+ forgotten+victims+with+video/6350524/story.html

548 https://link.springer.com/chapter/10.1007/978-3-319-736 21-1_8 (page 3)

549 http://humantraffickingsearch.org/wp-content/uploads/2017/06/ ManilaStreetWorkingBoys.pdf#page=13

550 https://www.academia.edu/17147312/I_thought_it_could _never_happen_to_boys (page 11)

551 https://www.academia.edu/35166715/Becoming_An_Anti _Human_Trafficking_Advocate (page 18)

552 https://link.springer.com/chapter/10.1007/978-3-319- 73621-1_8 (page 11)

553 https://link.springer.com/chapter/10.1007/978-3-319- 73621-1_8 (page 7)

554 https://jjie.org/2014/04/14/trafficked-boys-overlooked -underrepresented/

555 https://papers.ssrn.com/sol3/papers.cfm?abstract_id=2411017 (page 9)

556 https://papers.ssrn.com/sol3/papers.cfm?abstract_id=2411017 (page 8)

557 https://www.state.gov/wp-content/uploads/2019/02/ 271339. pdf#page=30

558 https://papers.ssrn.com/sol3/papers.cfm?abstract_id=2411017 (page 2)

559 https://papers.ssrn.com/sol3/papers.cfm?abstract_id=2411017 (page 3)

560 https://papers.ssrn.com/sol3/papers.cfm?abstract_id=2411017 (page 27)

561 https://papers.ssrn.com/sol3/papers.cfm?abstract_id=2411017 (page 24)

562 https://papers.ssrn.com/sol3/papers.cfm?abstract_id=2411017 (page 38)

563 https://papers.ssrn.com/sol3/papers.cfm?abstract_id=2411017 (page 39)

564 https://papers.ssrn.com/sol3/papers.cfm?abstract_id=2411017 (page 10)

565 https://web.archive.org/web/20160305091243/https://www. d1qkyo3pi1c9bx.cloudfront.nct/00028B1B-B0DB-4FCD-A991-219527535DAB/1b1293ef-1524-4f2c-b148-91db11379d11.pdf#page=14

566 https://papers.ssrn.com/sol3/papers.cfm?abstract_id=2411017 (page 46)

567 https://papers.ssrn.com/sol3/papers.cfm?abstract_id=2411017 (page 45)

568 https://www.academia.edu/17147312/I_thought_it_could _never_happen_to_boys (page 13)

ABOUT THE AUTHOR

Christopher Daniel Votey was born in Dayton, Ohio but currently resides in Mesa, Arizona. He has a B.S. in Computers and has primarily worked in Customer Support. In 2012, he realized his dream by becoming a self-published author and has since released several books.

Unfortunately, in 2012, he also suffered brain damage at work that left him permanently disabled. His condition is Post Concussion Syndrome. Unfortunately, he slipped through the cracks and was unable to get the medical help he needed, nor could he get on any financial assistance. Chris has spent the last decade slowly recovering, unable to work a regular job and finding ways to regain financial independence. In 2020, he became a Lyft driver after developing a therapy to heal his mind. Despite his mental and physical improvements, it's unlikely he'll ever make a full recovery.

After seeing a woman raise funds to do a series on why video games are sexist, Chris discovered the Men's Movement and started to make videos. In 2013 he had the idea to write what eventually became the Boys' & Men's Issues Handbook. While he wouldn't actually start writing it until 2019, he continued to do videos and help coordinate local meetups, sponsor a Red Pill screening in Philadelphia, do two pin-up calendars of women within the Men's Movement, created a Men's Magazine, and hosted the 2021 International Conference for Men's Issues for North America.

Chris now spends his time learning and mastering photography and photoshop, starting back writing fiction again, and working on the next book in this series. He hopes to do more for men in a vast variety of ways, not just to raise awareness, but be part of projects to be of direct and indirect help to people as a whole.

Made in the USA
Columbia, SC
26 June 2023